*Booktalks Plus*

# *Booktalks Plus*

## *Motivating Teens to Read*

**Lucy Schall**

2001
LIBRARIES UNLIMITED, INC.
Englewood, Colorado

Libraries Unlimited, Inc.
P.O. Box 6633
Englewood, CO 80155-6633
1-800-237-6124
www.lu.com

**Library of Congress Cataloging-in-Publication Data**

Schall, Lucy.
Booktalks plus : motivating teens to read / Lucy Schall.
p. cm.
Includes bibliographical references and index.
ISBN 1-56308-817-7 (pbk.)
1. Teenagers--Books and reading--United States. 2. Book talks--United States. 3. Reading promotion--United States. 4. Best books. 5. Teenagers--Books and reading--United States--Bibliography. 6. Young adult literature, English--Bibliography. I. Title.

Z1037.A1 S27 2001
028.5'35--dc21

00-066306

# Contents

# Introduction

When I began to research *Booktalks Plus*, my task was to find 100 quality books for young adults published between 1996 and 1999. My library cards now outnumber my credit cards. Librarians, book publishers, professional publications, and my editor, Betty Morris, have guided me to many quality works. The 100-plus books in *Booktalks Plus* illustrate the high quality of young adult literature available today.

I tried to choose books that are related to each other, to school curricula, and to older works. These booktalk books appeal to many ages and reading levels. Some of the related works also fall into the 1996–1999 range. The summaries, booktalks, and supplementary materials will help media specialists, librarians, classroom teachers, and home school instructors match kids with books. The related activities will help students further explore the ideas, examine the writers' techniques, and express their own ideas. All the books speak to universal concerns.

The world forces us to find out who we are. Very early, we learn that some people accept or reject us simply because of our looks. Our families, in trying to nurture us, show us that we should be independent. Nature's unrelenting patterns and powers test our will to survive. National conflicts remind us that we must reach out to others. And cosmic powers let us know that some puzzles are still beyond our understanding.

This battle with the world, called growing up, helps us realize our values, strengths, and weaknesses so that we can choose our society and our personal path within it. As we experience different groups and their values, we must decide which groups hold the values we admire. Our spiritual strength or commitment may call us to one group. Our physical strength may call us to another, but, in each decision, our minds help us examine our choices.

Just when we decide where we are going, something or someone seems to decide we aren't going to get there. We like to think of conflicts, decisions, or problems as being simple or clearly solvable, but life doesn't always mimic the myth or the movie. Physical or mental illness may limit us or make us stronger. Hate and prejudice may destroy us or give us understanding. Family plans may clash with our own dreams but then clarify them. We may think that we have no choice at all and then discover we have been making choices all along.

As we struggle with opposition, we help another traveler. We may entertain, extend loyalty or trust, contribute insight or perspective, and discover or inspire. In this search and in this struggle, we find ourselves. These messages organize the four chapters of *Booktalks Plus.*

Each chapter contains four or five subtopics. In the first chapter, "The World Reacts." Those reactions come in "First Impressions," "Family Decisions," "Nature's Pattern," "National Conflicts," and "Supernatural Forces." In the second chapter, "We Act." Our reactions are demonstrated "Socially," "Spiritually," "Physically," and "Mentally." Then, in Chapter 3, the forces do more than just react; the "Forces Try to Confound Us." We must deal with "Good Versus Evil," "Disease," "Hate and Prejudice," "Family Conflicts," and "The Supernatural." In Chapter 4, "We Struggle and Give." In this effort, we may "Entertain and Create," "Trust," or "Teach and Lead."

Each booktalk includes the author, book title, publisher and place of publication, year of publication, number of pages, price, and ISBN. (Citations for books published before 1990 do not include number of pages, price information, or ISBN.) The abbreviation "pa." indicates paperback. A summary/description follows this information. The summary allows the reader to quickly decide if this book will appeal to the audience. The booktalk follows the summary/description and provides a way to present the book, or it may suggest an idea for another presentation. The booktalk, geared to a live audience, is short enough to be adapted for the school's morning announcements or the school newspaper. It is also appropriate for a public service segment on the local radio station or in the local newspaper.

"Related Activities" presents individual and group projects based on the book and works related to the book. Statements or suggestions for discussion also provide writing assignments for journals, longer papers, poems, creative writing, panel discussions, or presentations. Some may even provide a basis for independent studies, portfolios, or senior projects. Activities also suggest alternative groupings for the books. Completion of any of the activities will improve reading, writing, and speaking skills.

The "Related Works" section includes books discussed within the volume, as well as related classics, short stories, plays, poems, articles, and videos. Consequently, these sections will help instructors organize theme presentations and will guide both instructors and parents to books and related works that speak to particular areas of interest. The indexes include authors, titles, and topics for a quick overview of a work's relationships to others mentioned in this volume.

Each book takes us on a journey, and, as Emily Dickinson pointed out, these "frigates" and "coursers" come free to every "human soul." I don't know if that statement was meant to be pro-library, but certainly libraries have enhanced many life journeys. I hope this book will help media specialists, librarians, instructors, and parents to encourage those journeys. Writing it has been a wonderful journey for me.

# 1

# The World Reacts

## FIRST IMPRESSIONS

Bennett, Cherie. **Life in the Fat Lane**. New York: Delacorte Press, 1998. 260p. $15.95. ISBN 0-385-32274-7.

### *Summary/Description*

Lara Ardeche, the perfect and most popular girl at her school, learns about *Life in the Fat Lane* when she develops Axell-Crowne Syndrome. She begins at 118 pounds and peaks at over 200. Her friends and boyfriends change. Her parents' marriage falls apart. Lara, her mother, and her brother all move to a new town and school. She must abandon her stereotypes, examine her life, and let go of her obsession with control. The chapter numbers indicate her weight and the crisis that each gain brings. By the end of the novel, Lara shows a slight weight loss, but the loss could be a false indication that her body is changing. Her journey makes her realize how society dehumanizes the fat and aging.

## Booktalk

Bring in advertisements for weight loss programs or several mainstream magazines that contain articles about losing weight. Ask what the assumptions are about each of the products and the results that those products promise. Ask about students' favorite television shows or movies. Are there any fat people in these programs? If so, how are they treated? Now show a work by Rubens. Is fat ugly or beautiful?

The modern monster—fat—attacks Lara Ardeche. At the beginning of the year, she is the 118-pound homecoming queen and by the end has peaked at 210. She can't control her weight or her life. Lara begins to see friends and family differently as she finds herself both "huge and invisible." *Life in the Fat Lane* answers the ultimate question: How can you be happy if the in group treats you "like a pile of puke?"

## Related Activities

1. In the acknowledgments, Cherie Bennett lists a series of factual sources for her novel. Locate these and other sources that discuss society's attitudes toward weight. Discuss the articles.

2. Describe a healthy eater. You might start with the source *Coping with Compulsive Eating* by Carolyn Simpson.

3. Construct a bulletin board displaying advertisements for or explanations of body enhancing foods, medicines, or programs. Group or classify the advertisements. Under each grouping, write the message the group sends.

4. In *A Fly Named Alfred*, Harper Winslow describes Mrs. Jewel, the school secretary. Read pages 100 and 101. Begin with the paragraph at the bottom of page 100. "Speaking of shape, maybe I'll write about Mrs. Jewel." What assumptions does Harper make about Mrs. Jewel? What does he reveal about himself in his description of her?

5. Read one selection per day from "Part One: The Body Under Assault," in *Ophelia Speaks.* The sections "Media Fed Images" and "Eating Disorders" are most applicable. After each day's reading, discuss the group's reaction. These selections seem to be appropriate for more mature audiences.

6. Finish the story. Does Lara become fat or thin? What effect does the result have on her life?

## *Related Works*

1. Abelove, Joan. **Go and Come Back**. See full booktalk in Chapter 2 (p. 61). In Alicia's society, where food is scarce, fat and generosity are marks of a person's beauty and humanity.

2. Carlson, Dale, and Hannah Carlson. **Girls Are Equal Too, 2d ed.** Madison, CT: Bick Publishing House, 1998. 231p. $14.95. ISBN 1-884158-18-8. The Carlsons present what some might consider a strongly feminist point of view. The following chapters are most applicable to *Life in the Fat Lane*: "Women's Image in Advertising and What They Do to You at the Mall" and "The Beautiful Imbecile."

3. Kahaner, Ellen. **Growing Up Female**. New York: The Rosen Publishing Group, 1997. 64p. (The Need to Know Library). $17.95. ISBN 1-884158-18-8. Chapters 5 and 6 are the most applicable.

4. Lipsyte, Robert. **One Fat Summer**. New York: Harper & Row, 1977. $5.95. Bobby Marks begins the summer as a passive personality who uses food to deal with his frustrations and ends it as an assertive young adult who takes charge of his life.

5. Shandler, Sara. **Ophelia Speaks**. See full booktalk in Chapter 2 (p. 126). "Media-Fed Images" and "Eating Disorders" are made up of writings from teenage girls about their own and their friends' reactions to weight. With some selections, the presenter may wish to judge the appropriateness of the language and images for the maturity of the audience.

6. Simpson, Carolyn. **Coping with Compulsive Eating**. New York: The Rosen Publishing Group, 1997. 89p. (Coping Series). $17.95. ISBN 0-8239-2516-1. Describing the compulsive eater, Simpson defines a healthy physical and emotional lifestyle. Like the other books in the Coping Series, *Coping with Compulsive Eating* provides further sources of information, a glossary, and an index. An excellent source, it provides a base for further research.

Grove, Vicki. **The Starplace**. New York: G. P. Putnam's Sons, 1999. 214p. $17.99. ISBN 0-399-23207-9.

## *Summary/Description*

*The Starplace* tells about the friendship of Francine Driscoll, a white girl who has lived in Quiver, Oklahoma, all her life, and Celeste Chisholm, a black girl who has just moved to Quiver. Francine Driscoll and her friends are beginning their eighth-grade year with a party. In 1961 Quiver, Oklahoma, the most controversial guest is Celeste. Celeste has chosen to attend the white school instead of the black school in the black area of town. Her father, a professor, has decided to research the death of his great-grandfather and the death of a judge who dared to fight the Ku Klux Klan. The popular girls try to intimidate Celeste and close her out. Their parents back the girls' efforts. Despite having the best voice in the chorus, Celeste is blocked from representing the school in national competition. When Francine and her friends decide to stick by Celeste, they learn about personal integrity, civil rights, peaceful protest, and the Klan. In this same year, Francine's mother scores the highest score on the real estate test but won't receive a promotion because she is a woman. Although Celeste must leave town and Mrs. Driscoll must quit her job, Francine has begun to ask about who makes the rules, and her parents are beginning to understand her questions. In the epilogue we learn that Celeste becomes a famous performer and Francine becomes a successful writer.

## *Booktalk*

What do Bosnia and Berlin have in common? If Oklahoma were added to that list, would you make the same connection? Francine Driscoll wouldn't have. In Quiver, Oklahoma, everyone follows the rules, and everyone gets along. But when Celeste Chisholm moves to town, the rules don't seem to apply anymore. Celeste is black, and she decides to go to the white school. Her father is looking around for some kind of charred evidence, and they move into a haunted house. The popular kids don't like this different and mysterious Celeste. Frannie, her classmate, would like just to plan a good party. She doesn't want any friction about who is and who isn't invited, but this is 1961. The Berlin wall is going up. Martin Luther King Jr. is crusading for equal rights. Frannie and Celeste find their own place in the world, called *The Starplace*, and Quiver, Oklahoma, will never be the same again.

## *Related Activities*

1. Research the Berlin Wall, then discuss the comparison Francine makes between segregation and the Berlin Wall.

2. Define and research affirmative action. Explain why affirmative action policies were passed into law and why they are so controversial today.

3. Research women's rights in the workplace over the last twenty-five to thirty years.

4. Investigate the recent resurgence in popularity of the Ku Klux Klan, especially among younger people.

5. Read "Between the World and Me" by Richard Wright in *Shimmy Shimmy Shimmy Like My Sister Kate: Looking at the Harlem Renaissance Through Poems*. Discuss the following questions: Who is the speaker? Why is he speaking? What details and images characterize the people he describes? What does Wright accomplish in each of the four parts of the poem? What is Wright's overall purpose? "Between the World and Me" is appropriate for a more mature audience.

## *Related Works*

1. Carlson, Dale, and Hannah Carlson. "Women at Work." In **Girls Are Equal Too, 2d ed**. Madison, CT: Bick Publishing House, 1998. 231p. $14.95pa. ISBN 1-884158-18-8. The chapter gives statistics about women's success in the workplace.

2. Hacker, Carlotta. **Great African Americans in the Arts**. New York: Crabtree Publishing, 1997. 64p. (Outstanding African Americans). $8.95pa. ISBN 0-86505-821-0. Hacker profiles black artists who have succeeded despite discrimination.

3. Hunter, Shaun. **Writers**. New York: Crabtree Publishing, 1998. 48p. (Women in Profile). $8.95pa. ISBN 0-7787-0027-5. Hunter profiles successful women writers.

4. McLuskey, Krista. **Entrepreneurs**. New York: Crabtree Publishing, 1999. 48p. (Women in Profile). $8.95pa. ISBN 0-7787-0034-8. McLuskey profiles successful women entrepreneurs.

5. Wright, Richard. "Between the World and Me." In **Shimmy Shimmy Shimmy Like My Sister Kate: Looking at the Harlem Renaissance Through Poems** by Nikki Giovanni. See full booktalk

in Chapter 4 (p. 236). The poem reviews the racism and hate that block an African American from the world.

Mikaelsen, Ben. **Petey**. New York: Hyperion Books, 1998. 280p. $15.95. ISBN 0-7868-0426-2.

### *Summary/Description*

*Petey* traces the life of a man born with cerebral palsy, labeled an idiot, and raised in a mental institution. Ben Mikaelsen uses characters in Petey's life to represent each of Petey's realizations: communication, language, friendship, romantic love, socialization, and rebirth. Esteban is the first attendant to recognize Petey's intelligence. Joe, another attendant, helps Petey learn to communicate. Cassie, a beautiful, young nurse, helps him to realize love. Calvin, another inmate, becomes his committed friend, and thirteen-year-old Trevor discovers that a friend who is the most different can make the biggest difference in life. A man imprisoned in a crippled and neglected body is able to reach out to inspire and support the people who walk into his life.

### *Booktalk*

Ask the following questions and allow time for answers: What does an evil monster look like? What does a hero look like?

Petey looks like both. When people first meet him, they see a monster. When people get to know him, they see a hero. Born with cerebral palsy in 1920, Petey Corbin is labeled an idiot and institutionalized. "Locked inside a defective body," Petey can't adjust the temperature to get a good night's sleep or eat without choking. He makes friends and even falls in love, but eventually everyone leaves him. He decides never to love anyone again and keeps his promise for thirteen years. Then he meets Trevor, a teenage boy. At first, Trevor sees only a "deformed" old man living in a "madhouse," and he doesn't like old people anyway. But when the same bullies push around both Petey and Trevor, the two join forces. In fighting back and sticking together, they teach each other what "quality of life" means.

## *Related Activities*

1. Ask a special education teacher or psychologist to speak to the class about the psychological as well as physical challenges of the handicapped as they relate to inclusion.

2. List the characters in the novel. Identify the quality or awakening each represents for Petey.

3. Discuss the following questions: Is Petey a hero? Why or why not?

4. In the novel *I Rode a Horse of Milk White Jade*, Oyuna describes her childhood. Read aloud the passage on page 8 that begins with, "That night, and for many days . . ." and ends with the chapter. Ask the students to describe Oyuna. Discuss what she shares with Petey.

5. Read aloud "Handicaps" by Bob Henry Baber in *Pierced by a Ray of the Sun*. Write a sentence expressing the idea of each section. What images in each section help express those ideas? Why are the ideas presented in a particular order? What is the speaker's point? How does the poem relate to Petey?

## *Related Works*

1. Baber, Bob Henry. "Handicaps." In **Pierced by a Ray of the Sun: Poems About the Times We Feel Alone** edited by Ruth Gordon. p. 28. New York: HarperCollins, 1995. 105p. $15.89. ISBN 0-06-023613-2. The poem reminds us that a person labeled handicapped has the same feelings and aspirations as everyone else.

2. Bobryk, Jim. "Navigating My Eerie Landscape Alone." *Newsweek* (March 8, 1999): 14. Bobryk tells how his life has changed since he became blind.

3. Johnson, Marilyn. "What Happens to Children Nobody Wants?" *Life* (May 1997): 11 pages beginning on 56. Johnson writes about Norma Claypool who, in spite of her blindness, cares for difficult-to-adopt children.

4. Powell, Bill, and Yana Dlugy. "Russia's Gulags for Children." *Newsweek* (December 21, 1998): 2 pages beginning on 40. The article describes the terrible conditions that Russian handicapped children experience.

5. Wilson, Diane Lee. **I Rode a Horse of Milk White Jade**. New York: Orchard Books, 1998. 232p. $17.95. ISBN 0-531-30024-2. See full booktalk below. The main character's grandmother helps turn a girl's handicap into an inspiration.

 Wilson, Diane Lee. **I Rode a Horse of Milk White Jade**. New York: Orchard Books, 1998. 232p. $17.95. ISBN 0-531-30024-2.

### *Summary/Description*

Oyuna is a handicapped twelve-year-old girl no one wants to marry. Her mother's death by lightning confirms to Oyuna that she is a jinx to her family and community. When Kublai Khan's army raids her *ail* (her family's group of herdsmen and their families), she masquerades as a boy to save her step-brother and follow the horse her father has given her, the magic horse she feels has called to her for help. With Bator, her cat, and Bayan, her horse, she carries a message to Kublai Khan. During her journey she faces death and capture, but she pushes on. Her grandmother has prophesied that she will find a swift white horse to win the festival race at Karakorum. Her physical journey is also a spiritual one. As she overcomes her fears and protects Bator and Bayan, even from the Khan, she discovers that each person chooses luck and that even a ruler as fearsome as the Khan is human. In the final chapter, she travels with her husband to the festival at Karakorum to win the race and complete the circle of life as her grandmother has prophesied. Oyuna tells this story to her granddaughter as they wait for the birth of yet another filly from the family's horses.

### *Booktalk*

Everyone has dreams that come true and dreams that fail, but all of Oyuna's dreams seem to fail. She is handicapped. Her mother dies. Her parents try to hide her in their tent. Her ail, the herdsmen with whom her family travels, says she is bad luck, and yet her grandmother has told her the future, a good one. When Oyuna takes pity on a horse as handicapped as she is and a cat as lonely as she is, she must forget her fears and protect them. Together, they journey to the fearsome Kublai Khan. Now, Oyuna must do what she can do, not worry about what she can't do. Can she choose luck? Can she change it? Can she find the wonderful horse her grandmother has promised? Oyuna answers those questions when she tells her granddaughter the story, *I Rode a Horse of Milk White Jade*.

## *Related Activities*

1. Oyuna's grandmother, in some ways, is a frightening and grotesque figure, and yet she helps Oyuna get control of her life. Read Chapter 9. Identify the frightening details, then identify the details that comfort Oyuna. Discuss why Wilson created this character and how she uses her throughout the story.

2. While reading books or watching movies or television programs, collect grotesque or undesirable-looking characters. Keep descriptions of them to read aloud or, if possible, create a bulletin board with their pictures. Discuss how and why each author used each character.

3. Read Chapter 10 aloud. The grandmother seems to give Oyuna conflicting messages. What are the messages? Does the grandmother believe Oyuna's life is controlled by choice or by fate?

4. Oyuna recalls her life journey. The events are magical and real. They teach her, build her confidence, and reveal her character. Divide the thirty chapters among small groups of students. Ask each group to identify the important events within the assigned section. As a large group, classify the important events as magical or real. Mark the magical events with asterisks. Discuss why this labeling is difficult.

5. Read the poem "Mother" by Bea Exner Liu on page 13 of *Pierced by a Ray of the Sun*. Describe the speaker. Why does she speak? How is her situation similar to Oyuna's? How is it different?

## *Related Works*

1. **Genghis Khan: Terror and Conquest**. Produced by A&E Television Networks, 1995. 50 min. Color. (Biography). $14.95. AAE-14011. Videocassette. The film tells the story of Genghis Khan, one of the most terrifying leaders in history. Several aspects of his life parallel Oyuna's life.

2. Liu, Bea Exner. "Mother." In **Pierced by a Ray of the Sun: Poems About the Times We Feel Alone** edited by Ruth Gordon. New York: HarperCollins, 1995. 105p. $15.89. ISBN 0-06-023613-2. The speaker returns to her mother's house after the mother's death. She realizes that they are separated forever and also that her mother would want her to take control of her own life.

3. Napoli, Donna Jo. **Sirena**. See full booktalk in Chapter 2 (p. 91). Sirena is definitely controlled by fate, but the personal choices she makes within that fate define her personality.

4. Sachar, Louis. **Holes**. See full booktalk below (p. 35). *Holes* deals with the idea of personal choice versus fate.

5. Stern, Jerome. **Making Shapely Fiction**. New York: Laurel, 1991. 283p. $6.50pa. ISBN 0-440-21221-9. Stern describes patterns and techniques used in fiction. "Journey" and "Visitation" from Part I and "Grotesque" from Part III would be helpful in understanding how these patterns and techniques are used.

Reybold, Laura. **The Dangers of Tattooing and Body Piercing**. New York: The Rosen Publishing Group, 1998 rev. ed. 64p. (The Need to Know Library). $17.95. ISBN 0-8239-2742-3.

### *Summary/Description*

*The Dangers of Tattooing and Body Piercing* warns people about the problems of making a permanent change to the body for a fashion fad. It gives the history of tattooing and body piercing, then explains the modern objections to it. Tattoos that identify gang members may keep a person from being hired. Some religions ban tattoos. In many states, tattooing is illegal, and in other states, it is illegal under a certain age. The biggest objections, however, are medical. Both tattooing and body piercing may cause infections, some of which are life altering or life threatening. The process and the healing are usually more painful and delicate than the person anticipates. The book offers temporary tattoos and non-piercing body jewelry as alternatives, but if tattooing or piercing is a "must," Reybold lists what to look for to get the safest and most hygienic job.

### *Booktalk*

Ask how many people in the group are considering being tattooed or having body piercing. Ask them why they are considering it. Ask also if anyone has experienced tattooing or body piercing. They may wish to share their experiences.

If you have never experienced tattooing or body piercing but are now considering it, you might want to read *The Dangers of Tattooing and Body Piercing*. A bad job may mean gangrene, hepatitis, or even HIV. Your body may reject the piercing. Your religion, the state, or your future employer may object. And you might change your mind later and have to live with the tattoo or scar. Removing a tattoo costs between $500 and $1,000 per inch. So, before you go through several hours with painful needles, read the book and check the health standards for a permanent job and some alternatives to the real thing.

## *Related Activities*

1. In Chapter 3 ("The Spouter Inn") of *Moby Dick*, Ishmael sees Queequeg for the first time. Ishmael also sees tattooing for the first time. The paragraph in which Ishmael gives his reaction begins, "Lord save me, thinks I, that must be the harpooner . . . ." Read Ishmael's description of Queequeg aloud. Before reading, divide the group in half. Ask the first half to list the details that reveal Queequeg and ask the other half to list the reactions, both inferences and judgments, that reveal Ishmael's attitudes about Queequeg and tattooing. Discuss the lists.

2. Examine the techniques Melville uses in Ishmael's first impression. Using the paragraph as a model, write a first impression paragraph. In describing the character, the speaker should reveal himself.

3. Ask a student or students to write to the agencies listed on page 60 of *The Dangers of Tattooing and Body Piercing* for information. Compare the information received on the basis of fact, inference, and judgment. Discuss which sources have more credibility and why.

4. In *Street Gangs* by Evan Stark, Stark cites a program that helps former gang members remove tattoos. After reading *Street Gangs*, write or discuss why having a tattoo might be a gang requirement.

5. Read selections from "Self-Inflicted Wounds" in *Ophelia Speaks*. Compare the purposes and effects of a tattoo and a self-inflicted scar.

## *Related Works*

1. Curran, Christine Perdan. **Sexually Transmitted Diseases**. See full booktalk in Chapter 3 (p. 142). Curran talks about the relationship between tattooing and sexually transmitted diseases.

2. Gard, Carolyn. "Think Before You Ink." *Current Health* 2 (February 1999): 2 pages beginning on 24. Gard gives reasons for teens opting for tattooing or body piercing and the problems they may encounter. An inset, "Body Art Without the Pain," describes an alternative to permanent tattooing or piercing.

3. Melville, Herman. **Moby Dick**. Edited by Charles Feidelson Jr. New York: Bobbs-Merrill Company, 1964. (The Library of Literature). Ahab hunts for the great white whale.

4. Seligson, Susan. "Permanent Ink." *Walking Magazine* (January/February 1999): 3 pages beginning on 34. Seligson describes the tattoo process, the popularity of the fad, and the possible physical and emotional results.

5. Shandler, Sara. **Ophelia Speaks**. See full booktalk in Chapter 2 (p. 126). The selections in "Self-Inflicted Wounds" are powerful and graphic. The presenter may wish to judge the appropriateness of the language and images for use with some audiences.

6. Stark, Evan. **Street Gangs**. New York: The Rosen Publishing Group, 1995 rev. ed. 64p. (The Need to Know Library). $17.95. ISBN 0-8239-2121-2. Stark emphasizes the gang's possession of a person. He then distinguishes between destructive and constructive gangs.

## FAMILY DECISIONS

Denenberg, Barry. **The Journal of William Thomas Emerson: A Revolutionary War Patriot**. New York: Scholastic, 1998. 152p. (Dear America: My Name Is America). $10.95. ISBN 0-590-31350-9.

### *Summary/Description*

When a storm kills his family, ten-year-old Will lives with and works for an abusive farmer for two years. He then runs away and meets Mr. Wilson, who takes him to Boston and finds him a job with Mrs. Thompson, an innkeeper. Will becomes a spy for Mr. Wilson and the other Revolutionaries. The book ends when the British army moves into town, and Will decides to stay and help Mrs. Thompson during the occupation. The book shows the daily life of the period, the cruelties, and the communications of both sides. It includes sample documents, notices, and pamphlets. The author also includes pictures illustrating the environments, punishments, and occupations described in the book. Maps, including a foldout map of Boston, show where the story takes place. An epilogue explains what happens to each of the characters, and an historical note explains the background. The story of Will's life in Boston begins in the summer of 1774 and ends in the spring of 1775.

## *Booktalk*

Ask how many people in the audience have held jobs. Ask them to explain their jobs, what kind of pay they received, and how many hours they worked per week.

William Thomas Emerson is a twelve-year-old boy looking for a full-time job. An orphan at ten and a runaway at twelve, he must support himself. Mr. Wilson who finds Will on the side of the road knows an innkeeper who needs a worker. The person hired will have a good basement room and three meals a day. But, really, Mr. Wilson has an even bigger job in mind for Will. The American Revolution is starting. The British have spies, and the rebels need spies also. Will can move quickly and keep quiet. People trust him, and the inn has many strangers passing through. Will listens to the secret meetings and reads the anti-British editorials. When he quietly decides to take his first assignment from Mr. Wilson, he knows that the wrong word or move can mean death, but, at that moment, William Thomas Emerson becomes "A Revolutionary War Patriot."

## *Related Activities*

1. Research the status of slaves, indentured servants, and apprentices at the time of the Revolutionary War. Discuss how these classifications apply to the novel.

2. Pages 81 and 83 show a letter written in code and deciphered. Ask students to write a code letter of their own.

3. Pages 30, 31, 48, 95, 105–6, and 115–17 are examples of the types of documents circulated during the revolutionary period. Discuss each in terms of its speaker, audience, technique, and purpose.

4. Compare the writing and meeting activities of Mr. Wilson with those of Samuel Adams. Discuss why the author would choose to write about the period before the actual fighting began.

5. *Come All You Brave Soldiers* describes the role of James Armistead in the Revolutionary War. Compare Armistead's role, described in a nonfiction account, with William Thomas Emerson's role, in a fiction account. Discuss why each spy was able to be so successful.

## *Related Works*

1. Collier, James Lincoln. **My Brother Sam Is Dead**. New York: Four Winds Press, 1974. A young man in New England is caught between loyalty to his brother, who is part of the Revolution, and his family, who wish to stay neutral.

2. Cox, Clinton. **Come All You Brave Soldiers**. See full booktalk in Chapter 3 (p. 155). Cox describes Armistead's role as a spy.

3. Fradin, Dennis. **Samuel Adams: The Father of American Independence**. See full booktalk in Chapter 4 (p. 234). Fradin describes Adams's controversial role in fueling the American Revolution.

4. The History Channel, in cooperation with the Smithsonian National Museum of American History. **The Star-Spangled Banner Project: Teacher's Manual**. New York: A&E Television Networks, 1998. 54p. (Save Our History). Free. This guide accompanies the History Channel' s *The Star-Spangled Banner*. The program discusses the composition of the "Star-Spangled Banner" during the War of 1812. The teacher's guide offers activities for students in grades K–8.

5. Rinaldi, Ann. **Cast Two Shadows**. See full booktalk below (p. 46). The main character is pulled by loyalties to two armies and two races.

6. Sterman, Betsy. **Saratoga Secret**. See full booktalk below (p. 21). The main character discovers her own strength and her true love as she carries a secret message to Benedict Arnold.

Peck, Robert Newton. **Cowboy Ghost**. New York: HarperCollins Children's Books, 1999. 200p. $15.95. ISBN 0-06-028168-5.

## *Summary/Description*

In *Cowboy Ghost*, Titus Timothy MacRobertson grows to manhood. The "Prologue" introduces the close relationship among Titus, Mrs. Krickitt (the housekeeper), and Micah (Titus's brother). When Titus's mother dies giving birth to Titus, Titus's father shuts himself off from both sons. Mrs. Krickett comforts Micah, and Micah, thirteen years older than Titus, becomes the father figure. Micah is the big, muscular son, for whom his father arranges boxing matches. Titus, the runt who favors his mother's side, his father ignores. In 1924, when Titus is sixteen, he and his brother join the ranch's cattle drive. They face hostile Indians, rugged storms, and robbers. When both the foreman and Micah are killed, only the unseasoned Titus can take over the drive. He accepts the responsibility, despite a bullet wound, proves to himself and his father that no man has to be big to be tough, and discovers that the toughest and biggest man can also be the loneliest.

## *Booktalk*

In *Cowboy Ghost,* Titus Timothy MacRobertson is "a skinny kid [who] owns a tree for a brother." Titus thinks he'd be better if he were bigger, like his brother, Micah. Then, at least, his dad would love him. But before he has time to grow, he must prove himself on a cattle drive to his father's cattle hands, the men who know the mysteries of The Bent Ace Saloon. With Micah as his guide, Titus faces Indians, storms, and robbers. During the journey, he finds out that the size of a man's heart is as important as the size of a man's fist. But more important, he discovers that each man must follow his own trail.

## *Related Activities*

1. Compare Micah's poem and Titus's writing assignment. What does each piece of writing reveal about the writer?
2. Titus learns about himself on his journey, but his brother and father have experienced journeys also. Discuss why Titus's is the most successful.

3. Research the ranches, cowboys and Indians of Florida. Mark ranching areas on a map.
4. Form four reading groups. Assign each reading group one of the following novels: *Cowboy Ghost*, *Holes*, *Transall Saga*, and *Sang Spell.* All four novels involve mystical survival journeys. Compare the physical journeys and how the mystical or magical influences each.
5. Read the prologue aloud. The prologue tells about Titus when he is seven years old, but the story starts when he is sixteen. Discuss why Peck includes the prologue.

## *Related Works*

1. Carter, Alden R. **Between a Rock and a Hard Place**. New York: Scholastic, 1995. 213p. $4.99. ISBN 0-590-37489-9. In a survival rite of passage, cousins gain respect for themselves, each other, and the wilderness.
2. Naylor, Phyllis Reynolds. **Sang Spell**. See full booktalk in Chapter 3 (p. 187). The main character learns to rely on his own sincerity and determination when he is trapped in a mystical world.
3. Paulsen, Gary. **The Transall Saga**. See full booktalk in Chapter 3 (p. 192). The main character learns manhood in an other-world survival adventure.
4. Sachar, Louis. **Holes**. See full booktalk below (p. 35). The main character believes that a gypsy curse controls his life. A survival journey convinces him of his own strengths.
5. Wynne-Jones, Tim. **Stephen Fair**. See full booktalk below (p. 56). Two brothers become closer as they deal with family mysteries and a distant father.

Bloor, Edward. **Tangerine**. New York: Scholastic, 1997. 294p. (An Apple Signature Edition). $4.99pa. ISBN 0-590-43277-X.

## *Summary/Description*

Paul and his family have just moved to an upper-class housing development in Tangerine County, Florida. Although legally blind, Paul wants the starting goalie position on the middle school soccer team. His mother wants to become part of the Homeowners' Association. His father wants to move up in the county engineer's office. Erik, Paul's older brother, wants to be a high school football star and eventually an NBA star. According to Erik, Paul's blindness developed when Paul stared at an eclipse for a full hour. Paul's diary, the format of the book, helps him sort out the real circumstances of the accident, his personal strengths, and the fear and sadness he feels about his family.

*Tangerine* is divided into three major parts. In Part One, Paul explains his family, meets the neighbors, and settles into Lake Windsor Middle School, where he is prevented from playing soccer because of his eyesight. Lightning strikes and kills a high school football player who is in competition with Erik, and a sinkhole swallows the school's portable classrooms. Paul wants to play soccer and so takes the opportunity to transfer to the poorer and tougher Tangerine Middle School. In Part Two, Paul makes friends at Tangerine. He shows his toughness, loyalty, and respect as a member of the Tangerine championship team, and develops his love of the land and nature. Erik shows his cruelty by mocking the grieving brother of the dead football player, but then finds himself the center of a humiliating blooper football play. Paul's mother deals with a theft ring and environmental problems in the housing development, and Paul's father becomes the head of the county office. In Part Three, Paul remembers Erik blinded him with spray paint, helps two Tangerine soccer players when they settle a score with Erik, and reveals Erik's role in what may be judged a murder. Paul's mother discovers that Erik and his friend are the housing development thieves. Paul's father loses his dreams.

## *Booktalk*

Ask how many people fight with their brothers or sisters. Ask when the fighting is funny and when it is not. Ask what usually starts the fights.

Paul doesn't really fight with his brother. Paul tries to avoid him; otherwise, Paul might be dead. When Paul transfers to Tangerine Middle School, the "gangsta" school, he is pulled into some tough talking and fist action, and he thinks living with Erik has taught him how to handle it. But this time Paul has to confront trouble, not dodge it. *Tangerine* tells a story about lies and terror, and about people who can't see and about people who won't see. It tells about people who *look* tough and about people who *are* tough. The story also tells about people who love money and fame, and people who love people and the land. Paul must choose a side and take a stand.

## *Related Activities*

1. *Tenderness*, *Making Up Megaboy*, and *Tangerine* present three distinct pictures of juvenile offenders. Ask each reader to describe the offender in each book. Discuss each author's purpose in the characterizations.

2. *When She Was Good* presents a picture of family abuse and violence between sisters. Compare this abusive situation with the abusive situation between Paul and his brother in *Tangerine*. You may wish to refer to "What Is Abuse?" in *Family Violence*.

3. Both *Tangerine* and *The Spirit Window* present the dangers developers pose to Florida. Ask readers to compare the environmental issues and each author's treatment of those issues.

4. In *The Great Eye* and *Tangerine* the main characters must, with the help of their families, become more independent. Trace the processes of independence in each novel and compare them.

5. Throughout *Tangerine* and *Stephen Fair*, the main characters struggle with a vague but troubling memory. The conclusion of each novel involves the clarification of that memory. Ask readers to describe the clarifications and the effect each clarification has on the characters.

## *Related Works*

1. Cormier, Robert. **Tenderness**. See full booktalk in Chapter 2 (p. 64). A serial killer is released because he committed the murders when he was a juvenile.

2. Mazer, Norma Fox. **When She Was Good**. See full booktalk in Chapter 3 (p. 176). An older, mentally ill woman abuses her younger sister.

3. Shalant, Phyllis. **The Great Eye**. New York: Puffin Books, 1996. 150p. $4.99pa. ISBN 0-14-130072-8. When the main character's family changes drastically, she must build her own life.

4. Stark, Evan. **Family Violence**. New York: The Rosen Publishing Group, 1997 rev. ed. 64p. (The Need to Know Library). $17.95. ISBN 0-8239-2293-6. The book defines abuse and explains what can be done about it.

5. Sweeney, Joyce. **The Spirit Window**. See full booktalk below. The main character's grandmother wishes to prevent irresponsible land development.

6. Walker, Virginia, and Katrina Roechelein. **Making Up Megaboy**. See full booktalk in Chapter 2 (p. 82). A young boy arrested for murder is represented sympathetically.

7. Wynne-Jones, Tim. **Stephen Fair**. See full booktalk below (p. 56). Dreams haunt the main character as he is troubled by family upheaval.

Sweeney, Joyce. **The Spirit Window**. New York: Delacorte Press, 1998. 243p.$15.95. ISBN 0-385-32510-X.

### *Summary/Description*

Miranda travels with her father and stepmother to visit her grandmother Lila, now diagnosed with a failing heart. Miranda discovers a deep spiritual kinship with Lila, from whom Miranda's father Richard has been estranged for ten years. During the family visit, the tensions that produced the rift resurface. These tensions intensify as Richard's friend, Skip, and Lila's friend, Adam, polarize the family. Finally, Miranda realizes her power to effect understanding and compromise. Her efforts save her father from losing his mother, wife, and daughter all at the same time.

### *Booktalk*

Our pictures remind us of good times, family, and friends. In *The Spirit Window,* Miranda tries to capture the reality of her family and their world with her camera. But her loving, flamboyant grandmother, self-conscious father, mysterious new boyfriend, and sprite-like stepmother all convince her that she can't just focus on pretty pictures. Miranda must take charge of the people and places in the pictures. Otherwise, she may lose her family, her boyfriend, and the land that they all hold dear.

## *Related Activities*

1. Build a collage that explains a turning point in your life. Choose black and white pictures and print to depict your situation before the turning point. Choose color pictures and print to depict your situation after the turning point. Then explain how the collage represents your experience and your new understanding.

2. Compare the characters of the novel with the characters of *The Tempest*. For example, why does the author use the names Ariel and Miranda? Which character in the play does Adam represent?

3. In Act 1, Scene 2 of *The Tempest*, Miranda and Prospero compare perceptions of his power as a father to calm the storm. How does their exchange apply to *The Spirit Window*?

4. One of the issues in *The Spirit Window* is people's responsibility for the preservation of nature and family. In Act 4, Scene 1 of *The Tempest*, Prospero speaks about the wedding masque or play. Read lines 168–85 aloud. How do these lines apply to the pictures Miranda takes? To the land deal Skip plans? To the death of Miranda's grandmother?

5. Construct a play, poem, message, joke, or short story around an allusion. You might use a modern version of Pip, Romeo, Juliet, or Madame DeFarge. You might speculate about what a modern George Washington, Franklin D. Roosevelt, or Lincoln would do in a modern-day situation.

6. In *The Spirit Window*, mother and son battle over the destruction of wildlife by developers. Are Lila's concerns based on knowledge or whim? Research the dangers of development in beach areas.

7. Read Chief Seattle's speech. (See *Dreamcatcher* in Related Works.) Ask students to apply the speech to *The Spirit Window*.

## *Related Works*

1. Bauer, Joan. **Backwater**. See full booktalk below (p. 28). Ivy Breedlow learns about the power and beauty of nature as she works to unify her family by writing a family history.

2. Hurwitz, Jane. **Coping in a Blended Family**. See full booktalk in Chapter 3 (p. 170). Hurwitz gives practical suggestions for building family closeness and trust.

3. Latimer, Jonathan P. (text), Karen Stray Nolting (text), and Roger Tory Peterson (illus). **Shorebirds**. New York: Houghton Mifflin, 1999. 48p. (Peterson Field Guides for Young Naturalists). $15.00. ISBN 0-395-95212-3. Latimer's guide lists birds that inhabit shore regions and a logical, simple method of observing them.

4. Maynard, Meredy. **Dreamcatcher**. Vancouver, BC: Polstar Press Ltd., 1995. 137p. $7.50. ISBN 1-896095-01-1. On pages 98 and 99, Jo reads an excerpt from Chief Seattle's speech of 1854. It talks about the relationship people should have with nature.

5. Shakespeare, William. **The Tempest: First Folio Edition** edited by Charlotte Porter and Helen A. Clarke. New York: Thomas Y. Crowell, 1908. The play includes magic, romance, and the pains of growing up.

6. Sterman, Betsy. **Saratoga Secret**. See full booktalk below. The main character finds true love on a journey to save her family and country.

 Sterman, Betsy. **Saratoga Secret**. New York: Dial Books for Young Readers, 1998. 249p. $16.99. ISBN 0-8037-2332-6.

### *Summary/Description*

Sixteen-year-old Amity Spencer lives near Saratoga, New York. Cheppa John, a peddler, brings news that the British, under Gentleman Johnny Burgoyne, are marching through New York to defeat the Continental Army. Amity's father leaves with the other men to join the rebels. Amity and her mother must care for the farm and Amity's baby brother. Their neighbor, Matt, seriously wounded, returns from battle with a letter stolen from Burgoyne's spy. The letter was intended for Cheppa John, whom Amity now fears is a spy. Amity must carry the letter to Benedict Arnold to warn the American troops of Burgoyne's attack. Through her journey and successfully delivering the letter, Amity discovers her own strength, Cheppa John's loyalty to his country, and his love for her. The novel ends with Burgoyne's surrender and the successful return of the men who left to fight.

In "A Note from the Author," Betsy Sterman explains France's involvement in the Revolution; General Burgoyne's perception of the colonies; the history of Tim Murphy, who shot General Fraser and may have decided the Battle of Saratoga; the plight of the German soldiers; and Benedict Arnold's decision to commit treason.

## Booktalk

Ask the following questions: How many people here have told a secret to someone and then found out that person told someone else? Do you want to talk about the consequences? Probably not. Amity Spencer has an entire country's fate in her hands. She alone knows when Burgoyne will attack the Continental Army. If she tells the wrong person, her father and friends will die. At sixteen, she must travel roads full of spies, robbers, and enemy soldiers to deliver a message to Benedict Arnold, a man she has never seen. In a "World Turned Upside Down," she must question friends, family, and even the man she hoped to marry. Her *Saratoga Secret* may either destroy her world or help her discover not only her love of country but also the love of her life.

## Related Activities

1. *Saratoga Secret* and *Cast Two Shadows* are both about girls on secret missions to save lives during the Revolutionary War. List the differences between the two novels. Discuss which novel is more serious, and why.

2. *Saratoga Secret* includes mercenaries. Compare the poems "Epitaph on an Army of Mercenaries" and "Another Epitaph on an Army of Mercenaries" in *War and the Pity of War*. Discuss each speaker's view of mercenaries.

3. Compare the view of the mercenaries in *War and the Pity of War* with Rinaldi's description of mercenaries in the Revolutionary period. Research mercenaries and their role in battle.

4. Benedict Arnold is usually associated with treason. In *Saratoga Secret*, he is the general who achieves the victory. Take on the role of Amity Spencer or Cheppa John. Write a letter or journal entry in which either reacts to the news of Arnold's treason.

5. After viewing *Benedict Arnold: Triumph and Treason*, choose one significant event or situation in Benedict Arnold's life. Write the journal entry you feel he would have written about that event or situation.

## *Related Works*

1. **Benedict Arnold: Triumph and Treason**. Produced by A&E Television Networks, 1995. 50 min. Color. (Biography). $14.95. AAE-14017. Videocassette. The video describes how Arnold grew up, how he became a successful and envied military man, and how his personal life influenced his tragic decision to commit treason.

2. Denenberg, Barry. **The Journal of William Thomas Emerson: A Revolutionary War Patriot**. See full booktalk above (p. 12). The main character serves as a spy for the Boston patriots.

3. Fradin, Dennis. **Samuel Adams: The Father of American Independence**. See full booktalk in Chapter 4 (p. 234). The book tells how Adams fueled the revolutionary fire through his writing.

4. Philip, Neil, ed., and Michael McCurdy (illus). **War and the Pity of War**. See full booktalk below (p. 44). "Epitaph on an Army of Mercenaries" by A. E. Housman and "Another Epitaph on an Army of Mercenaries" by Hugh MacDiarmid present contrasting views about soldiers for hire.

5. Rinaldi, Ann. **Cast Two Shadows**. See full booktalk below (p. 46). The main character is torn between nations and races as she works to help her entire family.

Trembath, Don. **The Tuesday Cafe**. Victoria, BC: Orca, 1996. 121p. $6.95pa. ISBN-55143-074-6.

## *Summary/Description*

In *The Tuesday Cafe*, Harper Winslow is a distant, angry teenager who expresses his anger by setting a fire in the school hallway. The judge sentences him to write an essay about his future, so his mother enrolls him in a writing class named The Tuesday Cafe. By mistake, Harper has enrolled in a class with adults who are having difficulty reading and writing. But Harper chooses to stay, and when he starts sharing his writing with his fellow students, he begins to talk with his guidance counselor and his parents as well. By the end of the book, Harper has learned that he can have a better life with better communication.

## *Booktalk*

Hold up a thermometer. Point to the thermostat. Ask the students to explain the difference between these two items.

Everything happens to Harper Winslow. He gets arrested when it isn't his fault. His parents constantly want to improve him. His classmates pick on him, and he never gets invited to a party. He is a thermometer just recording his own slow burn in reaction to the people around him. Finally, he heats up and then heats up the school by setting a fire. That fire sends him to court, and when the judge orders Harper to write a 2,000-word essay on how he's going to turn his life around, Harper composes his essay and himself in a very different school called The Tuesday Cafe.

## *Related Activities*

1. Complete the same writing assignments completed in *The Tuesday Cafe*.

   a. "My Sunday," chapter 6

   b. soap opera episode, chapter 7

   c. free write letter to Mom and Dad, chapter 9

   d. a turn-yourself-around essay, chapter 13; read the actual directions on page 104

2. Analyze the voice of the personal narrator, Harper Winslow. Start each class for sixteen days by reading a chapter aloud. Discuss who Harper Winslow is in each chapter. How does he reveal himself, and how does he change?

3. Compare other first-person voices. The narrator in each of the following novels describes his world and reveals himself.

   a. *Catcher in the Rye*: Read the passage beginning, "This book I was reading . . ." on pages 18 and 19 in Chapter 3.

   b. *Parrot in the Oven*: Read the passage beginning, "I wasn't like Nardo . . ." on pages 6 and 7 in Chapter 1.

   c. *Huckleberry Finn*: Read the passage beginning, "You read about them once . . ." on pages 382 and 383 in Chapter 23.

4. Analyze the journey. In *The Tuesday Cafe*, Harper Winslow experiences his journey through unexpected friendships. What insight or gift does each person bring to Harper? Discuss which character is most important to Harper's change.

5. Sean Parker, the main character in *Hero,* writes an essay about his hero. Compare the "turn-yourself-around" essay in Chapter 13 of *The Tuesday Cafe* and the "hero" essay of *Hero*. Read each essay aloud. Ask the students to describe what the essays reveal about each of the writers.

6. Many visitors in Harper Winslow's life change his thinking. Read "The Visitor" in *Making Shapely Fiction.* Then discuss the use of the visitor in *The Tuesday Cafe.*

## *Related Works*

1. Martinez, Victor. **Parrot in the Oven**. See full booktalk in Chapter 2 (p. 112). The main character describes his situation and sorts out his life.

2. Rottman, S. L. **Hero**. See full booktalk in Chapter 4 (p. 223). Through his court-assigned experience, the main character discovers the meaning of heroism.

3. Salinger, J. D. **The Catcher in the Rye**. New York: Bantam, 1945. The main character reveals his anger and fear through his description of his world.

4. Stern, Jerome. "Visitation." In **Making Shapely Fiction**. New York: Laurel Books, 1991. 283p. $6.50pa. ISBN 0-440-21221-9. Stern describes the visitation story, its relationship to the journey story, and its purpose.

5. Twain, Mark. "Adventures of Huckleberry Finn." In **The Portable Mark Twain**. New York: Viking Press, 1966. The main character decides where he belongs in the world after a journey filled with new people and places.

# NATURE'S PATTERN

Branford, Henrietta. **White Wolf**. Cambridge, MA: Candlewick Press, 1998. 96p. $16.99. ISBN 0-7636-0748-7.

### *Summary/Description*

*White Wolf* is the story of a wolf cub that moves back into the wild. Jim and his son Jesse capture White Wolf and raise him as a dog. Snap, a mother dog with new pups, nurtures him. The Native Americans, who come to the trading post, see White Wolf as a god, attack the father and son, and steal the wolf. With Jesse's help, White Wolf escapes, joins a pack, and eventually forms his own pack. Finally, White Wolf is able to reunite with Snap and save Jesse's life.

### *Booktalk*

The white man wants to raise the wolf as a dog. The Native Americans want to send his soul to "travel the spirit world." Men will kill him and each other to fit him into their world, but White Wolf wants his own world. He will join a pack, choose his mate, raise his cubs, and form his own pack Yet he owes his life to a boy and a dog. Each world calls to him, and White Wolf knows that his heart belongs to both.

### *Related Activities*

1. Read the opening paragraph on page 20 of Chapter 3 in *White Wolf.* Read two paragraphs in *Call of the Wild.* Begin with "And Buck was truly a red-eyed devil," in Chapter 1. Both describe training a wolf dog. What are the differences in the descriptions? Discuss which description has the greater emotional effect on the listener, and why.

2. Read the poem "Direction" by Alonzo Lopez. "Direction" talks about the assets people may acquire from each animal. Discuss what the Native Americans hope to acquire from the White Wolf. List several animals and the trait or skill each might contribute or teach to people.

3. Write a poem about or from the point of view of one of the animals or people shown in the tape *Cry of the Wild: Wolves, Fires and the Fight*.

4. Read pages 57–59 in *White Wolf.* Thin Moon's story explains the relationship between the seasons and the life cycle. Find a nature myth, such as the story of Proserpine. Read the nature myth you have selected and compare the techniques used in the myth with those used in Thin Moon's story. Then write a short nature myth of your own.

5. White Fang, Buck in *Call of the Wild*, and White Wolf each undergoes a change or metamorphosis. Compare the changes that occur and the circumstances that bring about the changes.

6. Different people in the novel classify White Wolf differently. Therefore, they treat him differently. Discuss how he is treated when he is classified as a pet, a wolf, and a god. Each of us also has many different classifications: a brother or sister, student, son or daughter, or worker. Select three ways in which you are classified. Explain how each classification affects how you are treated. Explain how the expectations of those three labels or classifications may conflict.

## *Related Works*

1. Branford, Henrietta. **Fire Bed and Bone**. See full booktalk in Chapter 2 (p. 68). This Branford novel tells the story of a dog pulled between people and the wild.

2. **Cry of the Wild: Wolves, Fires and the Fight**. Produced by A&E Home Video, 1996. 50 min. Color. (20th Century with Mike Wallace). $19.95. AAE-21537. Videocassette. The tape presents the battle to keep Yellowstone ecologically balanced and preserved as a national park. It presents people and their machines as the biggest threats.

3. London, Jack. "Call of the Wild." In **Jack London**. New York: Amaranth Press, 1984. (Masters Library). A dog is stolen and sent to the wild, where he learns to survive.

4. London, Jack. "White Fang." In **Jack London**. New York: Amaranth Press, 1984. (Masters Library). A half-dog, half-wolf pup learns to live with and love a man.

5. Lopez, Alonzo. "Directions." In **Life Doesn't Frighten Me at All** edited by John Agard. New York: Henry Holt, 1989. Lopez explains what people can learn from each of the animals listed.

Bauer, Joan. **Backwater**. New York: G. P. Putnam's Sons, 1999. 185p. $16.99. ISBN 0399-23141-2.

## *Summary/Description*

Sixteen-year-old Ivy Breedlow wants to be a historian, not a lawyer like the generations of Breedlows before her. In proving her own worth and researching the family history, she decides to interview Aunt Josephine, a hermit. According to the Breedlows, Josephine is "stuck in the backwater" of life. She is an embarrassment because she has chosen solitude over money, confrontation, and power. When Ivy begins her survivalist journey to interview Josephine, she seeks help from Mountain Mama, a local wilderness guide who is also writing a book. During the journey she meets Jack, a would-be ranger trying to make up for a "D" in Search and Rescue class. The encounters and disasters that follow prove to Ivy that different people are good people, good things and strong character come from taking risks and embracing hard work, and boyfriends show up when least expected.

## *Booktalk*

Ask how many people know what they want to do for the rest of their lives. Ask how many people want to do something different than their parents or family did.

Ivy Breedlow knows what she wants to do for the rest of her life, and her plans are different from the Breedlow plan. In the Breedlow family, being different is a bad idea. In fact, no one even talks about Ivy's Aunt Josephine, who has chosen to be a hermit. But Ivy is a dedicated historian, and a good historian talks about everybody. When Ivy hears about the mystery lady who shows up in the Breedlow garden and graveyard every year, she knows the lady is Aunt Josephine and knows she must find her. But during the journey Ivy learns that getting the whole story may mean risking her whole life.

## *Related Activities*

1. Interview a family member who is at least fifteen years older than you are. You may want to ask questions about education, friends, family, and work. Use report language only. Write a report about that person. In the report, place him or her in the context of the larger family's pattern of education, friends, family, and work. Note how the person has and has not followed the family pattern.

2. *Backwater* uses several nature images, including the title itself. Identify at least five nature images in the novel. Answer the following questions about each: What do you usually associate with the image? How is the image used in *Backwater*? How does it help Joan Bauer accomplish her purpose?

3. Mountain Mama tells Ivy that she is planning to write a bestseller, *One Mountain at a Time*. It will explain "how to" explore the wilderness and life. Choose one of the chapter titles and write a chapter for the book. Let the chapter deal with just physical survival, just emotional survival, or both. Discuss why the topics of wilderness survival and emotional survival can be so closely linked.

4. Both *Rules of the Road* and *Backwater* involve strong characters choosing a career. Both involve journeys. Both involve supporting characters who might be considered rugged individualists. Identify and discuss the differences between the two books.

5. Read "Dear Dad" by Sheila Gonzalez, aloud. Describe the speaker. Describe the situation. Explain the speaker's purpose in speaking. Describe the speaker's tone. What do you think the relationship between father and daughter was and will be? Compare the father/daughter relationship to the relationship between Mr. Breedlow and Ivy.

6. Write a poem or monologue in which Ivy Breedlow is the speaker. Decide to which relative she will speak and for what purpose.

7. Write a poem or monologue in which you are the speaker. Decide to which relative or authority figure you will speak and for what purpose.

## *Related Works*

1. Bauer, Joan. **Rules of the Road**. See full booktalk in Chapter 2 (p. 114). The main character makes a major career move and life change when the company's owner asks her to be the driver on a cross-country tour of all the company's stores.

2. Gonzalez, Sheila. "Dear Dad." In **Workplace Communication: Learner's Guide, Module 1**. Cincinnati, OH: Communication 2000, Agency for Instructional Technology and South-Western Educational Publishing, 1996. $11.00. ISBN 0-538-63495-2. A daughter confronts her father about their relationship.

3. Latimer, Jonathan P. (text), Karen Stray Nolting (text), and Roger Tory Peterson (illus). **Backyard Birds**. Boston: Houghton Mifflin, 1999. 48p. (Peterson Field Guides for Young Naturalists). $15.00. ISBN 0-395-95212-3. The guide describes and tells how to identify the birds for which Ivy Breedlow's aunt cares.

4. McCaughrean, Geraldine. **The Pirate's Son**. See full booktalk in Chapter 2 (p. 74). With his friends' help, the main character is able to throw off a seer's prediction that he too will become a ruthless pirate.

5. Peck, Robert Newton. **Cowboy Ghost**. See full booktalk above (p. 15). On a dangerous cattle drive, the main character discovers his strength and character.

6. Sachar, Louis. **Holes**. See full booktalk below (p. 35). The main character decides that he is free from the family curse and free to make his own luck and decisions.

Hesse, Karen. **Out of the Dust**. New York: Scholastic, 1997. 227p. $4.99. ISBN 0-590-37125-8.

## *Summary/Description*

In a series of poems, fourteen-year-old Billie Joe tells her story within the context of the Oklahoma Dust Bowl and the Great Depression. Bright and artistic, she is both inspired and thwarted by the bleak land and the struggles of the people who stay on it. Billie Joe and her father share the guilt of the accidental fire that kills her mother and unborn brother. She suffers with the pain of her burned hands, her destroyed dreams, and her mother's death. Her father turns his grief to fighting the dust and floods that destroy his crops. Both share the great loneliness of unexpressed desperation. But together or individually, each chooses a path that pulls them both *Out of the Dust.*

## *Booktalk*

Ask if any students have heard of the Great Depression and the Dust Bowl. Note the years these events took place. Show the area of the Dust Bowl on the map. Show pictures from the Depression and Dust Bowl.

Billie Joe is fourteen when the Dust Bowl begins to swallow her home, her parents, and her. The dust is so thick that the white milk turns chocolate and potatoes, just put on the table, look doused in pepper. Her father seems old and beaten. But Mad Dog, with a beautiful voice and a face to match, Arley Wanderdale, and the Black Mesa Boys offer her happiness and success. Will she stay with her father and the land he loves, or strike out on her own to the promises that music and education have given her? Dust and sorrow cloud her vision, but with the music of her poetry, she tells her story, and in telling it, tries to lead herself *Out of the Dust.*

## *Related Activities*

1. Research the Dust Bowl. Find out the causes that came from both nature and man.

2. Both Billie Joe from *Out of the Dust* and Josh from *No Promises in the Wind* are teenagers during the Depression. Both are alienated from their parents. Both lose a first love. Both deal with the grief of death. Both turn to music for comfort. List as many additional similarities as you can between the two novels. Choose two from the list and discuss how each element is used in each story.

3. Billie Jo writes a poem about each of her reactions. Choose one or two of her poem titles. Using the title as an idea, write about your own experiences. List as many pictures and sensations as you can remember and then organize your list into a poem.

4. Interview someone who lived during the Depression. Establish how old that person was during the Depression. Discuss how his or her experiences compare with those in *Out of the Dust* and *No Promises in the Wind.* For your interview, you may want to draw on the suggestions from *Telling Your Own Stories* by Don Davis.

5. Compare Billie Joe in *Out of the Dust* and Weak-One-Who-Does-Not-Last from *The Sacrifice*. Even though they live in different centuries, what struggles, realizations, and feelings do they share?

6. In Chapter 5 of *Grapes of Wrath* Steinbeck describes the families, tenants, and landowners of the Oklahoma Dust Bowl. Read from the beginning of Chapter 5 to the words, "The tractors came over the roads . . ." What do Billie Joe and her father have in common with these people? How is their situation different? Discuss what Steinbeck is trying to communicate in his description.

### *Related Works*

1. Davis, Donald. **Telling Your Own Stories**. Little Rock, AR: August House Publishers, 1993. 127p. (American Storytelling). $10.00pa. ISBN 0-8783-235-7. The author provides prompts and methods for getting people to tell their own stories.
2. Hunt, Irene. **No Promises in the Wind**. New York: Berkley Books, 1970. The main character, his brother, and a friend leave home to find work during the Depression.
3. Janeczko, Paul B. **How to Write Poetry**. See full booktalk in Chapter 4 (p. 215). Methods, tips, and examples help the starting poet experiment with and get control of verse.
4. Matcheck, Diane. **The Sacrifice**. See full booktalk in Chapter 2 (p. 89). The main character embraces struggle and pain as she travels away from her home and back again on a journey of self-discovery.
5. Steinbeck, John. **Grapes of Wrath**. New York: Penguin Books, 1967. An Oklahoma farming family seeks survival as it flees Oklahoma to find work in California.

## Steger, Will, and Jon Bowermaster. **Over the Top of the World: Explorer Will Steger's Trek Across the Arctic**. New York: Scholastic, 1997. 63p. $5.99pa. ISBN 0-590-84861-5.

### *Summary/Description*

Will Steger describes his *Over the Top of the World* trek with other team members. They face cold, snow, and frigid waters. The journey is a meeting of basic human needs and high technology. Steger explains the clothing, food, and navigational supplies that keep the team safe and alive in a world of emergencies. The detail of this narration shows both the preparation and daring required to earn the title "explorer." Steger includes biographical information about both the people and dogs in the expedition. Dark blue insets form a book within the book. These insets explain some Arctic history and geography; the group's shopping list, menu, wardrobe, and communication; and the Arctic population and pollution. Colored pictures throughout the book provide a good feel for the terrain and the men and women who selected the task.

## *Booktalk*

You can eat 5,000 calories a day for fifty-eight days and still lose nine pounds. Just follow the *Over the Top of the World* fitness and training program! Will Steger and his team literally walk on water as they trek across the Arctic Ocean—an ocean Steger describes as a "bucket of water with a thin layer of dust on the surface." As the first team to ever cross the Arctic in one season, they needed preparation, cooperation, and tenacity, plus 10,000 pounds of dog food. At any time, they could have drowned or frozen to death in a world that constantly shifts, cracks, and whistles as it freezes and melts. In his story, Stager tells how he cooperated with man, beast, and high technology to explore a land he would never truly know but would always love.

## *Related Activities*

1. Complete the simulation "Broken Squares." Discuss what the simulation teaches about cooperation. See number 5 in Related Works.

2. List the supplies for a typical school day and tell how the supplies should be prepared. Have members of the group exchange the lists and react to them in journals. Then discuss the lists and reactions in class. Ask each person to revise his or her original list and write a paragraph that explains why certain items were included or excluded.

3. Choose an event that requires cooperation, such as a school dance, a trip, or a sale. As a group, prepare a list of materials needed for this event. Exchange with another group. Ask the group to write down their reactions. Discuss the results in class. If opinions differ, discuss sources of information the students might use to clarify the task.

4. Chapter 5 of *The Call of the Wild* describes the disaster that befalls an ignorant and unprepared traveler in the Yukon. Read the description

of the preparation and trip. It begins on page 42 with the words "Buck heard . . ." and ends with the chapter on page 50. After reading the passage, ask students to write down their reactions. Then discuss their reactions in relation to cooperation, kindness, and respect.

5. Stager and Bowermaster include background inserts throughout the book. These include "The History of Arctic Exploration," "The Arctic Ocean," "The Dogs," "Food," "Keeping Warm in the Arctic," "Communicating with the World," "Pollution in the Arctic," "The Peoples of the Arctic," "The Canoe-Sleds," and "Animals of the Arctic." Choose one of these topics and find as much additional information about it as you can.

## *Related Works*

1. Dyer, Daniel. **Jack London: A Biography**. See full booktalk in Chapter 4 (p. 199). The biography tells the experiences that helped London develop his stories.

2. Hacker, Carlotta. **Explorers**. New York: Crabtree Publishing, 1998. 48p. (Women in Profile). $8.95pa. ISBN 0-7787-0004-6. The book describes women explorers of the world and outer space. It provides a good basis and format for factual reporting.

3. Hacker, Carlotta. "Matthew Henson." In **Great African Americans in History**. New York: Crabtree Publishing, 1997. 64p. (Outstanding African Americans). $8.95pa. ISBN 0-86505-805-9. The passage profiles Matthew Henson, the co-discoverer of the North Pole, and tells how he was denied credit until after his death.

4. London, Jack. "Call of the Wild." In **Jack London**. New York: Amaranth Press, 1984. The chapter cited in "Related Activities" describes a disastrous expedition fueled only by arrogance.

5. Pfeiffer, J. William, and John E. Jones. "Broken Squares." In **A Handbook of Structured Experiences for Human Relations Training, Volume I**. Iowa City, IA: University Associates Press, 1969. The exercise requires the group to assemble five squares. All members must share their puzzle pieces and participate in the placement for the squares to be completed correctly.

Sachar, Louis. **Holes**. New York: Farrar, Straus & Giroux, 1998. 233p. $16.00. ISBN 0-374-33265-7.

### *Summary/Description*

*Holes* is realistic fiction that combines three narratives. Stanley Yelnats is wrongfully convicted of stealing Clyde "Sweet Feet" Livingston's $5,000 tennis shoes. Actually, he picks the shoes up after they come flying at him. Stanley takes the shoes because his father is trying to invent a way to recycle old tennis shoes. Stanley is sentenced to Camp Green Lake, a desert camp for boys where each boy must dig a five-foot by five-foot hole each day. The assignment is supposed to build character, but Stanley figures out that the camp authorities are looking for something. While Stanley digs, he reflects on his family curse, which he feels is the real reason he has come to this camp. His great-great-grandfather broke his promise to a gypsy. She gave him a pig to pay for a bride. In return, he had to carry the gypsy up the mountain to the waters that run uphill. Deciding against the marriage, he left for America and forgot his promise. His family carried the gypsy's curse and Stanley now refers to him as his "dirty-rotten-pig-stealing-great-great-grandfather." The third narrative involves Stanley's great-grandfather. A notorious outlaw, Kissin' Kate Barlow, stole the great-grandfather's entire fortune and left him in the desert to die. He survived; however, without his fortune.

When Stanley is in the dormitory complex, he must think about the group pressure rather than his ancestor's misfortunes. He finds himself with streetwise boys whose nicknames tell their status. Afraid to make trouble and exhausted from the work, Stanley bows to the pressures. He becomes known as Caveman. When he finds an interesting clue in his hole, he gives it to the leader. But one boy, Zero, does not fit in with the group or the counselors. He asks Stanley to teach him to read. In return, Zero will dig part of a hole each day for Stanley. When this agreement produces fighting in the group, Zero runs away into the desert. The camp authorities decide that he will die in the heat, and because he is a ward of the state, they erase his records. Stanley goes after Zero. He figures out that he is in the area where his great-grandfather was robbed, and carries Zero up the mountain that saved his great-grandfather's life. Here they find water that runs uphill. They return to the camp, find the grandfather's fortune in the hole that contained the interesting clue, and discover that a lawyer and officer from the state are there to save them. Both Stanley and Zero become wealthy from the find. In addition, the father has secured a valuable patent on a tennis shoe deodorizer. Zero, coincidentally, is the great-great-grandson of the gypsy, and the one who stole Clyde's shoes in the first place. Clyde, whose smelly shoes sent Stanley to prison, endorses the product. Stanley gains friends, confidence, and wealth. The story explores how Stanley finds his own identity. His independence grows as his choices make him physically, morally, and psychologically stronger.

## *Booktalk*

The Warden wears rattlesnake venom nail polish; Mr. Sir tells the campers to run away whenever they want because they'll die in the desert; the counselor makes fun of the campers. Welcome to Camp Green Lake. But there really isn't a lake anymore, just miles of sand, rattlesnakes, tarantulas, lizards, and *Holes*. The campers dig the holes, and Stanley Yelnats is one of the campers. A gypsy cursed Stanley's "dirty-rotten-pig-stealing-great-great-grandfather," and the curse passed to the rest of the family. So, when a pair of tennis shoes flew at Stanley, he should have known they were nothing but bad luck, bad luck that sentenced him to Camp Green Lake for robbery. Now he digs a hole every day to build his character, but Stanley figures out that the captors, who will torture and kill, don't want good character. What Stanley figures out they do want will change lives, challenge the curse, and make everybody who reads *Holes* check the family history.

## *Related Activities*

1. Read "Envy" by Yevgeny Yevtushenko, aloud. You may want to discuss the following questions: Who is the speaker? Why does he speak about his envy? Do you think Stanley will someday feel the same way? In your own words, describe the boy the speaker envies.

2. *Holes* tells several stories at the same time. Diagram each plot and show how those plots meet. How do the multiple plots aid the author in accomplishing his purpose?

3. Read "The Onion," in *Making Shapely Fiction*. Is *Holes* an "onion" story? Try to plan your own onion story.

4. React to the title, *Holes*. Does it have one or more than one meaning in the story?

5. What ironies occur in the story? How do these ironies affect the novel's tone?

6. *Holes*, *Pirate's Son*, *Cowboy Ghost*, and *Backwater* all relate to a young person's relationship to family. Discuss the families in each novel and how they affect the main character's life.

## *Related Works*

1. Bauer, Joan. **Backwater**. See full booktalk above (p. 28). The main character decides to be an historian even though her family pressures her to be a lawyer.
2. Lipsyte, Robert. **One Fat Summer**. New York: Harper & Row, 1977. The main character loses weight and gains confidence as he tackles and succeeds at a job alone.
3. McCaughrean, Geraldine. **The Pirate's Son**. See full booktalk in Chapter 2 (p. 74). The main character must throw off what he believes to be his family fate to find his own place in the world.
4. Peck, Robert Newton. **Cowboy Ghost**. See full booktalk above (p. 15). The main character learns to make his own path rather than trying to be like his brother and father.
5. Stern, Jerome. "Onion." In **Making Shapely Fiction**. New York: 1991. 283p. $6.50pa. ISBN 0-440-21221-9. Stern describes the onion story and the effects it might produce.
6. Yevtushenko, Yevgeny. "Envy." In **Pierced by a Ray of the Sun: Poems About the Times We Feel Alone** edited by Ruth Gordon. New York: HarperCollins, 1995. 105p. $15.89. ISBN 0-06-023613-2. The speaker reflects on an imaginary boy who makes none of the mistakes in life that the speaker makes.

# NATIONAL CONFLICTS

Bartoletti, Susan. **No Man's Land: A Young Soldier's Story**. New York: The Blue Sky Press, 1999. $15.95. 169p. ISBN 0-0590-38371-X.

## *Summary/Description*

Fourteen-year-old Thrasher Magee goes into the swamp with his father to kill a bull alligator. In the hunt, a female alligator rams the boat. The father falls out of the boat, and Thrasher is unable to save him. Even though passing hunters do save the father's life, Thrasher feels the father's scorn. To prove his manhood, he enlists in the Southern Army. During his journey, he discovers that manhood means doing one's duty: marching in mud, digging trenches, and digging graves. He finds out that the enemy is just as human as himself, and that any man can lose his life or his nerve in battle. In fact, Thrasher discovers that Tim, the best soldier in the outfit, is really a woman. Thrasher does finally have the opportunity to fight bravely in the Gaines' Mill Battle. But when he shows compassion to a dying Yankee soldier, the soldier shoots him. Then Baylor, the irresponsible joker, who finds Thrasher, takes him to the field hospital, and stays with him through the amputation of Thrasher's arm. When Thrasher returns home, he has discovered that there is no one way to be brave or responsible. He respects himself enough to face his father, and his father welcomes him with affection rather than scorn.

## *Booktalk*

Alligators, snakes, war, and baseball—*No Man's Land* has them all. At fourteen, Thrasher Magee isn't strong enough or brave enough to please his father. When Thrasher can't wrestle an alligator to save his father's life, he decides to throw off his shame and his father's disapproval and join the Rebel army. In battle, Thrasher can prove he is a hero, but he must figure out if he is fighting the Yankees or his father. First, however, Thrasher finds out that fighting and duty may be two different things, and sometimes a deadly joke with snakes, a baseball game, or a good piece of chicken is more powerful than a fist, a knife, or a gun.

## *Related Activities*

1. Read "On Liberty and Slavery." Describe the speaker. Describe the situation. Discuss the following questions: What are the speaker's feelings about slavery? What are the speaker's feelings about liberty? How could the speaker's message apply to Thrasher?

2. After discussing "On Liberty and Slavery," read "The Funeral of Martin Luther King, Jr." How do Giovanni's reflections on the meaning of the word "free" affect your interpretation of "On Liberty and Slavery"?

3. Reread Timothea's letter on pages 155 and 156. What does Timothea's life have in common with a slave's life? What ironies are involved in her decision to fight for the South and her reasons for doing so?

4. Bartoletti includes a note to the reader and an extensive bibliography at the end of her novel. Choose one source and find information that supports or amplifies the details Bartoletti has included.

5. Compare the two journeys of the main characters in *Soldier's Heart* and *No Man's Land*. What idea does each journey illustrate? The books both tell the story of a young man coming to war, so why do the ideas differ?

6. Read pages 129–32. Thrasher describes the charge. Compare this description with Walt Whitman's "Cavalry Crossing a Ford." What impression of war does each description present? What effect might each scene have on the reader?

## *Related Works*

1. Clinton, Catherine. **I, Too, Sing America**. See full booktalk in Chapter 4 (p. 219). In "On Liberty and Slavery" by George Moses Horton, on page 22, a slave questions why he was born to slavery and calls on Liberty to save and cheer him. In "The Funeral of Martin Luther King, Jr." by Nikki Giovanni, on page 118, the speaker reflects on the inscription of Martin Luther King Jr.'s headstone and the meaning of "free."

2. Murphy, Jim. **The Journal of James Edmond Pease**. See full booktalk below (p. 42). Throughout the war, the main character builds his self-confidence.

3. Paulsen, Gary. **Soldier's Heart**: **Being the Story of the Enlistment and Due Service of the Boy Charley Goddard in the First Minnesota Volunteers**. New York: Delacorte Press, 1998. 106p. $15.95. ISBN 0385324987. A young soldier who enthusiastically enlists returns home, wounded both physically and emotionally.

4. Rinaldi, Ann. **Mine Eyes Have Seen**. See full booktalk in Chapter 4 (p. 243). The main character must deal with her conflict with her father, John Brown, as she helps him to carry out his mission.

5. Whitman, Walt. "Cavalry Crossing a Ford." Philip, Neil, ed., and Michael McCurdy (illus). **War and the Pity of War**. See full booktalk below (p. 44). In "Cavalry Crossing a Ford," Whitman presents a romantic view of Civil War soldiers crossing a stream.

Lobel, Anita. **No Pretty Pictures: A Child of War**. New York: Greenwillow, 1998. 193p. $16.00. ISBN 0-688-15935-4.

## Summary/Description

In *No Pretty Pictures*, Anita Lobel relates her experiences under the Nazis. She is five when she first leaves her parents to hide in the country. Her brother is three. They hide unsuccessfully in a convent, experience forced marches, live in concentration camps, and travel in cattle cars. When the war is over, she is ten. Her brother is eight, and they are both infected with tuberculosis. Her recovery in the Swedish sanitarium is heavenly, but her difficulties are not over. Even though all four members of the family have survived, they must learn to be a family again. Anita and her brother remember few, if any, good times, and this new world is fascinating, but Anita's parents have lost everything and must start over in a foreign world. Finally, the family immigrates to America, and here, Anita decides she will never look back. The book includes a prologue that sets the tone of the book, an epilogue that explains some of the confusing circumstances of the journey, and pictures that establish a strong context for the story.

## Booktalk

Ask if any students can remember what a typical day was like at the age of five. Ask them to describe it.

When the German persecution of the Jews begins, Anita Lobel and her brother begin their nightmare of typical days. She is five, and he is three. They are disguised, hide in a convent, live in concentration camps, escape a death sentence, survive forced marches, and travel in cattle cars. When the Allies arrive, Anita is ten and her brother is eight. The children begin to discover that a typical day does not mean terror, but parents, home, school, regular meals, and clean beds. They discover that they are not ugly, dirty, and repulsively different, but clean, lovable, and talented. Today, Anita Lobel is an illustrator of children's books. Her career grew from the talent she discovered after the war; during the war, there were *No Pretty Pictures*.

## Related Activities

1. Read and watch nonfiction accounts of European children threatened during World War II. From these accounts, develop a fictional character and a story with that character as the center. Follow the guidelines in Marion Dane Bauer's *What's Your Story?*

2. Map the travel of Anita Lobel during and after her period of hiding.

3. Now map the concentration camps. Compare the two maps. What does this comparison illustrate about the danger to those in hiding?

4. Research European Resistance movements during World War II.

5. Find examples of propaganda that fueled hate against the Jews. Identify the propaganda techniques the Germans used. Keep track of the techniques used most often.

6. Read "Don't Be Afraid," in *War and the Pity of War*, aloud. Why is the speaker's statement ironic? What effect does it have, and why?

## *Related Works*

1. Baer, Edith. **Walk the Dark Streets**. See full booktalk in Chapter 3 (p. 153). The main character lives through government-fueled Anti-Semitism and escapes Germany before she can be placed in a camp.

2. Bauer, Marion Dane. **What's Your Story? A Young Person's Guide to Writing Fiction**. New York: Clarion Books, 1992. 134p. $6.95pa. ISBN 0-395-57780-2. Bauer takes the writer step-by-step through the story writing process.

3. Kustanowitz, Esther. **The Hidden Children of the Holocaust**. See full booktalk in Chapter 3 (p. 158). Concentration camp survivors describe their experiences hiding from the Nazis.

4. **The Lost Children of Berlin**. Produced by A&E Television Networks, 1997. 50 min. Color. $19.95. AAE-16117. Videocassette. Students from the same Jewish school reunite and tell their stories.

5. Ungerer, Tomi. **Tomi: A Childhood Under the Nazis**. See full booktalk in Chapter 3 (p. 164). In this nonfiction account, a man recalls his life and indoctrination under the German occupation of Alsace.

6. Vogel, David. "Don't Be Afraid." In **War and the Pity of War** edited by Neil Philip and illustrated by Michael McCurdy. See full booktalk below (p. 44). A mother quiets the fears of her child by assuring the child that she will provide protection.

Murphy, Jim. **The Journal of James Edmond Pease**. New York: Scholastic, 1998. 173p. (My Name Is America). $10.95. ISBN 0-590-43814-X.

## *Summary/Description*

When James Edmond Pease loses his parents, he moves to his uncle's cold and unwelcoming home. He decides to strike out on his own, and eventually joins the Northern Army to get his "feet covered" and his "belly full." Sixteen-year-old Pease is the youngest man in the camp, and he sees himself as the Jonah Boy, one who has bad luck and carries it to others. One major piece of bad luck, according to Pease, is the lieutenant ordering him to keep the daily journal of brave deeds. The book is Pease's journal, which recounts not only brave deeds but also the details of daily camp life. Pease also records his friendships, his pen pal romance, and the personal histories of the other soldiers. Pease advances to corporal and then to sergeant. He is a good writer and a good fighter, and with his quiet ways, he is able to subdue even the most obnoxious soldier. Knocked unconscious by an explosion in battle, he finds that he is alone in enemy territory. Sally, a black slave, befriends him. With Sally's family, he makes his way back to the Union camp to join his friends. Finally he realizes that a man determines his own luck by the friends he makes and the people he loves. The action takes place in 1863. The Epilogue tells what happened to the characters after the war, the Historical Note explains the context of the story, and the Author's Note explains how Jim Murphy became involved in writing the book. The maps pinpoint where the action takes place, and the sketches and pictures illustrate the descriptions.

## *Booktalk*

Ask the audience if they have heard the story of Jonah and the Whale. If not, explain the story and why the crew threw Jonah overboard.

James Emerson Pease thinks he is a Jonah Boy. His parents are dead, and his aunt and uncle don't want him. When he joins the Northern Army at age sixteen, a fellow soldier even writes a song about him. (Read the song on pages 23 and 24 and show the artist's sketch on page 167.) One of the unluckiest things that Pease thinks happens to him is being assigned to write the company journal. The first two writers have died in battle. But if Pease wants to eat, he has to write, and the company journal really becomes *The Journal of James Edmond Pease*. The "Orphan Boy" must face the taunts of the other soldiers, the fear of battle, and his own self-doubt. He has to decide if he should listen to his friends and officers, who want to build him up, or some enemies, both Blue and Gray, who would like to see him fail. Is luck something somebody gives to him, or something he makes for himself?

## *Related Activities*

1. Compare James Edmond Pease's motivation to join the army with that of Thrasher Magee in *No Man's Land.* How are their situations similar and different?
2. Research the Battle of Gettysburg. Find out why the battle was so bloody and confusing.
3. Research the Underground Railroad and report on how it affected the Civil War.
4. The war was a topic even for the circus. Read the following speeches by the American humorist and Shakespearean circus clown, Dan Rice: "Things That I Like to See," and "Flag of Our Union Forever." What is Rice's stand on the war and slavery?
5. Research the Battle of Appomattox. What did it reveal about both Grant and Lee?

## *Related Works*

1. Bartoletti, Susan. **No Man's Land**. See full booktalk above (p. 37). The main character joins the service to prove he is a man and learns that manhood is much different than he thought.
2. Granfield, Linda. **Circus: An Album**. See full booktalk in Chapter 4 (p. 206). On page 73, a description of Dan Rice explains his place in politics and history.
3. Juleus, Nels, ed. **The Annotated Dan Rice: Dan Rice's Great Song Book of 1866**. York, PA: Nels Juleus, 1977 (photocopy). This booklet contains "Things That I Like to See" and "Flag of Our Union Forever." The speeches reveal the pressure to compromise about slavery to save the union. You may receive a copy by sending a letter of request and $5.00 to Dr. Nels Juleus, 74 Eisenhower Drive, York, PA 17402.

4. McKissack, Patricia C., and Fredrick McKissack. **Black Hands, White Sails: The Story of African-American Whalers**. See full booktalk in Chapter 2 (p. 103). The authors explain how the Underground Railroad often led into the sea.

5. Paulsen, Gary. **Soldier's Heart: Being the Story of the Enlistment and Due Service of the Boy Charley Goddard in the First Minnesota Volunteers**. New York: Delacorte Press, 1998. 106p. $15.95. ISBN 0385324987. The main character enthusiastically goes to war for adventure and returns physically and emotionally wounded.

6. Rinaldi, Ann. **Mine Eyes Have Seen**. See full booktalk in Chapter 4 (p. 243). The main character, John Brown's daughter, is assigned the task of telling her father's story.

Philip, Neil, ed., and Michael McCurdy (illus). **War and the Pity of War**. New York: Clarion Books, 1998. 96p. $20.00. ISBN 0-395-84982-9.

### *Summary/Description*

*War and the Pity of War* presents the universal problem of war through the poet's eyes. The book includes poems from ancient and modern times, and from countries around the world. Some poems are grouped by a particular war, but others are placed next to thoughts from completely different centuries. The black-and-white illustrations set a somber tone for the entire collection. The introduction provides a historical perspective and discusses the placement and pairing of poems within the volume. An index of poets and an index of titles and first lines make individual works easily accessible. The overall organization of the book is almost a poem itself.

### *Booktalk*

Push-button wars, antiseptic wars, no-casualty wars, no-consequence wars may be what politicians promise, but the poets in *War and the Pity of War* give a different picture. War poetry has changed as war consequences have become more horrifying. This collection also illustrates that although the weapons have changed, the same deadly attitudes arm them.

## *Related Activities*

1. Choose a quartet of poems from different wars. Read them aloud then discuss the similarities and differences in the poems.
2. Find another poetry collection built around another theme like love or nature. Compare the images of that collection to the images in the collection of *War and the Pity of War*.
3. Collect your own poems on a particular theme or build a particular collection with members of a group. Explain the order or groupings of the poems you have chosen. Illustrate the poems or ask someone in the group to illustrate them.
4. Write your own collection of poems on a particular theme. Organize and illustrate them.
5. Choose one poem. Research the poem and the poet. Research the war it is written about and then discuss the appropriateness of the images used.
6. Choose any one of the related works about war. Write poetry in reaction to the work or choose a quotation or situation from the work and build a poem around it.

## *Related Works*

1. Bartoletti, Susan. **No Man's Land**. See full booktalk above (p. 37). A young man learns the horrors of war and discovers his manhood.
2. Cox, Clinton. **Come All You Brave Soldiers**. See full booktalk in Chapter 3 (p. 155). Many black soldiers who fought for freedom are betrayed.
3. Denenberg, Barry. **The Journal of William Thomas Emerson: A Revolutionary War Patriot**. See full booktalk above (p. 12). The main character lives through the preparation for the Revolutionary War.
4. Hunter, Mollie. **The King's Swift Rider**. See full booktalk in Chapter 2 (p. 119). In his role as a soldier, a young man discovers he is a scholar.
5. Janeczko, Paul B. **How to Write Poetry**. See full booktalk in Chapter 4 (p. 215). Janeczko gives excellent tips and technical advice for writing poetry.
6. Kustanowitz, Esther. **The Hidden Children of the Holocaust: Teens Who Hid from the Nazis**. See full booktalk in Chapter 3 (p. 158). Nonfiction accounts relate experiences under the Nazis.

7. Lobel, Anita. **No Pretty Pictures**. See full booktalk above (p. 39). The narrator gives a nonfiction account of her experiences hiding from the Nazis.
8. Miklowitz, Gloria D. **Masada: The Last Fortress**. See full booktalk in Chapter 3 (p. 162). Zealots choose suicide rather than surrender to the Romans.
9. Murphy, Jim. **The Journal of James Edmond Pease**. See full booktalk above (p. 12). The main character learns about himself and war.
10. Paulsen, Gary. **Soldier's Heart: Being the Story of the Enlistment and Due Service of the Boy Charley Goddard in the First Minnesota Volunteers**. New York: Delacorte Press, 1998. 106p. $15.95. ISBN 0385324987. The main character is destroyed by the horrors of war.
11. Rinaldi, Ann. **Cast Two Shadows**. See full booktalk below (p. 46). The main character sees friends and family destroyed in the Revolutionary War.
12. Tito, Tina E. **Liberation: Teens in the Concentration Camps and the Teen Soldiers Who Liberated Them**. See full booktalk in Chapter 4 (p. 225). Nonfiction accounts tell the stories of both prisoners and soldiers.

 Rinaldi, Ann. **Cast Two Shadows**. New York: Gulliver Books, 1998. 276p. $16.00. ISBN 0-15-200881-0.

### *Summary/Description*

In *Cast Two Shadows*, Caroline Whitaker takes a journey with two purposes: to save her white Loyalist brother from the "tender mercies" of the British and to rediscover her true family roots with her black slave grandmother. In the turmoil of war, the lines between Loyalist and Patriot, owner and slave, blur. Caroline discovers that her real mother was sold when Caroline came to live in her father's house. Now she feels both love and resentment for her white family. The Revolutionary War frees family secrets as well as the colonies.

### *Booktalk*

You see your fourteen-year-old friends imprisoned or hanged, your family split by politics and race. Suddenly, everyone is telling you to follow your heart even as it is breaking.

Many personal wars were fought during the Revolutionary War, many as difficult as the one waged by Caroline Whitaker, the girl who casts two shadows—one black and one white. Should she go to the slave quarters with her black grandmother or stay in the big house with her white father? And can she ever forgive the secret treachery that brought her to that big, white house?

## *Related Activities*

1. Caroline's brother, grandmother, and mother-in-law give Caroline advice about life and maturity. Discuss the advice. Evaluate it. Start a journal section called "Advice." Write down advice given to you. Explain why it was given and how you applied it.
2. Ms. Rinaldi provides an extensive explanation of how she wrote *Cast Two Shadows*. She states that Miz Mindy is a "composite character." Define "composite character." Make up a composite character of your own. Follow the guidelines for character in Chapter 3 of *What's Your Story?* by Marion Dane Bauer.
3. Research about Greene, Marion, Sumter, Daniel Morgan, and Light Horse Harry Lee. Find out as much as possible about their functions and interactions during the war.
4. Ann Rinaldi claims that the Revolutionary War in the South was much different than the one fought in the North and planted the seeds for the American Civil War. Research the Revolutionary War in the North and the South. Agree and/or disagree with Rinaldi's claim. You may wish to refer to Ann Rinaldi's bibliography on pages 279–81.
5. Phillis Wheatley and Frances Ellen Watkins Harper wrote almost 100 years apart. Both were black, and both lived through war. Read "Liberty and Peace" and "Bury Me in a Free Land." Both speakers talk about liberty. Contrast the two speakers and their statements.

## *Related Works*

1. Bauer, Marion Dane. **What's Your Story? A Young Person's Guide to Writing Fiction**. New York: Clarion Books, 1992. 134p. $6.95pa. ISBN 0-395-57780-2. In Chapter 3, Bauer outlines the basic decisions a writer must make when building a character.

2. Clinton, Catherine. **I, Too, Sing America**. See full booktalk in Chapter 4 (p. 219). "Liberty and Peace" and "Bury Me in a Free Land" show the excitement about freedom that the Revolutionary War planted among slaves and the disappointment and bitterness the resulting betrayal produced.

3. Collier, James Lincoln. **My Brother Sam Is Dead**. New York: Four Winds Press, 1974. The main character tries to keep both his revolutionary brother and his neutral family safe.

4. Cox, Clinton. **Come All You Brave Soldiers**. See full booktalk in Chapter 3 (p. 155). Cox tells about the contribution blacks made to the American Revolution.

5. Denenberg, Barry. **The Journal of William Thomas Emerson**. See full booktalk above (p. 12). A twelve-year-old serves as a spy for the Boston Revolutionaries.

6. Sterman, Betsy. **Saratoga Secret**. See full booktalk above (p. 21). A sixteen-year-old girl becomes a messenger for the revolutionary forces in Saratoga.

## SUPERNATURAL FORCES

Branford, Henrietta. **The Fated Sky**. Cambridge, MA: Candlewick Press, 1999. 156p. $16.99. ISBN 0-7636-0775-4.

### *Summary/Description*

*The Fated Sky* is a historical fiction Viking tale of Ran's life journey. When Ran is sixteen, she lives with her grandmother, mother, and an elderly worker on the grandmother's farm. Her father and brother have been drowned at sea. Vigut, the warrior her mother always loved, comes to the farm and takes the mother and daughter with him. On the journey to Sessing Hall, wolves attack Ran's mother. Ran and the witch brought to save Ran's mother are accused of the mother's death. Ran is promised to Odin in sacrifice. As she is to die, raiders attack the hall. Toki, the blind musician, saves her. Because she has been promised to Odin, they flee to Iceland. There they find a hall and raise a family, but Vigut still pursues them. When Vigut raids the hall, Ran loses her husband and saves her children. But as her death nears, a huge wave destroys the hall and carries Ran to safety. The sea saves the girl named for the sea goddess, and she lives to see her children grow to adulthood. *The Fated Sky* shows the harsh and magical Viking world through one woman's eyes.

## Booktalk

Discuss the safety and danger of belonging to a group. Discuss how gangs are related to this safety and danger.

In Viking times, gangs could dictate one's entire life. People gathered in halls for protection and worked to pay for that protection. Still, larger gangs of Viking warriors could overcome these halls and kill or enslave the dwellers. Sixteen-year-old Ran has been isolated from this world, but one day, the warrior her mother has always loved appears to take them into the fierceness of nature and war. Suddenly, she must find protection from wolf attacks and human sacrifice. She must dare to love and trust in the goddess who is her namesake. In *The Fated Sky*, the Viking gods will decide whether happiness or death will control each day.

## Related Activities

1. Vigut was a *scop*, a storyteller who entertained and inspired the Vikings with story poems of their heritage. A *griot* was an African minstrel who entertained and informed his people in much the same way. Both were part of the oral tradition that preserved history and carried the news. Using the guidelines and prompts in *Telling Your Own Stories*, ask members of the group to tell stories from their own experiences.

2. After practice with personal experiences, ask members of the class or audience to tell a story that will strengthen the glory and identity of a particular group. They might choose a political party, a school, or a spiritual group. Use *Telling Your Own Stories* as a reference.

3. Make a list of things about yourself over which you feel you have had no control. Beside each item on the list, tell how you have reacted to this lack. Combine each characteristic and your reaction into a line of a poem. At the end, write two lines that describe the person you have become as a result.

4. *The Fated Sky*, *The Sacrifice*, *Sirena*, and *I Rode a Horse of Milk White Jade* are stories about women who must balance their lives between choice and fate. Assign each book to a different person or group. Then discuss the main characters' personal choices and the factors influencing those choices.

5. Personify a small part of nature: a wave, a raindrop, a leaf, or perhaps a single dandelion. Tell its story as it tries to work with the other elements of nature that are bigger and stronger than it is.

6. After viewing *The Vikings*, discuss the appropriateness of the time and place setting for *The Fated Sky.*

## *Related Works*

1. Davis, Donald. **Telling Your Own Stories**. Little Rock, AR: August House, 1993.128p. (American Storytelling). $10.00pa. ISBN 0-87483-235-7. Davis explains how to tell stories and how to draw them out of others. He also provides several prompts for oral storytelling or journal writing.
2. Elmer, Howard. **Blues: Its Birth and Growth**. See full booktalk in Chapter 4 (p. 201). Elmer tells how the Blues are rooted in an oral culture and includes a description of the griot.
3. Matcheck, Diane. **The Sacrifice**. See full booktalk in Chapter 2 (p. 89). A girl believes she has been selected to be a great leader in her tribe.
4. Napoli, Donna Jo. **Sirena**. See full booktalk in Chapter 2 (p. 91). A mermaid runs away from her fate, but her fate finds her anyway.
5. **The Vikings**. Produced by A&E Television Networks, 1996. 50 min. Color. (Foot Soldier). $19.95. AAE-13913. Videocassette. With humor and present-day comparisons, *The Vikings* depicts the lifestyle and war style of the Northern Invaders.
6. Wilson, Diane Lee. **I Rode a Horse of Milk White Jade**. See full booktalk above (p. 8). Like Ran, Oyuna believes her life to be controlled by fate. She fights soldiers in a harsh land and lives to tell her story to her grandchildren.

Yolen, Jane, and Bruce Coville. **Armageddon Summer**. New York: Harcourt Brace, 1998. 266p. $17.00. ISBN 0-15-201767-4.

## *Summary/Description*

Fourteen-year-old Marina and sixteen-year-old Jed become swept up in a religious group's journey to Armageddon during their *Armageddon Summer*. Going to the mountaintop with their parents, who have committed themselves to Reverend Beelson's vision, they find themselves uncertain members of the chosen 144. Their commitment to their families forces them to clarify their own spiritual beliefs in relation to their parents' beliefs. In the process, they discover each other and renew their commitment to their families. The chapters alternate between Marina and Jed as the book records two personal journeys that eventually meet. The themes of personal clarification and discovery transcend the year 2000.

## Booktalk

What did you do last summer? Marina and Jed can tell a story of danger and discovery. Marina's mother and Jed's father go to the mountaintop with Reverend Beelson. Armageddon is upon them, and their families may be divided between the "Believers" and the "Fried." But are all the members of this chosen 144 good enough to be saved? Why do they need electrified fences, strict schedules, and "Angels" who carry semi-automatic weapons? In this safe-haven, Marina must protect her brothers from disease and violence. Jed must struggle to save his father from his father's own self-destructive sorrow and hate. In their personal journeys during their *Armageddon Summer*, Marina and Jed find each other and start to discover what they really believe.

## Related Activities

1. Using *The Millennium* by David Cohen, find parallels to Reverend Beelson's plan. Try to explain why this Armageddon reaction repeats itself.

2. Emily Dickinson's poetry provides Marina with comfort and support. Examine the poems she uses. Choose two or three that you feel are especially appropriate and explain why you chose them.

3. Find or develop a profile of cult behavior and organization. Use written sources, interviews, or film.

4. Reverend Beelson prohibits technology such as television and computers from his community. Is there any reasonable basis for his rules?

5. The film *The Apocalypse: The Puzzle of Revelation* defines Armageddon and explains the confusion surrounding it. Discuss the plausibility of the explanations.

## *Related Works*

1. **The Apocalypse: The Puzzle of Revelation**. Produced by Multimedia Entertainment and A&E Television Networks, 1994. 50 min. Color. (Mysteries of the Bible). $14.95. AAE-95064. Videocassette. The film explains why the Apocalypse is open to so many different interpretations.
2. Cohen, Daniel. **The Millennium**. New York: Pocket Books, 1998. 115p. $3.99pa. ISBN 0-671-01562-1. Cohen reports on plans and prophecies for the millennium.
3. Frost, Robert. "Fire and Ice." In **Mindscapes: Poems for the Real World** edited by Richard Peck. New York: Delacorte Press, 1971. Frost discusses two possible disasters that will end the world.
4. Johnson, Thomas, ed. **The Complete Poems of Emily Dickinson**. Boston: Little, Brown, 1960. This edition provides Emily Dickinson's poems in addition to those included in *Armageddon Summer.*
5. Levitin, Sonia. **The Singing Mountain**. See full booktalk in Chapter 2 (p. 86). This novel presents parallel spiritual journeys in alternating chapters.

Rylant, Cynthia. **The Heavenly Village**. New York: The Blue Sky Press, 1999. 95p. $15.95. ISBN 0-439-04096-5.

## *Summary/Description*

*The Heavenly Village* tells about the village between heaven and Earth. Here are homebodies who have unfinished business on Earth. Everett, the bank teller, is learning to appreciate the quality of life as well as its quantities. The baker, Violet Rose, is learning that she was loved on Earth and that she can trust in the future. Fortune and his master Harold are renewing their faith in Fortune's skill as a rescue dog. Isham Taylor, the magician, is learning the difference between the magical and the miraculous as he makes amends for killing Violet Rose. Raphael Blake, the doctor, is learning the difference between the healing of science and the healing of spirit. Cordie, the runner, decides to stop awhile for love, and God asks Thomas, the potter, to stay for conversation and collaboration. The message of the novel is realization of wrong rather than punishment for it. An Old Testament quotation introduces each story. *The Heavenly Village* will have a wide audience of many ages and beliefs.

## *Booktalk*

What happens after we die? If there is a heaven, who gets in? (You might want to discuss the answers before moving on.)

*The Heavenly Village* brings up some new possibilities. It suggests what might happen to the man who can find out how much but never how beautiful, or the lady who worries about everything, or the hit-and-run driver who gets away. With one foot in heaven and one foot on Earth, they all live together and learn about all the things they missed or wondered about in life. The village gives them a little more time and a better view. Reading *The Heavenly Village*, we may recognize the people we love, the people we don't want to be around, and ourselves.

## *Related Activities*

1. *The Heavenly Village* is a frame story. Read Jerome Stern's definition of a frame story on pages 139–41 of *Making Shapely Fiction*. Make up a plan for a frame of your own. Possible topics: reactions to a help wanted ad, the quarterbacks of your high school over a ten-year period, all the valedictorians over a ten-year period, every business on the main street of your town, the passengers on a bus or a plane.

2. The afterlife has puzzled and worried people for ages. Find another description of an afterlife. You might read about Greek, Viking, or Egyptian societies. Compare it to *The Heavenly Village*. Discuss what the afterlife reveals about the values of its society.

3. Choose a quotation from Bartlett's *Quotations*. Write or tell a story to which it applies.

4. *Armageddon Summer*, *The Boxes*, *A Door Near Here*, *The Harry Potter Series*, *King Arthur*, *Sang Spell*, and *Transall Saga* all include a world beyond the physical, everyday world. Ask each reader to describe the world in one of the novels and explain its purpose in relation to the total story.

## *Related Works*

1. Kerven, Rosalind. **King Arthur**. See full booktalk in Chapter 3 (p. 131). Arthur and Merlin disappear into a different world to sleep and wait for their return to the physical world.

2. Naylor, Phyllis Reynolds. **Sang Spell**. See full booktalk in Chapter 3 (p. 187). The main character finds himself living in a village suspended in time.

3. Paulsen, Gary. **The Transall Saga**. See full booktalk in Chapter 3 (p. 192). A young man comes of age by surviving an other-world experience.

4. Quarles, Heather. **A Door Near Here**. See full booktalk below (p. 54). The youngest child tries to escape to Narnia because of the stress in the household.

5. Rowling, J. K. **The Harry Potter Series**. See full booktalks in Chapter 3 (pp. 181–87). Harry battles the evil spirits and learns about himself.

6. Sleator, William. **The Boxes**. See full booktalk in Chapter 3 (p. 189). The main character opens up a completely different reality, which threatens to control and destroy her life.

7. Stern, Jerome. "Frame Story." In **Making Shapely Fiction**. New York: Laurel Books, 1991. 283p. $6.50pa. ISBN 0-440-21221-9. Stern defines the frame story, gives examples, and explains its uses and forms.

Quarles, Heather. **A Door Near Here**. New York: Delacorte Press, 1998. 231p. $13.95. ISBN 0-385-32595-9.

### *Summary/Description*

Fifteen-year-old Katherine tells the story of her family's disintegration and possible rebirth. As the oldest daughter, she tries to keep the family together by hiding her mother's alcoholism. Her father left the family ten years ago. He now has a new wife and young family and rarely communicates with his original family. Tracey, thirteen, and Douglas, fourteen, support Katherine so that they can protect Alisa, their eight-year-old half-sister, whose father is unknown. They fear that their father will reject Alisa, and that she will be assigned to a foster home. Their struggles lead them into lies, fear, and near-starvation. Alisa, in reaction to the stress, retreats to the fantasy of Narnia. Katherine's teacher tries to help the situation, but Katherine, to keep him from interfering, falsely accuses him of molesting her. When Alisa tries to run away to Narnia, the accused teacher finds and rescues her. Because he has been forbidden to have any contact with the family, he loses his job. The father finds out about his children's situation, and with his new wife's support, accepts all the children into his family. Katherine learns that she must believe and trust in someone or something beyond herself.

## *Booktalk*

Mom is an alcoholic. Dad is rich but moved out ten years ago. Now he has a new family. That leaves three sisters and a brother to survive and keep their secrets from the world, especially social services. What can they use to wage the war? How many lies can they tell? How much money can they steal? How long can they hide? Are there any good guys, including themselves? Finally, eight-year-old Alisa becomes so confused that she seeks another world at *A Door Near Here*. Heather Quarles shows how hard it is to love, believe, and forgive.

## *Related Activities*

1. Read one or all of the books in The Chronicles of Narnia. Discuss why Quarles chooses to allude to that world in *A Door Near Here.*

2. Read the first and last paragraphs of Chapter 1. Read the last three paragraphs and the last page, beginning, "I have something important to tell you . . ." through the end of Chapter 23. Examine the word choice, images, and allusions. What does Katherine reveal about herself? Is she cruel, defensive, confused? Explain your answer.

3. Connect each character in the novel with an idea that the character might represent. Explain your choices.

4. Read "Lies" by Yevgeny Yevtushenko, on page 21 of *Pierced by a Ray of the Sun: Poems About the Times We Feel Alone*. You might want to answer the following questions: Who is the speaker? Who is his audience? Ask if the audience agrees/disagrees with what the speaker says about lies. How were lies central to *A Door Near Here*?

5. Read "Divorce" by Tove Ditlevsen in *Life Doesn't Frighten Me at All.* You might want to answer the following questions: How does the speaker feel about divorce? Why doesn't the speaker use more emotional language?

## *Related Works*

1. Ditlevsen, Tove. "Divorce." In **Life Doesn't Frighten Me at All** edited by John Agard. New York: Henry Holt, 1989. The speaker talks about the division of property in a divorce and implies that the child is ripped apart also.

2. Gormley, Beatrice. **C. S. Lewis: Christian and Storyteller**. See full booktalk in Chapter 2 (p. 84). Gormley tells how Lewis came to write the Narnia stories and how his own life reflected their spirit. A bibliography of Lewis's works is included.

3. Lewis, C. S. **The Chronicles of Narnia**. New York: HarperCollins, 1994. 7 vol., $34.65pa. ISBN 0-06-447119-5. Lewis's fantasy world communicates his spiritual beliefs.

4. McFarland, Rhoda. **Drugs and Your Parents**. New York: The Rosen Publishing Group, 1997 rev. ed. 64p. (The Drug Abuse Prevention Library). $17.95. ISBN 0-8239-2603-6. *A Door Near Here* follows the profile of the drug abusing family and illustrates the mistakes that continue to trap its members, especially the children. McFarland offers practical advice on how to avoid those problems.

5. Rottman, S. L. **Hero**. See full booktalk in Chapter 4 (p. 223). An alcoholic mother abuses the main character, but through a court placement he finds responsibility and hope.

6. Yevtushenko, Yevgeny. "Lies." In **Pierced by a Ray of the Sun: Poems About the Times We Feel Alone** edited by Ruth Gordon. New York: HarperCollins, 1995. 105p. $15.89. ISBN 0-06-023613-2. The speaker feels that adults should admit the pain and obstacles of life. They should not lie to make life seem pleasant.

 Wynne-Jones, Tim. **Stephen Fair**. New York: DK Ink, 1998. 218p. $15.95. ISBN 0-7894-2495-9.

## *Summary/Description*

When Stephen is eleven years old, he is recording his brother's nightmares in a notebook called The Dreamcatcher. When he is fifteen, he is having nightmares of his own; his brother has run away; and his father has deserted the family. His mother seeks help for Stephen from Hesketh Martin, an alternative health-care practitioner who eventually concludes that the parents need to resolve their own problems before Stephen can resolve his. Virginia Elizabeth Dulcima Skye, Stephen's girlfriend, seems to have the perfect family, but Stephen must rescue her when he discovers that she, too, has parents who need to solve their problems first. Finally, when Stephen, his brother, his mother, and his grandmother reunite, Stephen discovers that his troubled mother had stolen him from his birth parents, whose neglect threatened his life. *Stephen Fair* explores the meaning of family and the importance of adults acting like adults.

## *Booktalk*

Stephen Fair has nightmares. Four years ago his brother had nightmares. Are they catching?

They may come from his home life. He lives in an ark instead of a house, his parents won't let him call them Mom and Dad, his brother has run away, and his father has deserted the family. But when he begins to make friends with some "perfect" people from "perfect" families, Stephen discovers that their lives aren't so perfect after all. As Stephen tries to help his friends and search his world of dreams, he discovers family lies and secrets that change him to a "Stephen Dark" and threaten to destroy families.

## *Related Activities*

1. *Tangerine*, *A Door Near Here*, *The Spirit Window*, *Belle Prater's Boy*, *Bull Catcher*, and *Stephen Fair* all involve family secrets that could destroy families. Ask individuals or groups to choose one of the novels. Ask the readers to identify the family secrets. Explain why each is dangerous. Then discuss whether the secrets would have been as dangerous if they had not been kept secret.

2. *Dreamcatcher* and *Stephen Fair* deal with loss of a father, mysterious dreams, and dreamcatchers. Even though these novels share these elements, how do they differ?

3. Page 34 of *Depression* lists symptoms of depression. Who exhibits these symptoms in *Stephen Fair*, *A Door Near Here*, *Tangerine*, and *Bull Catcher*? How do these people affect others in the novel?

4. Read *Coping in a Blended Family*. List the myths that prevent families from blending. Watch television programs about families. How do you think these programs help or hinder coping in a family unit?

5. Stephen's health-care practitioner concludes that Stephen's parents must solve their problems before he can solve his. *P.S. Longer Letter Later*, *A Door Near Here*, *The Spirit Window*, *Belle Prater's Boy*, *Bull Catcher*, *Tangerine*, *Cowboy Ghost*, *Life in the Fat Lane*, *The Great Eye*, *Out of the Dust*, *Cast Two Shadows*, *Parrot in the Oven*, and *No Promises in the Wind* involve problem parents. Ask individuals or groups to choose one of the books. Then ask the readers to identify the problems the parent or parents present. Discuss which problems are the most difficult and how the children can cope with the problems.

## *Related Works*

1. Bennett, Cherie. **Life in the Fat Lane**. See full booktalk above (p. 1). The main character must deal with parents who concentrate on physical appearance.

2. Bloor, Edward. **Tangerine**. See full booktalk above (p. 16). Blinded by his brother, the main character tries to overcome his handicap, recall the reason for it, and establish himself as independent and capable.

3. Carter, Alden R. **Bull Catcher**. See full booktalk in Chapter 2 (p. 96). The main character has grown up with his grandparents because his mother preferred to pursue a career.

4. Danziger, Paula, and Ann M. Martin. **P.S. Longer Letter Later**. See full booktalk in Chapter 3 (p. 172). The two main characters use letters to share their concerns about their shaky family lives.

5. Hesse, Karen. **Out of the Dust**. See full booktalk above (p. 30). The main character's father becomes distant after her mother's death.

6. Hunt, Irene. **No Promises in the Wind**. New York: Berkley Books, 1970. $10.30. Permabound. Because they are tired of their father's abuse, the main character and his brother leave home.

7. Hurwitz, Jane. **Coping in a Blended Family**. See full booktalk in Chapter 3 (p. 170). Hurwitz talks about the new definitions of family and how to build a family unit based on more than birth.

8. Martinez, Victor. **Parrot in the Oven**. See full booktalk in Chapter 2 (p. 112). The main character decides that with his family, even with all its problems, is where he wishes to be.

9. Maynard, Meredy. **Dreamcatcher**. Vancouver, BC: Polestar Press, 1995. 137p. $7.50pa. ISBN 1-896095-01-1. The main character must cope with his father's death and his mother's remarriage.

10. Naylor, Phyllis Reynolds. **Sang Spell**. See full booktalk in Chapter 3 (p. 187). The main character is trying to deal with his mother's recent death.

11. Peck, Robert Newton. **Cowboy Ghost**. See full booktalk above (p. 15). The main character's father ignores the son he feels is too weak.

12. Quarles, Heather. **A Door Near Here**. See full booktalk above (p. 54). The main character tries to help her family deal with divorce and alcoholism.

13. Rinaldi, Ann. **Cast Two Shadows**. See full booktalk above (p. 46). The main character discovers that her white family sold her black mother.

14. Shalant, Phyllis. **The Great Eye**. New York: Puffin Books, 1996. 150p. $4.99pa. ISBN 0-14-130072-8. The main character's parents are separated and her sister has a new boyfriend.

15. Silverstein, Alvin, Virginia Silverstein, and Laura Silverstein Nunn. **Depression**. See full booktalk in Chapter 3 (p. 150). The book defines depression and proposes ways to prevent and treat it.

16. Sweeney, Joyce. **The Spirit Window**. See full booktalk above (p. 19). The main character must deal with the poor relationship between her father and her grandmother.

17. White, Ruth. **Belle Prater's Boy**. New York: Farrar, Straus & Giroux, 1996. 196p. $16.00. ISBN 0374-306-680. Cousins admit the family secrets and begin to build their own lives.

# 2

# We Act

## SOCIALLY

 Abelove, Joan. **Go and Come Back**. New York: DK Ink, 1998. 177p. $16.95. ISBN 0-7894-2472-2.

### *Summary/Description*

In *Go and Come Back*, twelve-year-old Alicia tells about one year in her Peruvian village. During this year, two New York anthropologists visit Alicia's village to observe the people's customs. To the villagers, these women visitors appear old and unmarried, yet they want to study babies, family life, and agriculture. Soon, Alicia concludes that they are alone because they are stingy and lazy. They only ask questions and write. They do not till the soil or take care of families. She concludes that the village must teach the women to be human and generous. With the baby she has adopted, Alicia tries to help them be both. Everyone learns. Alicia sees her own village from a perspective she never anticipated. The anthropologists learn about the village and themselves, and the reader learns about the great emotions, which could join us, and the petty cultural differences, which could separate us.

## *Booktalk*

Ask how old a person should be before getting married. Ask each person to write the number on a sheet of paper. Then ask the students to read their numbers and find people who agree with them. Ask them for their reasons.

Twelve-year-old Alicia may be married. She really doesn't know if she is or isn't. But she decides to adopt a girl baby anyway. The women, not the men in her village, decide about the children, and at twelve, Alicia is a woman. Old white ladies come to her jungle village and ask about her baby, her crops, and her life, and Alicia thinks she knows why they ask so many questions. These women don't know how to work; they don't have babies; they are stingy. Her village must teach them about beauty, love, and sharing life. Alicia is a wise teacher. Her pupils learn. She learns, and their sharing makes them want to *Go and Come Back.*

## *Related Activities*

1. Tell a story about a new person entering your school. What social "mistakes" might that person make? What would the consequences be?
2. Read the opening chapter of *Go and Come Back.* Discuss what the first chapter reveals about the village.
3. As you are reading the book, record in your journal the customs and beliefs of the village. Group these customs and beliefs. Give each group a title. Some may be birth, friendship, eating, or marriage customs. After you are finished reading, report on the village customs. Use the group titles to organize your report.
4. The Star Wars series by DK presents an archeologist's view of *Star Wars* civilization. *Go and Come Back* presents an anthropologist's view of Alicia's culture. Discuss the differences that you observe between what an archeologist studies and what an anthropologist studies.
5. *A Hope in the Unseen* and *Buried Onions* present problems rooted in cultural differences. Describe the cultures in these books and the resulting clashes.
6. *A Hive for the Honeybee* is an allegory about a woman's place in society. After reading *Go and Come Back,* discuss how the story would apply to Alicia's society.

7. In *Ophelia Speaks*, teenage girls from our culture express their concerns about life. Discuss the topics about which Alicia and her friends might speak. Then state or write an expression about one of their concerns.

## *Related Works*

1. Bennett, Cherie. **Life in the Fat Lane**. See full booktalk in Chapter 1 (p. 1). Our culture rejects a young girl because of her uncontrollable weight gain.

2. Lally, Soinbhe. **A Hive for the Honeybee**. See full booktalk in Chapter 3 (p. 179). The allegory shows the female bees questioning their place in society.

3. Reynolds, David West. **Star Wars, Episode I: Incredible Cross-Sections**. See full booktalk in Chapter 3 (p. 138). The book explains and illustrates in detail the craft of *Star Wars*.

4. Reynolds, David West. **Star Wars, Incredible Cross-Sections: The Ultimate Guide to Star Wars Vehicles and Spacecraft**. See full booktalk in Chapter 3 (p. 138). The book illustrates and explains the main vehicles in the Star Wars trilogy.

5. Reynolds, David West. **Star Wars: The Visual Dictionary**. See full booktalk in Chapter 3 (p. 140). The book defines and illustrates the characters, creatures, and equipment in the *Star Wars* society.

6. Shandler, Sara. **Ophelia Speaks**. See full booktalk below (p. 126). Adolescent girls write about their concerns.

7. Soto, Gary. **Buried Onions**. See full booktalk below (p. 124). A young man discovers that he must leave his community to have a successful life.

8. Suskind, Ron. **A Hope in the Unseen**. See full booktalk below (p. 94). A young man must adjust to the demands and customs of another culture to accomplish his goals.

Cormier, Robert. **Tenderness**. New York: Bantam Doubleday Dell, 1997. 229p. $16.95. ISBN 0-385-32286-0.

## *Summary/Description*

*Tenderness* is an ironic thriller about a runaway teenager, Lori Cranston, and a teenage serial killer, Eric Poole. Lori has lived with her mother and a series of her mother's boyfriends. She runs away because of the unwanted advances of her mother's current boyfriend and her own obsession with a rock star named Throb. When she sees Eric in the paper, she remembers him from a previous encounter, and her obsession shifts. She posts herself outside the house where he lives and hides in his van. She has always used her looks and lies to get what she wants and has always been in control. Eric has just been released from juvenile detention for killing both of his parents. He claimed that abuse provoked his parents' murder. The police have not been able to connect him to the murder of three teenage girls. He plans to take the insurance money and investments that his aunt has made for him, buy a van, and pursue more young victims. Lieutenant Proctor believes that Eric is a psychopathic serial killer. Proctor is haunted by the memory of a previous serial killer who escaped him. He does not want Eric to escape. While Eric is in detention, Proctor plants a decoy who fits the murdered girls' profile. Eric intends to see this girl first. When he discovers Lori in his van, he knows she may explode his plan. She had first met him after he had just killed his third victim. Her testimony could tie him to that murder. He decides to kill her. Lori persuades Eric not to kill her and encourages him to seek out and kill other girls. When he arranges to meet the decoy, Lori discovers the police plot and warns Eric. They then reunite and decide to celebrate with a canoe ride in a park. Lori falls overboard and panics. Eric cannot save her. As Eric approaches the shore he sees the police waiting for him. Ironically, Proctor realizes that Eric did not commit this crime. His co-workers, however, decide to pursue a conviction for murder in the first degree.

## *Booktalk*

Lori Cranston runs away from her mother's boyfriend. She wants a more exciting man, a rock star, even a convicted killer. Eric Poole killed his parents and three teenage girls when he was fifteen. He admitted killing his parents, but claimed they had abused him. He believes no one will ever prove he murdered the girls. At eighteen he is free, but Lieutenant Proctor doesn't believe Eric's abuse plea. He suspects that Eric is a serial killer and decides to try and prove it. Both Lori and Eric have always done what they wanted. After all, they wanted just a little *Tenderness.* When they meet, are their chances for success twice as good?

## *Related Activities*

1. The word "tender" has several definitions. Discuss which definitions fit the novel *Tenderness.*

2. Cormier's conclusion is ironic. He could have ended the novel with a successful arrest at the carnival. Discuss why Cormier does not end the novel with this event and why he has Eric arrested for a murder he did not commit.

3. The novel is based on a teenager being released because of his age at the time of his crime. Now some legislation requires teens to be tried as adults. Research which states have passed such legislation, what the legislation specifies, and what specific cases inspired the legislation.

4. Debate the following issue: Adult crime deserves adult punishment.

5. Proctor calls Eric Poole a psychopath. Find a clinical definition of that word and examples of criminals who have been labeled psychopathic. Discuss how the definition and the examples apply to the novel.

## *Related Works*

1. Bloor, Edward. **Tangerine**. See full booktalk in Chapter 1 (p. 16). The main character's brother maims, steals, and murders. The main character must stop him.

2. Cooney, Caroline B. **Hush Little Baby**. See full booktalk in Chapter 3 (p. 168). In this mystery, the teenagers are the heroes, but they need some help from adults to get out of a situation created by adults.

3. Cooney, Caroline B. **The Terrorist**. See full booktalk in Chapter 3 (p. 135). In this mystery, international terrorists try to use a naive American teenager to carry out their plans.

4. Cooney, Caroline B. **Wanted!** See full booktalk below (p. 117). In this mystery, a teenage girl thinks the police want to arrest her for her father's murder, and she feels driven to find the real murderer.

5. Rottman, S. L. **Hero**. See full booktalk in Chapter 4 (p. 223). Through his court placement, the main character builds good relationships with positive adults and begins to turn his life around.

6. Walker, Virginia, and Katrina Roechelein. **Making Up Megaboy**. See full booktalk below (p. 82). A young boy kills a shopkeeper. The reactions of people who know the boy and of people who are pulled into the event build a sympathetic picture for the reader.

Hautman, Pete. **Stone Cold**. New York: Simon & Schuster, 1998. 163p. $16.00. ISBN 0-689-81759-2.

### *Summary/Description*

Denn Doyle changes from a conscientious, hardworking, and loving son into a "stone cold" gambler able to face off even the toughest opponent. When the story begins, sixteen-year-old Denn owns a landscaping business, has a girlfriend, works with his good friend Murky, and values the friendship of Father O'Gara. After Denn starts playing poker, his skill and obsession cause him to leave his business, alienate his friends, and detach himself from his family. He starts to trust dropouts and gamblers more than his friends, his girlfriend, his parents, and his priest. He is able to challenge Mr. Kingston, "The King," and win the casino, but he is unable to face Father O'Gara's challenge. Father O'Gara believes that Denn Doyle is an addict, not a winner who can walk away at anytime. Because he can pick up on his opponent's "tells" and win from the big guys, Denn sees himself as a winner, not a loser who has to attend Gambler's Anonymous meetings. Denn thinks that only a crazy man would walk away from the kind of money he is making. But, ultimately, he has more than enough money and no one with whom to share it.

### *Booktalk*

How much do you think you can make in a summer? Denn Doyle has a successful lawn business and does fairly well. But one summer he changes careers and makes $50,000. He learns to play cards and read people. He knows when they're happy, sad, or excited. *Stone Cold* he can beat the wanna-be's, the hustlers, and the loan sharks, even "The King." He's so good that he wouldn't even call what he does gambling.

Cookie, a gambling man, tells him that the cards keep "opening doors," but the cards are closing some, too. What does it mean to win? Can winning also mean losing?

## *Related Activities*

1. Read "Gambler" by Elma Stuckey in *Life Doesn't Frighten Me at All*. How do the details of the poem bring you to your conclusion about gambling? Compare the speaker to Denn.

2. Father O'Gara introduces the idea that a person can turn anything into an obsession: gambling, drinking, or even being a priest. Research the addictive personality.

3. *Stone Cold* ends with a surprise. At sixteen, Denn owns a restaurant. How has Hautman prepared us for the ending? Discuss the ending. Is it happy?

4. Write one more chapter.

5. On page 106, Cookie explains to Denn what cards mean. Discuss whether the group agrees or disagrees with the explanation.

6. After reading the articles by Joan Caplin and Kevin Cook, write a short story or poem about the teenager who loses. You may wish to refer to *What's Your Story? A Young Person's Guide to Writing Fiction* by Marion Dane Bauer.

## *Related Works*

1. Bauer, Marion Dane. **What's Your Story? A Young Person's Guide to Writing Fiction**. New York: Clarion Books, 1992. 134p. $6.95pa. ISBN 0-395-57780-2. Bauer takes the writer through the process of writing the story, from planning to polishing.

2. Bridgers, Jay. **Having an Addictive Personality**. New York: The Rosen Publishing Group, 1998. 64p. (The Need to Know Library). $17.95. ISBN 0-8239-2777-6. The author defines addiction, its process, its effects on the family, and the process of recovery. Like the other books in The Need to Know Library, it includes sources of help, a bibliography, and an index.

3. Caplin, Joan. "Gambling in the USA." *City Family* (Summer 1996): 2 pages beginning on 48. Caplin discusses gambling as a long shot and lists questions that helps the reader distinguish problem gamblers from players.

4. Cook, Kevin. "Wanna Bet?" *React* (December 11-17, 1995): 3 pages beginning on 12. Cook describes a teenager addicted to gambling, warns about the growth of teenage gambling, and lists questions that teenagers can ask themselves about their attitudes about gambling.

5. **Gambling Mania**. Produced by A&E Television Networks, 1996. 50 min. Color. (20th Century with Mike Wallace). $19.95. AAE-21531. Videocassette. The film discusses America's growing preoccupation with gambling and the effect this preoccupation may be having on teenagers.

6. Stuckey, Elma. "Gambler." In **Life Doesn't Frighten Me at All** edited by John Agard. New York: Henry Holt, 1989. The poem describes the life of an unsuccessful gambler whose gambling kills him.

Branford, Henrietta. **Fire Bed and Bone**. Cambridge, MA: Candlewick Press, 1998. 122p. $15.99. ISBN 0-7636-0338-4.

## *Summary/Description*

*Fire Bed and Bone* is told by the dog of Rufus and Comfort, peasants living during the Peasants' Revolt in 1381. The story tells about one family in one village caught up in the revolt. Rufus and Comfort, revolutionaries, are betrayed and imprisoned. Their hunting dog sees their trials and does the best she can to help them while she is raising her own puppies. The story explains the historical context while portraying fully developed characters whose emotions and dreams transcend the time period. The narrator knows, better than her humans do, that greed, generosity, love, hate, cruelty, and kindness are integral parts of nature.

## *Booktalk*

Ask how many members of the audience own a dog. Ask them to tell about times when the dog showed loyalty or devotion.

Tied to *Fire Bed and Bone*, an old hunting dog tries to help her humans overcome the struggles and betrayals of revolution. As she gives birth to and raises her own puppies, she is constantly pulled into protecting those who have protected her. Like them, she is betrayed and imprisoned, and like them she must fight to be free. *Fire Bed and Bone* is cast in 1381. The Plague has left bodies piled on the roadsides. Labor is scarce, and the workers are beginning to demand better working conditions and more money. The Peasants' Revolt is a human revolution, but the animal who has tied herself to humans is part of it, too. And this animal knows, better than people do, that no life or revolution is clean, easy, or free of pain.

## Related Activities

1. Read the "Invitations" on page 77 of *Just People & Paper/Pen/Poem: A Young Writer's Way to Begin.* Apply the questions to both "Swifts," on page 22, and *Fire Bed and Bone.*

2. Research the Plague and present your findings in an oral or written report to the group.

3. Research the Peasants' Revolt and present your findings in an oral or written report to the group.

4. Research the changing role of women during and after the Plague.

5. In *I Rode a Horse of Milk White Jade*, Oyuna tells the story through her own eyes. Choose one incident from the novel and retell it through the eyes of either Bator the cat or Bayan the horse.

## Related Works

1. Appelt, Kathi (text), and Kenneth Appelt (photographs). **Just People & Paper/Pen/Poem: A Young Writer's Way to Begin**. See full booktalk in Chapter 4 (p. 195). Ms. Appelt presents suggestions for writing with each poem that she has written. Thus she helps the writer discover and organize thoughts and impressions.

2. Bauer, Marion Dane. **What's Your Story? A Young Person's Guide to Writing Fiction**. New York: Clarion Books, 1992. 134p. $6.95pa. ISBN 0-395-57780-2. The most useful chapter for activity 5 may be "Choosing Your Point of View," Chapter 7, on pages 57–67.

3. Branford, Henrietta. **White Wolf**. See full booktalk in Chapter 1 (p. 26). Branford again tells the story of an animal torn between man and the wild.

4. Farrell, Jeanette. **Invisible Enemies**. See full booktalk in Chapter 3 (p. 146). Farrell tells how ignorance and prejudice spread the Plague and describes some major changes the disease made in the world.

5. Wilson, Diane Lee. **I Rode a Horse of Milk White Jade**. See full booktalk in Chapter 1 (p. 8). The main character rides a magical horse to carry out the fate her grandmother has outlined for her.

Ferris, Jean. **Love Among the Walnuts**. New York: Harcourt Brace, 1998. 215p. $16.00. ISBN 0-15-201590-6.

## *Summary/Description*

*Love Among the Walnuts* begins with the romance of Horatio-Alger Huntington-Ackerman (HAHA) and Mousey Malone. Wealthy Horatio and the lovely young actress, Mousey, marry, build a mansion next to Walnut Manor (a home for "distressed" patients), and have a son, Alexander Huntington-Ackerman (AHA). They live in isolation and bliss with their loyal Bentley and Flossie, who eventually marry. Bartholomew and Bernie, Horatio's evil brothers, try to poison the group to inherit the company. The poison puts all family members into a coma except Bentley and Alexander. Bentley and Alexander are forced to hire a nurse and move the victims to the deteriorating Walnut Manor. Alexander, his faithful nurse Sunnie, the hospital staff, and the other Walnut Manor residents work together to foil the evil brothers, find themselves, and face the outside world. The novel is filled with nostalgia, plays on words, and triumphs of good and love over evil.

## *Booktalk*

Would you like to get away from it all? Have enough money so that you would never have to work again? Surround yourself with people you can love and trust? Learn whatever you like whenever you like? Be accepted for who you really are instead of what you wear, how you look, or how you talk? Horatio-Alger Huntington-Ackerman and his wife Mousey build that kind of world, but they learn they "can't have their cake and eat it" when Horatio's evil and greedy brothers poison them into a coma. Then Alexander, their son, and Bentley, their loyal butler, must join forces with the distressed next-door neighbors. They must find out if the *Love Among the Walnuts* is strong enough to overcome the forces of evil.

## *Related Activities*

1. Choose a section of the novel and convert it into a scene from a play. You might wish to view the movie *Harvey* or read the play *Harvey* before doing so.

2. Read pages 210–11 in *Love Among the Walnuts*. Using puns, rename the courses or books in your own school.

3. Discuss Horatio's reading choices. What do his choices reveal about him? Choose another character from another novel. Make up a reading list for that character and explain your choices.

4. The allusion to *The Chronicles of Narnia* appears in both *Love Among the Walnuts* and *A Door Near Here*. Discuss its use in both novels.

5. Character names reveal personalities. Discuss the name choices and how actions reinforce the impression given by the name. You may wish to refer to "Character . . . The Key to Good Stories" in *What's Your Story?*

6. Jean Ferris draws on the tradition of the wise misfit or fool to solve the problems in the novel. Discuss how wisdom and sensitivity make these "different" characters appealing and humorous.

7. Compare *Ethan Between Us*, *Kissing Doorknobs*, and *Love Among the Walnuts.* All deal with the line between eccentricity and mental illness. Discuss and account for the differences in tone.

## *Related Works*

1. Bauer, Marion Dane. **What's Your Story? A Young Person's Guide to Writing Fiction**. New York: Clarion Books, 1992. $6.95pa. ISBN 0-395-57780-2. Bauer presents a step-by-step guide to creating a story. Chapter 3, "Character . . . The Key to Good Stories," focuses on building and naming characters.

2. Chase, Mary. **Harvey**. New York: Oxford Press, 1953. Elwood P. Dowd is guided by the advice of a large, wise, invisible rabbit.

3. **Harvey**. Produced by Universal, 1950. 104 min. Black and White. $14.98. 80321. Videocassette. The film keeps very close to the play.

4. Hesser, Terry Spencer. **Kissing Doorknobs**. See full booktalk in Chapter 3 (p. 148). The main character battles obsessive-compulsive disorder.

5. Lewis, C. S. **The Chronicles of Narnia**. New York: HarperCollins, 1994 ed. 7 vol. $34.65pa. ISBN 0-06-447119-5. Lewis's fantasy explores Christian thought.

6. Myers, Anna. **Ethan Between Us**. See full booktalk in Chapter 4 (p. 221). Voices direct Ethan in writing a masterpiece of music.

7. Quarles, Heather. **A Door Near Here**. See full booktalk in Chapter 1 (p. 54). The youngest sister tries to retreat to the land of Narnia to escape her stressful family life.

8. Stern, Jerome. **Making Shapely Fiction**. New York: Laurel, 1991. $6.50pa. ISBN 0-440-21221-9. In the definitions of "Comedy" and "Satire," Stern explains the techniques and purpose of comedy and satire.

## Hesse, Karen. **The Music of Dolphins**. New York: Scholastic, 1996. 181p. $4.99pa. ISBN 0-590-89798-5.

### *Summary/Description*

In *The Music of Dolphins*, Mila, a feral child, describes her capture and education. Mila is left an orphan through a plane crash at the age of four and becomes part of a dolphin family. When Mila is a teenager, the Coast Guard discovers her and brings her back to the United States. Here, doctors teach her language, music, and supposedly what it means to be human. Competition and politics, however, interfere with the human side of the study. Mila has left the world of experience and been thrown into the world of analysis. She finds that she has become an oddity and as a result, a prisoner. She finds herself overwhelmed physically and emotionally. Justin, the head doctor's son, decides to return her to the sea. Although she is torn between the sea and the land, she finally returns to her loving dolphin family and the ocean's freedom.

## *Booktalk*

Write "feral" on the board. Ask the students to define the word. If they are not familiar with it, define it for them.

Mila, a feral child, is raised in the sea with *The Music of Dolphins*. Discovered by the Coast Guard on an island near Cuba, she returns to the human community—to become a human. She must learn the language, the feelings, and the relationships. Like Shay, an abused and isolated child, she becomes a protected experiment, a focus of study.

Mila reaches out to her doctors and their assistants to build her human family. She must decide if she can leave the dolphin's music and the sea's freedom, her natural family. She must learn what civilization will stir in her and what it will kill as she tries to blend her human mind and her natural spirit.

## *Related Activities*

1. *Dolphin Talk* explores the dolphin's ability to learn human language. Discuss how the research presented in the film is related to *The Music of Dolphins*.

2. *Go and Come Back* is about the meeting of two human cultures. Identify two misconceptions that occur in the meeting. Compare these to the misconceptions in *The Music of Dolphins*. Which misconceptions would be easier to deal with?

3. Compare Victor from *Victor* and Mila from *The Music of Dolphins* as feral children. Discuss how the point of view the writer has chosen affects your perception of each of the characters.

4. Read "Voices" in *Where I'm From: Where Poems Come From*. Mila has two voices: the dolphin voice and the school or study voice. Choose a character or person. You might choose Victor from *Victor*. Write a chapter or a poem through that person's or character's voice.

5. Mila describes herself on pages 89–100. Discuss what kind of world she has experienced with the dolphins. Compare it to the kind of world she experiences with people. Discuss Hesse's purpose in using different print for Mila's different worlds.

6. The poem "De Profundis" by Alan Bold, talks about a disturbing part of being "human." Discuss what that part is. Discuss when and if Mila encounters it.

## *Related Works*

1. Abelove, Joan. **Go and Come Back**. See full booktalk above (p. 61). A young girl observes two scientists who are observing her.

2. Bold, Alan. "De Profundis." In **The Lyric Potential** edited by James E. Miller, Jr., Robert Hayden, and Robert O'Neal. New York: Scott, Foresman & Company, 1974. 408p. (The Fountainhead Series). Man finds monsters of the deep ready to take over the world when he destroys himself with his nuclear tools.

3. **Dolphin Talk**. Produced by National Geographic, 1986. 14 min. Color. (EDVENTURES). $49.00. Y58015. Videocassette. This brief film shows language experiments conducted with dolphins.

4. Gerstein, Mordicai. **Victor**. See full booktalk below (p. 79). The novel is based on the education and life of the Savage of Aveyron, who was discovered in the mountains after the period of the French Revolution.

5. Lyon, George Ella (text), and Robert Hoskins (photographs). **Where I'm From: Where Poems Come From**. See full booktalk in Chapter 4 (p. 217). In the "Voices" section, Lyon gives directions and examples for letting a person or character speak in the form of a poem.

6. **Nell**. Produced by 20th Century Fox, 1994. 113 min. Color. $19.98. 8737. Videocassette. A woman, raised in the woods, is discovered by a doctor, who then takes on the responsibility of protecting her from researchers and publicity seekers. Part of the doctor's research includes the Savage of Aveyron. The film, rated PG-13, includes strong language and nude scenes, but both are appropriate for the context of the situation. The story echoes many of the themes explored in *Victor*.

McCaughrean, Geraldine. **The Pirate's Son**. New York: Scholastic, 1998 American ed. 294p. $16.95. ISBN 0-590-20344-4.

## *Summary/Description*

*The Pirate's Son* tells the story of three eighteenth-century teenagers: Nathan Gull, Maud Gull, and Thomas White. Nathan and Thomas are students at Graylake, an austere London boarding school. The headmaster tells Nathan that his father, a poor minister, has died without paying two terms of Nathan's tuition. Both the headmaster and the students, despite the kindness of Nathan's teacher, drive him in disgrace from the school. Thomas White, the son of a pirate, befriends and defends Nathan. Thomas decides that he too, does not belong in the meanness of Graylake, and they set off with "Mousey Maud," Nathan's thirteen-year-old sister, to Madagascar, Thomas's homeland. On their journey, they encounter the treacherous Captain Sheller, Thomas' guardian, who would sell them all into slavery; the upright Charles Hardcastle, shanghaied into a pirates' crew; King Samson, the scurrilous and repulsive pirate captain; and Queen Delilah, Thomas's mother, who has married Samson.

Thomas, now Tamo, guides Nathan and Maud through the pirate and island worlds. When the three arrive in Madagascar, Nathan sees the world through schoolboy literature and a strong biblical orientation. Tamo sees it through his religion, superstition, and childhood memories. Maud blends her strict religious background and lessons of obedience with the island world. Together, they must survive. They help each other deal with the deaths of loved ones, prejudices, and the clash of cultures, through storms, sickness, and pirate attacks. Finally, Maud saves the day against the pirates and understands that she must stay with Tamo, and her brother Nathan must return with Hardcastle to England.

## *Booktalk*

Pirates are the bad guys. Civilized people are the good guys. Islanders are savages. Men are the strong, intelligent protectors. Women are the weak, not so intelligent, protected.

In 1717, many people saw the world in these neat categories. People knew where they fit; well, maybe not. Nathan and Maud Gull thought they were respectable, middle-class children protected by their father's good heart, kind church, and modest means. But they find themselves on a pirate ship with Tamo, *The Pirate's Son*. He should give them protection when their father can't, but storms, pirates, and even the dead rising from their graves threaten safety and sanity. Nathan, the romantic, Maud, the mouse, and Tamo, the pirate, each has to find who he or she really is, who to trust, where he or she can be happy, and what to believe. Together, they try to solve the problems their parents have given them and stay alive in the bargain.

## *Related Activities*

1. *The Pirate's Son*, *Holes*, *I Rode a Horse of Milk White Jade*, *The Sacrifice*, and *Fated Sky* all deal with the role of fate or the supernatural. Ask five groups or five individuals within one group to read each of the novels. Then ask all the readers to come together and compare the authors' use of fate or the supernatural in each novel.

2. Discuss the name Mousey Maud and how it helps to develop Maud's character.

3. Define "Good Guys" and "Bad Guys" in the novel. Use the specifics from the novel that clarify the good and bad characters.

4. Choose one day described in the novel. Write a journal entry of one of the following characters: Nathan, Maud, or Tamo.

5. The following works deal with young people taking charge: *Cowboy Ghost*, *Saratoga Secret*, *Holes*, *Cast Two Shadows*, *Armageddon Summer*, *Rules of the Road*, *The Terrorist*, *Summer Soldiers*, *Hero*, and *The Pirate's Son*. Ask each member of the group to choose one of the books and discuss the following: the situation, the crisis, and the quality of the decisions made.

## *Related Works*

1. Bauer, Joan. **Rules of the Road**. See full booktalk below (p. 114). The main character takes on more and more responsibility in the business world.

2. Branford, Henrietta. **The Fated Sky**. See full booktalk in Chapter 1 (p. 48). The main character believes she has been promised in sacrifice to the gods.

3. Cooney, Caroline B. **The Terrorist**. See full booktalk in Chapter 3 (p. 135). The main character decides to take on international terrorists by herself.

4. Lindquist, Susan Hart. **Summer Soldiers**. See full booktalk in Chapter 3 (p. 160). The main character and his friends must make their own cattle drive when their fathers go to war.

5. Matcheck, Diane. **The Sacrifice**. See full booktalk below (p. 89). The main character believes she is destined to be The Great One in her tribe and must prove it to her community and herself.

6. Peck, Robert Newton. **Cowboy Ghost**. See full booktalk in Chapter 1 (p. 15). When his brother dies on a cattle drive, the main character must take over and prove his manhood.

7. Rinaldi, Ann. **Cast Two Shadows**. See full booktalk in Chapter 1 (p. 46). A young girl must save her family, split by politics and race, during the Revolutionary War.

8. Rottman, S. L. **Hero**. See full booktalk in Chapter 4 (p. 223). The main character risks his life to take charge of it.

9. Sachar, Louis. **Holes**. See full booktalk in Chapter 1 (p. 35). The main character believes his life is controlled by a gypsy curse.

10. Sterman, Betsy. **Saratoga Secret**. See full booktalk in Chapter 1 (p. 21). A young girl must warn the revolutionary troops about the British army's plans.

11. Wilson, Diane Lee. **I Rode a Horse of Milk White Jade**. See full booktalk in Chapter 1 (p. 8). The main character must discover if her handicap is a curse or a blessing.

12. Yolen, Jane, and Bruce Coville. **Armageddon Summer**. See full booktalk in Chapter 1 (p. 50). Two teenagers find themselves guiding their parents when they enter a cult.

McKee, Tim (interviews), and Anne Blackshaw (photographs). **No More Strangers Now: Young Voices from a New South Africa**. New York: DK Ink/Melanie Kroupa, 1998. 107p. $19.95. ISBN 0-7894-2524-6.

### *Summary/Description*

*No More Strangers Now* contains fourteen interviews with South African teenagers. Each young man or woman represents a different aspect of South African life. McKee and Blackshaw include the urban and rural poor, the privileged, the militant, the segregated, the integrated, and the traditional voices. The book may be read with the interviews and pictures, but the pictures and text under the pictures form a book themselves. Archbishop Desmond Tutu wrote the foreword. A map of South Africa precedes the introduction, and excerpts from Mangane Wally Serote's poem, "No More Strangers," frame the interviews.

### *Booktalk*

Show some of the contrasting pictures from the book. For example, the picture on page 57 contrasts with page 65. Page 57 shows the privileged son, and page 65 shows the challenging one.

Nelson Mandela made world headlines when he and his supporters fought to end apartheid, but laws don't change hearts. *No More Strangers Now* lets those hearts speak. Teenagers from poverty and privilege, city and country, apathy and activism see a better world for Africa, their families, and themselves. They tell how they have lived and how they hope to live together. Their voices and pictures show us many countries now trying to merge into one.

## *Related Activities*

1. In "If My Right Hand" by Zinzi Mandela in *Life Doesn't Frighten Me at All*, the speaker talks about a meeting of white and black hands on one person, a seemingly impossible combination. What do the hands stand for? How does this poem apply to the racial makeup of South Africa?

2. In "The Cage" by Savitri Hensman, in *Life Doesn't Frighten Me at All*, what does the cage stand for? Why does the speaker call fear and hate a cancer? Why does the builder find himself inside the cage? Do you agree with the speaker?

3. Read the opening poem in *No More Strangers Now: Young Voices from a New South Africa.* Discuss how the poem applies to the interviews. What or who is "freedom" in the poem?

4. Read Chapter 9 of *Cry the Beloved Country*, beginning with the words "This night they are busy . . ." and read to the end of the chapter. Discuss what these brief passages suggest about life in Shanty Town. Relate these passages to "Out of the Shacks" in *No More Strangers Now.*

5. Discuss how the characters in the novel *Cry the Beloved Country* parallel the speakers in the nonfiction *No More Strangers Now.*

6. *Apartheid: Calibrations of Color* uses fiction and nonfiction works to communicate the effects of Apartheid. Choose one person or character and write an interview the person might give.

## *Related Works*

1. Achebe, Chinua. **Things Fall Apart**. New York: Fawcett Crest Books, 1959. The book describes the problems that come with the disintegration of the tribes. It requires a mature and insightful audience.

2. Agard, John, ed. **Life Doesn't Frighten Me at All**. New York: Henry Holt, 1989. $14.95. ISBN 0-8050-1237-0. "If My Right Hand" talks about a meeting of white and black hands on one person in prayer. They are uncomfortable in the pocket. The speaker asks why they exist on one person. "The Cage" describes a racist building a cage, which he finds ultimately imprisoning him.

3. Fugard, Athol. **"Master Harold". . . and the Boys**. New York: Penguin Books, 1982. This play explores the complicated relationship between a white boy and the black servants who have served as his father figures as well. The play requires a mature audience.

4. Hacker, Carlotta. **Nobel Prize Winners**. New York: Crabtree Publishing, 1998. 48p. (Women in Profile). $8.95pa. ISBN 0-7787-0029-1. The book includes a profile of South African writer and Nobel Prize winner Nadine Gordimer.

5. **On the Trail of Mark Twain with Peter Ustinov**. Produced by William R. Grant, Channel 13, WNET, NY, 1999. 4 hours. Color. $29.98. OTM 900-WHEB HBV. 2 Videocassettes. In the last section of the film, Peter Ustinov visits South Africa. He talks to people from all levels of society, and his interviews clearly depict the hopes and problems faced by the youth of South Africa. You may order the film by calling 1-800-336-1917.

6. Paton, Alan. **Cry the Beloved Country**. New York: Charles Scribner's Sons, 1948. Through a train robbery and murder, two fathers, one black and one white, learn about their sons and the deep-rooted problems of South Africa.

Gerstein, Mordicai. **Victor**. New York: Farrar, Straus & Giroux/ Francis Foster Books, 1998. 258p. $17.00. ISBN 0-374-38142-9.

### *Summary/Description*

*Victor* is about a feral child discovered in the hills of France shortly after the French Revolution; the man who attempted to educate Victor, Jean-Marc-Gaspard Itard; and a young girl who wished to learn but was ignored. Gerstein describes his nonfiction sources in the "Acknowledgments." When two woodcutters discover Victor, they capture him, tie him to a pole, and carry him into the village. He escapes and is recaptured a year later. While in captivity the second time, he is analyzed by two experts: a pioneer in the humane treatment for the mentally insane and a leader in education for the deaf. Both conclude that the wild boy is an idiot. But Itard, a young teacher of the deaf, decides that he can educate the boy by awakening his senses. He believes that the boy is an idiot or a noble savage with all the basic human instincts. Itard experiences some successes but is finally defeated by Victor's puberty and Itard's own unwillingness to acknowledge personal feelings of love or desire. Obsessive masturbation blocks Victor's desire to learn, and Itard fears what Victor would do with or to other human beings if he were taught how to redirect those sexual urges. Itard chooses work over any personal happiness. Neither Victor nor Itard can find the bridge between the sensual and the intellectual.

The parallel story is about Julie, the daughter of workers at the institute. She lives with her married sister's family. Only boys attend the institute, and the teachers fear that a girl would be a disruptive influence. At eleven, Julie sews with her sisters at home. In that environment, she is denied the opportunity to learn anything but domestic tasks and is sexually molested by her brother-in-law. Her mother helps Itard, dotes on Victor, and ignores Julie. As Julie and Victor mature, Victor finds Julie fascinating. When Julie feels repulsed by Victor's appearance and advances, her mother reproaches her. When Julie makes up her own alphabet so that she might learn as Victor learns, her mother dismisses the effort. When the brother-in-law impregnates Julie's other unmarried sister, Julie is the one who must leave her sister's house, but she is not allowed to return home. She is sent into domestic service. Here her employer promises Julie that she will learn to read and write. Finally, Itard abandons his project and Victor, but Victor continues to live with Julie's mother. Only when Victor dies does Julie's mother ask her to come home. The novel explores justice, prejudice, and the meaning of being human.

## *Booktalk*

When he is about nine, Victor is first dragged from the wilderness. Someone has abandoned him and tried to cut his throat. He wears dirt for clothes. He can live in the bitter cold and thrust his hands in the fire without pain. He can't speak and doesn't seem to hear. When he is tied to a pole and carried into civilization, his presence raises some haunting questions for civilization. Itard, a teacher of the deaf, feels that he and Victor, together, can answer those questions. But in their journey together, they raise new questions that are even more difficult and painful.

## *Related Activities*

1. Compare the teachers in *Victor* and *The Miracle Worker.* Compare the students and the situations. Using those comparisons, discuss the definition of a "feral" or wild child.

2. Compare Julie in *Victor* and Maud in *The Pirate's Son*. What do the characters reveal about women's roles during those time periods?

3. *The Music of Dolphins* and *Victor* occur in very different time periods. How do those time periods affect the stories? Discuss how you feel Mila would have been treated in *Victor's* time period.

4. Choose one chapter from *Victor*. Retell it from Julie's point of view. You may wish to refer to "Choosing Your Point of View" in *What's Your Story? A Young Person's Guide to Writing Fiction.*

5. Research the life and thinking of Jean Jacques Rousseau. How did his thinking affect people in Itard's time period?

## *Related Works*

1. Bauer, Marion Dane. **What's Your Story? A Young Person's Guide to Writing Fiction**. New York: Clarion Books, 1992. 134p. $6.95pa. ISBN 0-395-57780-2. Bauer provides practical guidelines for developing a story. Chapter 7 discusses the advantages and disadvantages of choosing different points of view.

2. Dickens, Charles. **A Tale of Two Cities**. New York: Dell, 1963. The story depicts both the excesses of the French Revolution and the conditions that produced it.

3. Gibson, William. **The Miracle Worker**. New York: Bantam, 1959. Annie Sullivan leads Helen Keller out of the world of deafness and blindness.

4. Hesse, Karen. **The Music of Dolphins**. See full booktalk above (p. 72). A young girl who has lived with the dolphins is discovered and brought back to civilization to be studied.

5. McCaughrean, Geraldine. **The Pirate's Son**. See full booktalk above (p. 74). Maud travels with her brother and *The Pirate's Son* to a distant island, where she and they learn about her strength and intelligence.

6. Mikaelsen, Ben. **Petey**. See full booktalk in Chapter 1 (p. 6). The novel demonstrates how a severely handicapped boy (and man) is treated by an ignorant society.

7. **The Miracle Worker**. Produced by Warner Home Video, 1962. 98 min. Color. $59.95. 34012V. Videocassette. This is the film version of the play, *The Miracle Worker.*

8. **Nell**. Produced by 20th Century Fox, 1994. 113 min. Color. $19.98. 8737. Videocassette. A woman, raised in the woods, is discovered by a doctor, who then protects her from publicity seekers and researchers. The doctor includes the Savage of Aveyron in his research. The film, rated PG-13, includes strong language and nude scenes, but both are appropriate for the situations and characters. The story reflects many of the themes from *Victor.*

Walker, Virginia (text), and Katrina Roechelein (graphics). **Making Up Megaboy**. New York: DK Ink/Richard Jackson, 1998. 63p. $16.95. ISBN 0-7894-2488-6.

### *Summary/Description*

Robbie Jones, on his thirteenth birthday, shoots the elderly owner of a liquor store. Witnesses, friends, acquaintances, police, and family give their perceptions of the event, Robbie, and the old man. Robbie does not speak. Robbie and his friend Ruben have created a cartoon character, Megaboy. Robbie's parents distrust Ruben because he is Mexican, and his father rejects writing and drawing as sissified.

Robbie draws a picture of Megaboy rescuing Tara Jameson, a very popular girl Robbie follows at school. Tara and her friend Tiffany used to buy cigarettes at the liquor store. The new owner refuses to sell them the cigarettes, and they complain about his rudeness. The accounts imply that Robbie killed the storeowner to save and impress Tara. In fact, Megaboy is the powerful, respected character Robbie wants to be. Tara discounts Robbie and the picture, until the shooting. Then she thinks she might sell the picture to a tabloid. The book is a very sympathetic picture of Robbie Jones. The graphics and printing amplify the characters and settings.

## Booktalk

Show pictures of superhero cartoon characters. Ask students what these characters stand for. Ask students why they think superheroes are popular.

Robbie Jones is into superheroes. He and his friend create Megaboy. Megaboy can right every wrong. He fears no one, and all who know him love him. But Megaboy draws Robbie farther and farther from reality and finally to murder. Now his parents, the police, the psychiatrists, and his fellow students are trying to figure out what happened to Robbie, that quiet kid no one wanted around, while he was *Making Up Megaboy.*

## Related Activities

1. Research superheroes from comic strips such as those produced by Marvel Comics. Identify hero patterns. For instance, what are the heroes like before and after transformation? For a start, refer to pages 18–20 in *How to Draw and Sell Comic Strips . . . for Newspapers and Comic Books.*

2. Create a superhero character. Describe him or her. Follow the step-by-step advice in "Mastering the Comic Strip," from *How to Draw and Sell Comic Strips . . . for Newspapers and Comic Books.* Create one part of the strip or the entire strip.

3. Analyze the media information surrounding Robbie Jones for report, inference, and judgment statements. What are your conclusions?

4. *Tenderness*, *Tangerine*, *Hero*, *A Door Near Here*, and *Making Up Megaboy* all present teenagers who challenge society. Ask five groups or five individuals to choose a novel. Ask each individual or group to describe the person at odds with society, and the cues for acceptance or condemnation of the character each author uses. State the message the author seems to be sending about that character.

5. The five items listed on pages 48–49 of *Depression* are the areas researched by a doctor diagnosing depression. How much of this information is a reader able to collect about Robbie Jones? Upon what problem areas in Robbie's life does the author seem to focus?

### *Related Works*

1. Bloor, Edward. **Tangerine**. See full booktalk in Chapter 1 (p. 16). The teenage criminals are presented as deliberate and threatening.
2. Cormier, Robert. **Tenderness**. See full booktalk above (p. 64). The young criminals are presented as sinister.
3. Mckenzie, Alan. **How to Draw and Sell Comic Strips . . . for Newspapers and Comic Books**. Cincinnati, OH: North Light Books, 1987. Mckenzie gives a short history of comics that explains the development and popularity of certain characters.
4. Quarles, Heather. **A Door Near Here**. See full booktalk in Chapter 1 (p. 54). The youngest sister of the family retreats to the fantasy world of Narnia when her family situation becomes too stressful.
5. Rottman, S. L. **Hero**. See full booktalk in Chapter 4 (p. 223). The main character turns his life around when the court sentences him to work on a farm.
6. Silverstein, Alvin, Virginia Silverstein, and Laura Silverstein Nunn. **Depression**. See full booktalk in Chapter 3 (p. 150). The book outlines the history, causes, and methods of prevention for depression.

## SPIRITUALLY

Gormley, Beatrice. **C. S. Lewis: Christian and Storyteller**. Grand Rapids, MI: Eerdmans Books for Young Readers, 1998. 182p. (Men of Spirit). $8.00pa. ISBN 0-8028-5069-3.

### *Summary/Description*

*C. S. Lewis: Christian and Storyteller* tells about Lewis's somewhat tumultuous boyhood, his spiritual and emotional growth, and his life as a scholar and writer. Experiencing the death of his mother and the emotional distance of his father, Lewis first declared himself an atheist and then converted to Christianity. As he sorted out the mythological characters, which he loved, found the strength to forgive his father, and established a place in Oxford's intellectual community, he also discovered his belief in a Christian God. His writings, for both children and adults, reflect that combination of the mythological, emotional, and intellectual. His life demonstrates the responsibility and kindness that his faith inspired. This biography includes pictures of Lewis, his friends, and family; a bibliography of books by Lewis and about Lewis; and a name and topic index.

## *Booktalk*

Ask the audience what they think would make their lives happy. Ask them to write down answers. Then ask them to read the answers out loud.

As a young man, C. S. Lewis didn't do much or have much that we would see as fun or happy. His mother died when he was very young. His father was too busy to pay attention to him. He was separated from his brother, and he went to a school directed by an insane headmaster. Yet he made wonderful friends, built his own family, and wrote some of the most memorable books in the English language. This man who didn't strike anyone as heroic, muscular, attractive, or rich managed to find more success and happiness than most people could manage in two lifetimes. Beatrice Gormley tells about a thinker who learned to love in *C. S. Lewis: Christian and Storyteller*.

## *Related Activities*

1. Select a character from mythology. Identify the character's traits. Discuss the ideas or ideal that character might represent. Create or select a modern cartoon character that has those same traits.

2. Place the character you created in Activity 1 in a conflict situation. Explain what the character would do and why.

3. Read at least one selection from *The Chronicles of Narnia*. Choose one character from that selection and explain C. S. Lewis's purpose in constructing that character.

4. In *A Door Near Here*, eight-year-old Alicia and Mr. Dodgson, a high school teacher and then a graduate student, discuss the Lion from *The Chronicles of Narnia*. What do their discussions tell us about C. S. Lewis's work?

5. *Making Up Megaboy* is the story of a young man who makes up a fantasyland, which harms him. How does his land differ from Narnia?

6. *Love Among the Walnuts* also deals with a land of retreat. Discuss how this place of isolation or land differs from Narnia. Discuss each author's purpose is using the retreat.

7. C. S. Lewis and J. R. R Tolkien were friends and belonged to Kolbitar, a group devoted to exploring Old Icelandic sagas. Both men wrote fantasies inspired by mythology. Like Lewis, Tolkien's writing reflected his religious and moral beliefs. Read "The Hoard" in *Poems and Stories* by J. R. R. Tolkien. Discuss the purpose of the work and how the characters aid that purpose.

## *Related Works*

1. Ferris, Jean. **Love Among the Walnuts**. See full booktalk above (p. 70). The characters retreat into an isolated world but find they can work with each other and the outside world to help others and build happy lives.
2. Lewis, C. S. **The Chronicles of Narnia**. New York: HarperCollins, 1994. 7 vol. $34.65pa. ISBN 0-06-447119-5. Lewis creates a fantasy world that expresses his spiritual beliefs.
3. Quarles, Heather. **A Door Near Here**. See full booktalk in Chapter 1 (p. 54). A young girl who is stressed by her dysfunctional family plans to run away to the land of Narnia.
4. Tolkien, J. R. R. "The Hoard." In **Poems and Stories**. New York: Houghton Mifflin, 1994. ISBN 0-395-68999-6. The poems tell how the dwarf, the dragon, the warrior, and the king are overcome by greed.
5. Walker, Virginia, and Katrinia Roechelein. **Making Up Megaboy**. See full booktalk above (p. 82). A young boy who is too shy to handle the real world retreats into a superhero fantasy and kills a shopkeeper.

 Levitin, Sonia. **The Singing Mountain**. New York: Simon & Schuster Books for Young Readers, 1998. 261p. $17.00. ISBN 0-689-80809-7.

## *Summary/Description*

*The Singing Mountain* tells the story of twin journeys. Mitch Green goes on vacation to Israel and discovers a rebirth in Orthodox Judaism. He decides to learn about his Jewish heritage by staying at an Orthodox

Yeshiva. He supports himself by making jewelry, a plan that he sees as being rejected by his materialistic U.S. community.

Carlie, his cousin, has lived with the Greens since her parents were killed in an automobile accident. When Mitch leaves and then calls home for money, she and her aunt travel to Israel. Her Aunt Vivian fears that Mitch is the victim of a cult. On this journey, Carlie must sort out her feelings about Mitch, her family, and her new boyfriend.

Both Mitch and Carlie strive to find out where and how they fit in their family and spiritual lives. The chapters alternate between Carlie's view and Mitch's view. Carlie returns to southern California after she discovers the closeness and devotion of a family she doubted. Mitch stays at the Yeshiva to continue his spiritual journey.

## *Booktalk*

The trip to Israel promises to be a "cultural experience," a break before college at UCLA. But Mitch does not come back. Thinking her son has been captured by a cult, Mitch's mother travels with Mitch's cousin to Israel. Here, all three journey on long forgotten spiritual and family paths as they share forbidden secrets, feelings, and fears. Carlie searches for the parents she has lost. Vivian searches for the dreams she has given up. Mitch searches for his identity. The glitzy world of southern California meets the stark, spiritual world of Israel, and Mitch, Carlie, and Vivian find that there are no perfect people but just humans journeying toward personal truths.

## *Related Activities*

1. *Masada: The Last Fortress* and *The Singing Mountain* are both written with alternating chapters. One chapter is the secular, pragmatic view, and the other is the spiritual view. Discuss how this format suits each author's purpose.

2. Read *Voices in the Park* aloud and show the pictures. This picture book tells the same event through four different sets of eyes. Discussing the differences in these perceptions should prepare the class or audience for discussing the different perceptions of similar events discussed in *The Singing Mountain.*

3. Identify the sections of *The Singing Mountain* that show how the characters differ in their perceptions of the same event. Discuss what elements produce these differences.

4. After viewing *The Lost Children of Berlin* and *Israel: Birth of a Nation*, discuss why the country of Israel draws so much emotional response.

5. Cults are an issue in both *Armageddon Summer* and *The Singing Mountain.* Discuss whether that definition applies in each novel.

6. Read and discuss "The Road Not Taken" by Robert Frost, in relation to *The Singing Mountain.*

7. Write a "Where You're From" poem for one of the characters in *The Singing Mountain.* Then write a "Where You're From" poem about yourself. *Where I'm From: Where Poems Come From* is listed in Related Works.

## *Related Works*

1. Browne, Anthony. **Voices in the Park**. New York: DK Publishing, 1998. 30p. $15.95. ISBN 0-7894-2522-X. Four different people give their perceptions of a chance meeting in the park. The book illustrates that what is beautiful to one may be quite threatening to another.

2. Frost, Robert. "The Road Not Taken." In **Robert Frost's Poems**. New York: Washington Square Press, 1946. This poem expresses the difference that taking the less traveled road makes in one's life.

3. **Israel: Birth of a Nation**. Produced by A&E Television Networks, 1996. 100 min. Color. $29.95. AAE-40403. Videocassette. The film explains the geographical, religious, and historical background of Israel.

4. **The Lost Children of Berlin**. Produced by A&E Television Networks, 1997. 50 min. Color. $19.95. AAE-16117. Videocassette. The film reunites the members of a Jewish school who were persecuted during Hitler's regime.

5. Lyon, George Ella. "Where You're From." In **Where I'm From: Where Poems Come From**. See full booktalk in Chapter 4 (p. 217). Lyon guides the poet through the process of writing a poem that forces the writer to define a personality.

6. Miklowitz, Gloria. **Masada: The Last Fortress**. See full booktalk in Chapter 3 (p. 162). *The Singing Mountain* alludes to Masada, a literal battle between the spiritual and materialistic worlds.

7. Yolen, Jane, and Bruce Coville. **Armageddon Summer**. See full booktalk in Chapter 1 (p. 50). Two teenagers must help their parents face a religious crisis and in the process, define their own beliefs.

Matcheck, Diane. **The Sacrifice**. New York: Farrar, Straus & Giroux, 1998. 198p. $16.00. ISBN 0-374-36378-1.

## *Summary/Description*

*The Sacrifice* explores two sacrifices. Fifteen-year-old Weak-One-Who-Does-Not-Last is an Apsaalooka maiden destined by a mystical dream to be the Great One. A twin, Weak-One has lived in the shadow of her dead brother, who was originally thought to be the Great One. Orphaned and rejected by her tribe, she decides to join the young braves and prove to everyone, including herself, that the destiny is hers. On her journey, she burns herself in the hot springs of Yellowstone and loses part of her hand fighting and killing a grizzly. Trying to recover her runaway horse, she is captured by the Pawnee. At the camp, the Pawnee give her to the kind young brave Wolfstar. Left together when many tribe members embark on a hunting expedition, they build friendship and love. When the tribe returns, Weak-One finds she is the human sacrifice of the Morning Star Ceremony. She feels her escape will endanger Wolfstar, and so she cooperates. At the climax of the ceremony, she runs in panic with Wolfstar behind her. He has prepared and hidden her horse. When he is fatally wounded in the flight, Weak-One takes him with her, tries to save him, and eventually buries him with her grizzly hide and necklace that might secure her claim to greatness. Wolfstar's sacrifice shows Weak-One the worth of her own life and causes her to reflect on the sacrifices others have made for her. She decides to return to the guidance of the tribe so that she might learn how to contribute her strength to the community, and someday grow into a Great One. The Author's Note provides background information about the Crow and Pawnee.

## *Booktalk*

Ask how many people would like to change their names. Ask them what the change might be and why they would like to change.

*The Sacrifice* tells the story of Weak-One-Who-Would-Not-Last. After naming his children, her father discovers that he has made a mistake. The girl should have been named Great One. Her twin brother should have been named Weak-One. But names and the judgments names carry are difficult to change. Orphaned and rejected by the tribe, Weak-One decides she must change her name, her vision of herself, and the way others see her. At fifteen, she must prove herself on a lonely, dangerous journey that challenges nature, man, and finally the gods. She must discover her destiny and perhaps shape it.

## *Related Activities*

1. Read "Direction" by Alonzo Lopez in *Life Doesn't Frighten Me at All.* Discuss how the poem applies to *The Sacrifice.*

2. View only the wolf segment of *Cry of the Wild: Wolves, Fires and the Fight.* Compare the way the wolves are regarded today and the way they are regarded in *The Sacrifice* and *White Wolf.* Explain the difference through the voice of a wolf.

3. After viewing *Cry of the Wild: Wolves, Fires and the Fight*, tell what difficulties today's tourist would face in contrast to the difficulties faced by Weak-One-Who-Does-Not-Last.

4. Read "The Sacred Bear of Hokkaido" by Kathi Appelt in *Just People & Paper/Pen/Poem: A Young Writer's Way to Begin*. Complete the related "Invitations."

5. The main characters in *The Sacrifice* and *Fated Sky* believe their lives are controlled or at least influenced by fate. Is there evidence in the books for their beliefs? How does each character bow to or fight her fate?

6. Discuss how Weak-One-Who-Does-Not-Last changes her definition of bravery or heroism by the end of the novel. Compare her definition with the definitions presented in *Hero*, *The King's Swift Rider*, and *No Man's Land.*

## *Related Works*

1. Appelt, Kathi. "The Sacred Bear of Hokkaido." In **Just People & Paper/Pen/Poem: A Young Writer's Way to Begin**. See full booktalk in Chapter 4 (p. 195). The haiku describes the walk of the bear in winter.

2. Bartoletti, Susan. **No Man's Land**. See full booktalk in Chapter 1 (p. 37). A young soldier changes his definition of bravery after fighting in the Civil War.

3. Branford, Henrietta. **The Fated Sky**. See full booktalk in Chapter 1 (p. 48). A young girl has been told that she must be sacrificed, but she runs away from her fate.

4. Branford, Henrietta. **White Wolf**. See full booktalk in Chapter 1 (p. 26). Native Americans pursue a wolf that they wish to sacrifice.

5. **Cry of the Wild: Wolves, Fires and the Fight**. Produced by A&E Television Networks, 1996. 50 min. Color. (20th Century with Mike Wallace). $19.95. AAE-21537. Videocassette. The tape may be viewed in the three separate parts: wolves, fires, and tourism. All three have become serious problems for the Yellowstone area.

6. Hunter, Mollie. **The King's Swift Rider**. See full booktalk below (p. 119). A young soldier finds that devotion to a cause is the most important part of heroism.

7. Lopez, Alonzo. "Direction." In **Life Doesn't Frighten Me at All** edited by John Agard. New York: Henry Holt, 1989. The poem explains how each part of the Earth gives us a particular power.

8. Rottman, S. L. **Hero**. See full booktalk in Chapter 4 (p. 223). A boy with no heroes decides he can define one after he is sentenced to work with a crusty farmer.

Napoli, Donna Jo. **Sirena**. New York: Scholastic, 1998. 210p. $15.95. ISBN 0-590-383-38388-4.

### *Summary/Description*

Sirena's name means to bind or attach. But she does not want to hurt sailors by seducing them with her siren song. Instead she isolates herself so that she will bring no harm. In doing so, she meets the human Philoctetes, saves his life, and falls in love with him. In mating with him, she makes herself immortal, but also attaches herself to the pain of human love. Even as their love grows, Sirena and Philoctetes realize the differences that draw them apart. One day, the Greeks who abandoned Philoctetes to die on the island return. Human loyalty and honor call him. Without Philoctetes, the Greeks cannot win the Trojan War. When Sirena protests his leaving, she discovers that she is arguing against destiny. She releases him. Both then realize that their love will never die even though their lives will now be separate. The novel carries out the theme that no one can run from fate. It does show, however, that within that fate each person is free to build personal character. The Trojan War and Greek mythology frame the novel. If readers are familiar with both they will recognize and enjoy how these allusions are used. If readers are unfamiliar with the Trojan War and Greek mythology, they will learn a great deal about both, even if they do not research the allusions.

## *Booktalk*

The citizens of Olympus never rest. Gods and goddesses constantly plot human destruction. Sirena decides to fight her destiny even if she must sacrifice immortality. She will not join her sister sirens and lure sailors to their death. When she finds a royal warrior abandoned and almost dead, she unselfishly tries to save him, but then falls in love with him. Now she is trapped. Unlike her sisters who love and reject on a whim, she dedicates her life to a human and must suffer the human doubts and pains of love. But the warrior has a destiny also. The Trojan War has brought them together, and now the Trojan War and mortality promise to separate them. Can either the mythical female or the mortal male shape love or fate?

## *Related Activities*

1. Chapter 14, "The Debate," reveals the different points of view Sirena and Philoctetes bring to the hero stories. Discuss what experiences may influence these points of view. Is there a right or a wrong view?

2. Read another hero story aloud. Ask the listeners to construct objections to it from the point of view of the hero's victim.

3. Read "The Mermaid" by W. B. Yeats in *Life Doesn't Frighten Me at All.* Is Yeats speaking about a mermaid only or about all people who love? Whom does he see as the victim?

4. In the A&E Home Video, *The Odyssey of Troy*, the narrator observes that Troy symbolizes the world and that the Trojan citizens symbolize all people. Discuss the following questions: If Sirena and Philoctetes are symbols, who or what do they represent? Do they find themselves in a human or mythical conflict?

5. Who is the woman the speaker addresses in Poe's poem "To Helen"? How does he feel about her? Use information from the poem's text, especially the allusions, to support your answers.

6. In "Ulysses," Tennyson shows an old Ulysses who has returned to his homeland and is now longing for the adventure of his youth. What does this "idle King" reveal about himself and his relationship to destiny?

## *Related Works*

1. Hamilton, Edith. "The Heroes of the Trojan War." In **Mythology**. New York: Mentor, 1940. Hamilton tells the story of Philoctetes and his interaction with the other heroes of the Trojan War.

2. **The Odyssey of Troy**. Produced by Multimedia Entertainment, 1995. 50 min. Color. (Ancient Mysteries). $14.95. AAE-95064. Videocassette. The film investigates the existence of an actual Troy and explores the symbolic meaning of the epic. In its explanation, it utilizes the relationship among fact, myth, and truth.

3. Poe, Edgar Allan. "To Helen." In **Literature: Reading Fiction, Poetry, Drama, and the Essay** by Robert DiYanni. New York: Random House, 1986. Poe speaks to a beautiful Helen.

4. Rees, Ennis, trans. **The Odyssey of Homer**. New York: Modern Library Books, 1960. The translation is quite readable and has an index of proper names.

5. Tennyson, Alfred Lord. "Ulysses." In **Literature: Reading Fiction, Poetry, Drama, and the Essay** by Robert DiYanni. New York: Random House, 1986. Ulysses speaks about his desire to continue his quests and adventures.

6. Yeats, W. B. "The Mermaid." In **Life Doesn't Frighten Me at All**. New York: Henry Holt, 1989. This one-line poem describes the mermaid finding a young man and then thoughtlessly drowning him.

Suskind, Ron. **A Hope in the Unseen**. New York: Broadway Books, 1998. 372p. $25.00. ISBN 0-7679-0125-8.

### *Summary/Description*

*A Hope in the Unseen* tells about Cedric Jenning's life from his junior year in high school to the end of his freshman college year. Cedric's world is made up of barriers and limits: not enough money, too little education, and a father in jail for drug dealing. Accepted first at a MIT summer school program and finally at Brown University, Cedric enters a world where people live almost without barriers. Cedric can experiment with nothing without facing possibly destructive consequences. The upper-class students seem to have endless second chances. Cedric's discipline, based on religious faith, has helped him build success even with the poor classes and hostile classmates at Ballou High School, where the honor roll is the gang hit list. Now he must learn to live in the "everything is accepted" world of an Ivy League school that challenges not only his intellect but also his moral resolve. Cedric must deal with problems of drugs, violence, sex, faith, and identity as he tries to build a bridge between the two worlds. Sometimes the language and images are shocking and threatening, but his inspiring nonfiction story speaks to the importance of individual strength nurtured by strong family, religious faith, and dedication to excellence.

### *Booktalk*

The Honor Role is the gangs' hit list. If you show up to accept an award, you'll probably be beaten up. As you walk through the halls, you'll probably see blood. Your advanced classes are another school's middle track. Welcome to Ballou High School, Washington, D.C.

Twelve hundred board scores are average. Parents fly into campus on their own jets. The buildings are classic, carpeted, and fully computerized. Your fellow students are used to soft carpets and maid service. Welcome to Brown University, the Ivy League.

Cedric Lavar Jennings wants to move from the world of Ballou to the world of Brown. He may never really be part of either, but if he doesn't work harder than everyone else he may always be held prisoner by the first. To ignore the fear, the jealousy, the unpaid bills, and the fragmentation in his own family, he must build on *A Hope in the Unseen.*

## *Related Activities*

1. After reading *A Hope in the Unseen*, research and debate voucher proposals for schools.

2. Research summer school programs, mentor programs, and scholarship programs for minorities and inner-city youth.

3. Read *Psalm Twenty-Three* illustrated by Tim Ladwig. Show the pictures while you are reading. Discuss how the psalm and the pictures would or would not apply to Cedric's life.

4. Establish three long-range goals and three short-term goals. (You may wish to refer to "Goals and Plans" in *Strategies for Studying.*) Map a plan for achieving those goals.

5. A fictional presentation, *Make Lemonade*, shows how a girl's baby-sitting job forces her to struggle against negative expectations and strengthen her resolve to go to college. Compare the obstacles Cedric finds with those the main character in *Make Lemonade* finds.

6. Read "Dinner Guest: Me" by Langston Hughes. Describe the speaker. Why does he speak at this time? How does he feel about his situation?

7. Read "Theme for English B" by Langston Hughes. Describe the speaker. Are his feelings like Cedric's? Are these concerns only black/white concerns or universal?

## *Related Works*

1. Giovanni, Nikki. **Shimmy Shimmy Shimmy Like My Sister Kate: Looking at the Harlem Renaissance Through Poems**. See full booktalk in Chapter 4 (p. 236). "Dinner Guest: Me" and "Theme for English B" communicate the loneliness and anger that the speakers feel in these situations.

2. Ladwig, Tim (illus). **Psalm Twenty-Three**. Grand Rapids, MI: Eerdmans Books for Young Readers, 1993. 30p. $15.00. ISBN 0-8028-5160-6. Illustrations show two children protected from the dangers of the streets.

3. Stark, Evan. **Street Gangs**. New York: The Rosen Publishing Group, 1995 rev. ed. 64p. (The Need to Know Library). $17.95. ISBN0-8239-2121-2. *A Hope in the Unseen* illustrates why young

people would choose to join a gang and participate in the behavior described in *Street Gangs*.

4. University of Victoria's Counseling Services. **Strategies for Studying: A Handbook of Study Skills**. Victoria, BC: Orca Book Publishers, 1996. 150p. $12.95pa. ISBN 1-55143-063-0. The section "Goals and Plans" focuses on setting specific, realistic study goals and managing one's time to meet them.

5. Wolf, Virginia Euwer. **Make Lemonade**. New York: Henry Holt, 1993. 208p. $15.95. ISBN 0-8050-2228-7. Written in verse, this journal tells about a young girl's hopes and fears as she works to earn money so that she can go to college.

# PHYSICALLY

Carter, Alden R. **Bull Catcher**. New York: Scholastic, 1997. 279p. $15.95. ISBN 0-590-50958-6.

### *Summary/Description*

Neil Larsen, nicknamed Bull, has decided to write his senior project about his junior high and high school career. *Bull Catcher* is a combination of those events and the reflections that clarify his life. Bull lives with his grandfather. His mother has never married, works in a high-powered city job, and sends money back to the grandfather to support Neil. Neil's best friend Jeff lives with his mother, stepfather, and new little sisters. Billy, a good friend to both, is a victim of an abusive father. In junior high, Ngo Huynh Phuong (pronounced No Win Fong), the star pitcher, joins the group. Jeff, driven by baseball, pushes and leads the others to be a winning team. In the drive, Bull supports and advises as he manages the plays. But off the diamond, Bull sorts out his personal life. Billy begins to date Sandi, the girl Bull loves. Bull then separates himself from Billy, and carries the guilt when Billy dies in a drunk driving accident. Jeff wants to steamroll all the way to a school championship, but Bull sacrifices two summers of baseball to work at a camp and to spend some time with his mother. Both Jeff and Bull plan on No Win leading them to a championship, but Phuong graduates early so that he can help his father set up a medical clinic in Vietnam before Phuong starts medical school. Through this all, Bull is trying to decide what romantic love means. He loves Sandi, and she loves him at her convenience. He's smitten with Jenna, but Jenna is smitten with everybody. He really feels comfortable with Bev, but she just isn't glamorous enough. Meanwhile, his grandfather is dating, and his mother is developing a love life. By the end of the story, he decides that his brain may help him more than his muscles and that love has more to do with trust and support than glamour. The situations and characters in *Bull Catcher* are very realistic, but the language is strong.

## *Booktalk*

Bull Larson, *The Bull Catcher*, loves baseball. All his friends love baseball. They run the team, and want a championship, maybe a career in the majors. But can the game be Bull's life? He's pretty good in school. There is this girl he likes. Well, maybe a couple of girls. His career-driven mother wants him to move to California, and the grandfather who raised him is developing a love life. To add to the confusion, Bull is the man people turn to in a crisis. Some people even want to hire him, the big Bull, to work with little kids. He has to sort it all out. Will going for the game make him miss all the important action off the field? Is there a difference between wanting to play and having to play? Is it better to think for the team or to think for himself?

## *Related Activities*

1. In *The Bull Catcher*, *Slam*, *Buried Onions*, *Hero*, *Parrot in the Oven*, and *Safe At Second*, young men must decide the direction of their lives. Ask six individuals or six groups to choose and read the books, one book for each individual or group. Then ask them to compare the characters on the basis of their goals, obstacles, and degree of success.

2. Debate the value of sports programs in schools.

3. Neil Larson uses his journal as his senior project. To do this, he must edit and condense events. Write a daily journal for one week. Then write a personal essay that focuses on the significant events of that week. You might want to refer to *Telling Your Own Stories* for help in finding a focus.

4. Take the role of each character. From that character's point of view, explain what baseball would mean to the character. You might want to use the suggestions for object poems on pages 12–17 in *Where I'm From: Where Poems Come From.*

5. Bull Larson's problems may come from having too many talents. Discuss these talents and how they might work together. Write the resume that you think Bull will write when he is thirty years old.

## *Related Works*

1. Davis, Donald. **Telling Your Own Stories**. Little Rock, AR: August House, 1993. 127p. $10.00pa. ISBN 0-87483-235-7. Davis explains methods and presents prompts that will help a storyteller get started and develop a focus.

2. Johnson, Scott. **Safe at Second**. See full booktalk below (p. 101). The main character decides that he must seek his own life instead of following the goals, successes, and tragedies of his friend.

3. Lyon, George Ella. "Objects." In **Where I'm From: Where Poems Come From**. See full booktalk in Chapter 4 (p. 217). The chapter explains how to express ideas and feelings by focusing on an object. She includes suggestions and sample poems.

4. Martinez, Victor. **Parrot in the Oven**. See full booktalk below (p. 112). The main character finally decides that his family, with all its problems, is his base.

5. Myers, Walter Dean. **Slam**. See full booktalk below (p. 110). The main character finds that getting his game together off the court improves his game on the court.

6. Rottman, S. L. **Hero**. See full booktalk in Chapter 4 (p. 223). The main character decides to make his life mean something by facing up to responsibility.

7. Soto, Gary. **Buried Onions**. See full booktalk below (p. 124). The main character must break out of the cycle of gang violence and vendetta.

8. Stark, Evan. **Family Violence**. New York: The Rosen Publishing Group, 1997 rev. ed. 62p. (The Need to Know Library). $17.95. ISBN 0-8239-2296-6. The author defines abuse and tells what to do about it. The book includes a glossary; names, addresses and phone numbers of abuse organizations; lists of books for further reading; and an index.

Corbett, Sara. **Venus to the Hoop**. New York: Anchor Books, 1997. 341p. $12.95pa. ISBN 0-385-49352-5.

### *Summary/Description*

*Venus to the Hoop* chronicles the Gold Medal Year of the U. S. Olympic Team. It profiles each of the players and the coach. Eight black women and three white women made up the team. The youngest was Rebecca Lobo, age twenty-one. The oldest was Teresa Edwards, age thirty-one. Some came from poverty, and some came from privilege. All faced grueling physical, mental, and emotional challenges. One player, Carla McGhee continued to "go for the Gold" even after a near-fatal accident. *Venus to the Hoop* discusses how these talented, feminine, and dynamic women acted and interacted on and off the court. Each woman had a vision of herself and her relation to her country and home. This vision motivated her to rise above petty differences and focus on the Gold Medal Game. Sara Corbett also gives a blow-by-blow account of the team's major games and their challenges from cultural differences as well as competition.

### *Booktalk*

Venus was the goddess of love and beauty. (Show pictures of Venus.) She doesn't look very athletic or energetic.

*Venus to the Hoop* doesn't talk about beauty in terms of small, wispy, or languid girls but about beauty in terms of women who are over six feet tall and weigh between 170 and 190 pounds. They run, elbow, and sweat to get the job done on a basketball court and then model for and charm their public off the court. As the 1996 Olympic Gold Team, they redefined beauty and basketball. These women weren't afraid of their power, their brains, or their size. Sara Corbett tells the story of fourteen classy ladies, like four-time medal winner Teresa Edwards and rookie Rebecca Lobo, whose pride and drive carried them through bone-crunching accidents and ego-crushing experiences to eventually eclipse the much-touted men's Dream Team at the 1996 Olympics.

### *Related Activities*

1. Apply the "Invitations" on page 81 of *Just People & Paper/Pen/Poem: A Young Writer's Way to Begin* to both "The Swimmer" and *Venus to the Hoop*.

2. Expand on the reports given in *Athletes*. Then find a woman athlete not mentioned. Research and report about her. Use the format of *Athletes* (Women in Profile).

3. Read the reports given in *Great African Americans in the Olympics.* Then find an African American Olympic athlete not mentioned. Research and report about the athlete. Use the format of *Great African Americans in the Olympics.*

4. Research the men's Olympic basketball team. Compare the media's treatment of the men's basketball team with that of the women's basketball team. Discuss when and how this attention and attitude might change.

5. Read "Catalogues," "Looking Through a Magnifying Glass," and "Mirrors," in *Ophelia Speaks.* Compare those reflections with the self-concepts expressed by the members of the Olympic team. Discuss the differences in attitude.

6. Write a sports article for the first women's team to make the slam dunk their signature play.

## *Related Works*

1. Appelt, Kathi. "The Swimmer." In **Just People & Paper/Pen/Poem: A Young Writer's Way to Begin**. See full booktalk in Chapter 4 (p. 195). The swimmer's struggle communicates the pressure and effort of other athletes' experiences also.

2. Bandrapalli, Suman. "Can Slam Dunk Find Spot in Women's Game?" *Christian Science Monitor* (February 24, 1998): 14. Bandrapalli explains the emotional issue of the slam dunk in women's basketball.

3. Hunter, Shaun. **Great African Americans in the Olympics**. New York: Crabtree Publishing, 1997. 64p. (Outstanding African Americans). $15.96pa. ISBN 0-7787-0037-2. The book provides seven full profiles of African American Olympic athletes and shortened profiles of six more.

4. McKissack, Jr., Fredrick. "Black Women in Basketball." In **Black Hoops: The History of African Americans in Basketball**. See full booktalk below (p. 106). McKissack traces the participation of women in basketball, especially black women. He begins with the first woman's college team at Smith College and concludes with the Women's National Basketball Association.

5. Shandler, Sara. **Ophelia Speaks**. See full booktalk below (p. 126). "Part One: The Body Under Assault" offers essays and poems that discuss body image.

6. Strudwick, Leslie. **Athletes**. New York: Crabtree Publishing, 1999. 48p. (Women in Profile). $15.96pa. ISBN 0-7787-0037-2. Strudwick fully profiles six athletes and briefly profiles ten athletes.

## Johnson, Scott. **Safe at Second**. New York: Philomel Books, 1999. 254p. $17.99. ISBN 0-399-23365-2.

### *Summary/Description*

Todd Bannister is the star pitcher of the high school team. College and professional teams have been scouting him since junior high. Todd doesn't have to study or play by the rules off the field because he is a star. Everyone except Melissa, Todd's ex-girlfriend, bows to his wishes.

Paulie, Todd's best friend, loves baseball so much that he makes up games to announce. He's a poor to mediocre athlete, but Todd and Paulie plan on going to the big leagues together. Paulie will be Todd's "personal assistant." Like Todd, Paulie studies as little as possible, and although he admires Melissa, he doesn't ask her out. Paulie's parents are pressuring him to apply to a school and make up his mind about a career. Adding to that pressure is his little brother's high academic ability and his whole family's "doer" mentality.

Then Todd gets hit by a batted ball and loses an eye. Inspired by the story of Herb Score, Todd plans a comeback. Paulie decides he'll help Todd make that comeback. They practice secretly at night, but cannot get Todd back to what he was. Todd turns to drinking and partying, and Paulie goes along to take care of him. Melissa, editor of the school paper, asks Paulie to write a sports column. After a few half-hearted attempts, Paulie starts to turn out some good columns, and he and Melissa work together to stage a comeback for Todd. Todd fails to live up to the publicity. Then Paulie finds out that he is on the team only because of Todd's influence. He begins to think his whole life is a lie. In the last game of the season, however, Paulie throws the pitch that wins the championship. Finally, he realizes that everyone has separate talents, problems, and lives. He must work with his own ability instead of being content to be *Safe at Second.*

## *Booktalk*

Picture yourself winning game after baseball game. Picture yourself so popular and skilled that even the coach is afraid to contradict you. Picture yourself scouted by the biggest teams in the country. Picture yourself on the cover of *Sports Illustrated.* Todd Bannister, star pitcher, was in all of those pictures, and then one batted ball put out his eye. The pictures would never be as bright or clear again.

Paulie Roy Lockwood tells Todd's story. Paulie isn't a star, but at second base; he will always be Todd's loyal back-up man on and off the field. In fact, he is so loyal that the accident threatens Paulie's future as much as it threatens Todd's. What will Paulie do with his life if he can't be Todd's personal assistant in the big leagues? Paulie has the guts to back a friend. Does he have the guts to star on his own, or will he always be willing to be *Safe at Second*?

## *Related Activities*

1. *Safe at Second* deals with the pressure of success. Research outstanding people in sports, entertainment, business, or politics. Find explanations of how they handle or fail to handle the pressure.

2. Refer to *Coping with Stress* by Gwen K. Packard. Identify a situation in which you feel stress and plan your own personal stress prevention program.

3. *Slam*, *Safe at Second*, and *Bull Catcher* all deal with the combination of academics and sports. Explain the characters' balance or lack of balance between the two and the pressures that determine their choices.

4. Make a weekly calendar. Keep track of the time you spend on academics, extracurricular activities, and personal recreation. Describe the pattern that you have developed. Then explain if you would like to revise it and why. You may wish to refer to *Strategies for Studying.*

5. Write the column that you think Paulie would write about the championship game. You might wish to use a story format. Refer to the techniques suggested in *Telling Your Own Stories.*

6. *Safe at Second* alludes to Herb Score. Research Mr. Score's career and life. Explain the appropriateness of the allusion. Then choose another athlete and build a story around his or her life. You might wish to refer to *What's Your Story? A Young Person's Guide to Writing Fiction.*

## *Related Works*

1. Bauer, Marion Dane. **What's Your Story? A Young Person's Guide to Writing Fiction**. New York: Clarion Books, 1992. $6.95pa. ISBN 0-395-57780-2. Bauer outlines the writing process and story construction.
2. Carter, Alden. **Bull Catcher**. See full booktalk above (p. 96). The main character finds that his other abilities are stronger than his athletic ability.
3. Davis, Donald. **Telling Your Own Stories**. Little Rock, AR: August House, 1993. 127p. $10.00pa. ISBN 0-87483-235-7. Davis provides prompts and techniques for telling stories about personal experiences.
4. Myers, Walter Dean. **Slam**. See full booktalk below (p. 110). The main character must learn to balance athletics, academics, and personal relationships.
5. Packard, Gwen K. **Coping with Stress**. New York: The Rosen Publishing Group, 1997. 153p. (Coping Series). $17.95. ISBN 0-8239-2081-X. Packard explains how to deal with stress in very practical ways. Like the other books in the series, *Coping with Stress* provides a glossary of terms, a list of support groups, and a bibliography.
6. University of Victoria's Counseling Services. "Managing Time Effectively." In **Strategies for Studying: A Handbook of Study Skills**. pp. 9–31. Victoria, BC: Orca Book Publishers, 1996. 150p. $12.95. ISBN 1-55143-063-0. The handbook tells how to plan and monitor a time schedule.

McKissack, Patricia C., and Fredrick L. McKissack. **Black Hands, White Sails: The Story of African-American Whalers**. New York: Scholastic, 1999. 147p. $15.95pa. ISBN 0-590-48313-7.

## *Summary/Description*

*Black Hands, White Sails* ties the history of the whaling ship to the history of the slave ship. So many runaway slaves and freemen signed into the whaling service that whalers became a significant part of the Underground Railroad. With the help of Quaker taskmasters, these men and women formed their own communities and successful businesses. *Black Hands, White Sails*, a nonfiction account, includes the stories of Prince

Boston of revolutionary times, Captain Paul Cuffe of the Back to Africa movement, and Frederick Douglass, an outstanding leader for human rights. It explains the social life, superstitions, music, and overwhelming danger of the sea. *Moby Dick* is a central reference. The appendix includes descriptions of the whales hunted; important dates in whaling and slave history; and a bibliography of books, journals, pamphlets, and videos. The index provides easy reference.

## Booktalk

In a racist world that wanted you to be a slave, where could you go? Often, it was back to the same place that carried you into slavery: the sea. *Black Hands, White Sails* tells the story of one of the most successful slave emancipation systems in history, the whaling industry. It tells about a New England dependent on the ingenuity and strength of a black whaling population and a Quaker population that controlled it. Whaling was an industry so vital and dangerous that only skill, not skin color, counted. In such a dangerous democracy, the strong and intelligent man succeeded, so former slaves became wealthy and respected. Black hands, holding the white sails, helped steer our country to economic freedom and prosperity.

## Related Activities

1. Read "Heritage," on pages 64–69 of *Shimmy Shimmy Shimmy Like My Sister Kate: Looking at the Harlem Renaissance Through Poems.* Discuss the following questions: What is the speaker's heritage? How does he feel about it? How does he see the world he is in? How does this poem apply to the Back to Africa movement?

2. Read "Frederick Douglass" by Robert Hayden in *Shimmy Shimmy Shimmy Like My Sister Kate: Looking at the Harlem Renaissance Through Poems.* Discuss the following questions: Who is the speaker? What is the speaker's purpose? How is Frederick Douglass related to that purpose?

3. Read aloud "The Chapel," "The Pulpit," and "The Sermon" from *Moby Dick.* Discuss why Melville includes "The Chapel" and "The Pulpit." Discuss the purpose of Father Mapple's sermon and the techniques he uses to accomplish that purpose.

4. Read "The Gam" from *Moby Dick* aloud. Discuss what "The Gam" reveals about whalers. When reading, ask students to identify the techniques used by Melville to define a gam.

5. Read the "Rime of the Ancient Mariner" aloud. What is the lesson of the Albatross? How does it parallel Melville's lesson of the whale?

## *Related Works*

1. Coleridge, Samuel Taylor. "The Rime of the Ancient Mariner." In **British Poetry and Prose**, 3d ed., Vol. 2, edited by Paul Robert Lieder, Robert Morss Lovett, and Robert Kilburn Root. Cambridge, MA: Houghton Mifflin, 1950. Like Melville's *Moby Dick*, "The Rime of the Ancient Mariner" illustrates that man should live in harmony with nature.

2. Elmer, Howard. **Blues: Its Birth and Growth**. See full booktalk in Chapter 4 (p. 201). Black whalers brought the African rhythms, the basis of blues, to the whaling industry.

3. Giovanni, Nikki. **Shimmy Shimmy Shimmy Like My Sister Kate: Looking at the Harlem Renaissance Through Poems**. See full booktalk in Chapter 4 (p. 236). In the poem "Heritage," the speaker wrestles with his anger at being snatched from his land, heritage, and gods. The speaker in "Frederick Douglass" realizes that the true salute to Douglass is gaining freedom.

4. Melville, Herman. **Moby Dick** edited by Charles Feidelson Jr. New York: The Bobbs-Merrill Company, 1964. (The Library of Literature). Ahab's crew represents the multicultural world of whaling.

5. **Moby Dick**. Produced by CBS/Fox, 1956. 116 min. Black and White. $49.98. 4635 B. Videocassette. The film dramatizes Melville's novel.

6. Murphy, Jim. **Gone A-Whaling**. See full booktalk below (p. 108). Murphy includes a chapter about African American whalers, but his main focus is the transitions in whaling history.

7. Reybold, Laura. **The Dangers of Tattooing and Body Piercing**. See full booktalk in Chapter 1 (p. 10). Reybold explains the history of tattooing and some of the implications in choosing a tattoo.

McKissack, Fredrick. **Black Hoops: The History of African Americans in Basketball**. New York: Scholastic, 1999. 154p. $15.95. ISBN 0-590-48712-4.

## *Summary/Description*

*Black Hoops* tells the story of basketball in the larger context of race relations in America and America's sports. The book begins with basketball's origin and its contribution to "muscular Christianity." Initially, the black basketball experience was for the college elite. Intramural competition grew to intercollegiate and then to professional competition. Throughout the growth of basketball, teams and leagues formed around race, gender, and academics. *Black Hoops* addresses that focus and the bitter ironies it produced. James Naismith, Robert L. Douglas, Abe Saperstein, Paul Robeson, Walter Brown, Kareem Abdul-Jabbar, Magic Johnson, Larry Bird, Michael Jordan, Ruth Bolton-Holifield, Sheryl Swoopes, and Tara VanDerveer are all part of the dynamics that have made basketball a significant part of black history. *Black Hoops* contains pictures of founders, promoters, and early and current players. It includes a glossary, bibliography of books and Internet sources, and name index.

## *Booktalk*

How did basketball get its name? When did African Americans first begin to play the game? Who were the first African American female players? Why was basketball a segregated sport?

What historical, social, and financial pressures gave African Americans a chance to play? How have women made their mark in professional competition?

*Black Hoops* has all the answers. Starting with the rules of the game, *Black Hoops* traces the history of basketball in a racist America. It shows how the game started in the black community with the intellectual elite and developed into an open college door for underprivileged black youth. It even talks about the women's challenge to the male-dominated game. *Black Hoops* records a significant chapter in black history and concedes that the chapter on both American basketball and race relations is still being written.

## *Related Activities*

1. Compare *Black Hoops* and *Sky Kings*. Discuss the focus of each author. How does that focus affect the work?

2. View *The Harlem Globetrotters*. Describe Abe Saperstein. Discuss why he is a controversial figure in black basketball. Discuss why the Globetrotters are so important to black basketball.

3. In *Slam*, Walter Dean Myers creates a character who feels basketball may be more important than academics. Given the history of black basketball, discuss why this view is ironic.

4. Write a poem of address (described on pages 59–62 in *How to Write Poetry*) to one of the people described in *Black Hoops*, *Sky Kings*, *The Harlem Globetrotters*, or *Venus to the Hoop*. Make a poster of the poem and include a picture of the person you have addressed. Display it with other poster poems written to basketball celebrities.

5. Research athletes' endorsement packages. Chart which sports and which accomplishments bring the most endorsements.

## *Related Works*

1. Bayne, Bijan C. **Sky Kings**. Danbury, CT: Franklin Watts, 1997. 144p. $9.95. ISBN 0-531-11308-6. Bayne tells about the black players who made today's celebrity explosion possible.

2. Corbett, Sara. **Venus to the Hoop**. See full booktalk above (p. 99). Corbett reports on the Olympic year for the Women's 1996 Olympic team.

3. **Harlem Globetrotters**. Produced by A&E Television Networks, 1999. 50 min. Color. $14.95. AAE-17449. Videocassette. The film explores the joy and controversy surrounding the Harlem Globetrotters.

4. Janeczko, Paul B. **How to Write Poetry**. See full booktalk in Chapter 4 (p. 215). Janeczko proposes many forms and techniques for poems. The address poem is just one choice.

5. Myers, Walter Dean. **Slam**. See full booktalk below (p. 110). The main character learns the relationship between life and the game.

6. Starr, Mark. "The $16 Million Man. Sports: In the Really Big Game—Money—Shaquille O'Neal Could Be King." *Newsweek* (May 1, 1995): 5 pages beginning on 72. Starr compares O'Neal's earnings to Michael Jordan's.

Murphy, Jim. **Gone A-Whaling: The Lure of the Sea and the Hunt for the Great Whale**. New York: Clarion, 1998. 208p. $18.00. ISBN 0-395-69847-2.

### *Summary/Description*

*Gone A-Whaling* spans the history of whaling from the earliest times to the present. It also explains how the meaning of the word has changed from hunting the whale for kill to hunting the whale for study and enjoyment. Murphy describes the tough life of whalers, many of whom signed on before they were even in their teens. He includes the special roles of African Americans and women and the contributions that whalers made to navigation and eventually war-time mapping and navigation. Insets within the chapters focus on different types of whales and how each has been affected by the whaling industry. Pictures and drawings throughout the book depict whales, ship owners, living conditions at sea, maps, and historical documents. A glossary defines nautical and whaling terms. An extensive bibliography provides the reference materials relevant to each chapter and the subject in general. The addresses of whale conservation and research organizations and an index provide easy access to information.

### *Booktalk*

You have the opportunity to work for four years and owe your employer money. You can spend your day navigating through blood and vomit. You can lose a leg, an arm, or an eye while chasing a multiple-ton monster that can turn and sink your boat. Oh for the life of a whaler!

Whaling wasn't for the soft or fearful, but many boys, men, and women boarded the ships to see the world and know adventure. *Gone A-Whaling* tells about the people, the prejudices, the whales, and the boats that shared the sea. It tells about the families who sailed together and the sperm whale that stove the *Essex* and drove its men to cannibalism. It tells about the thrifty, shrewd Quakers who prospered and the crews constantly hungry for diversion and human companionship. But Murphy also points out that people, who have seen the whale as a monster of destruction and a product for profit, are finally beginning to realize that it may be one of the smartest, most valuable, and most persecuted creatures on the planet.

## *Related Activities*

1. In *Moby Dick*, in the chapter "The Ship," read the passage that begins on page 114 with the words "I thought him the queerest Quaker" and ends on page 118 with the words "for the three hundredth lay." Analyze the "argument" between Bildad and Peleg. Does Ishmael win? What is going on in the negotiation?

2. In *Moby Dick*, read the chapter "The Advocate." What evidence does the speaker use to support the importance or integrity of the whaler? What does the speech reveal to us about the status of the whaler in society?

3. In *Gone A-Whaling*, Jim Murphy tells about the young men aboard ship who find comfort in writing their journals. Jim Murphy uses that journal format in his book *The Journal of James Edmond Pease*. Using the journal format, write about your school or community. Include any announcements, documents, maps, or pictures a reader might need to understand your environment or time period.

4. Much of Murphy's description comes alive through sensory details. One of the pastimes of whalers was storytelling. Tell a story about an experience you have had. In telling about your experience, concentrate on sensory details. You might wish to refer to pages 24–29 in *Telling Your Own Stories*.

5. Using *Black Hands, White Sails: The Story of African-American Whalers*, find five additional facts that expand the information given in Chapter 4 of *Gone A-Whaling*.

## *Related Works*

1. Davis, Donald. **Telling Your Own Stories**. Little Rock, AR: August House, 1993. 127p. $10.00pa. ISBN 0-87483-235-7. Davis provides prompts and techniques for using sensory details in telling stories.

2. **Humpbacks of Hawaii**. Produced by National Geographic Television: Educational Films, 1986. 19 min. Color. $69.00. 522635. Videocassette. The film shows how scientists go whaling to understand the migration patterns of an animal such as the humpback whale.

3. McKissack, Patricia, and Fredrick L. McKissack. **Black Hands, White Sails: The Story of African-American Whalers**. See full booktalk above (p. 103). The book explains why the African American played such a central part in the whaling industry.

4. Melville, Herman. **Moby Dick** edited by Charles Feidelson Jr. New York: The Bobbs-Merrill Company, 1964. (The Library of Literature). Many of the chapters may be used individually to depict a whaler's life.

5. Murphy, Jim. **The Journal of James Edmond Pease**. See full booktalk in Chapter 1 (p. 12). Murphy uses the journal of James Edmond Pease to depict the life of a Civil War soldier. This is the same form of communication used by young whalers.

Myers, Walter Dean. **Slam**. New York: Scholastic, 1996. 267p. $15.95. ISBN 0-590-48667-5.

### *Summary/Description*

Greg Harris, AKA Slam, transfers from his neighborhood school to a magnet school. His new school's academics are tougher and the basketball team is weaker than Slam's home school's. His teachers are going to fail him, and his coach doesn't like him. Slam has problems in his home and neighborhood, too. His dad is drinking and out of work. His little brother loses the video camera the school lent to Slam, his grandmother is sick, and his best friend is selling drugs. Slam asks why he should even try. But his girlfriend and his assistant coach point out that he, himself, may be part of his problems. He finally decides that getting through life means getting his game and his attitude together both on and off the court.

### *Booktalk*

When Slam goes to a magnet school and leaves the old neighborhood, he thinks winning is all about the numbers on the scoreboard.

So Slam has problems. His new school is tough, but the other kids seem to make the grades. He's the best man on the basketball team, but his team doesn't seem to care, especially the coach. His brother bugs him, his girlfriend seems more interested in math problems than partying, his mom and dad are fighting, and his best friend may be dealing. His new school brings new friends, and his fame offers him new girls. With pressure from home, school, and the old neighborhood, Sam must choose his teams on and off the court and decide how hard he'll work to make them all winners.

## *Related Activities*

1. After reading *Black Hoops*, decide what facts about the history of basketball might change Slam's attitudes about his basketball team and the classroom.

2. In *Bull Catcher*, *Safe at Second*, and *Slam* the main characters deal with how sports affect their lives. Discuss how the characters are similar and different.

3. *Make Lemonade* deals with the distractions a young urban girl must face in preparing for college. Compare those distractions to Slam's.

4. Read the poem "Foul Shot." What does the poem communicate about the importance of basketball?

5. Read the poem "Ex-Basketball Player." Discuss the character Flick Webb. In what ways is he like Slam? Write a paragraph about what you think Slam will be like in ten years. Compare your paragraph with another person's in the group. If you disagree, defend your opinions.

## *Related Works*

1. Carter, Alden R. **Bull Catcher**. See full booktalk above (p. 96). The main character decides he is too slow to be a professional athlete and decides to develop his other talents.

2. Hoey, Edwin A. "Foul Shot." In **The Lyric Potential: Arrangements and Techniques in Poetry** edited by James E. Miller, Robert Hayden, and Robert O'Neal. p. 355. Glenview, IL: Scott, Foresman, 1974. The poem expresses the tension of making the shot.

3. Johnson, Scott. **Safe at Second**. See full booktalk above (p. 101). The narrator decides that he needs to make his own life plans instead of reacting to the decisions of his best friend.

4. McKissack, Fredrick, Jr. **Black Hoops**. See full booktalk above (p. 106). The book traces the participation of African Americans in basketball.

5. Updike, John. "Ex-Basketball Player." In **Mindscapes: Poems for the Real World** edited by Richard Peck. New York: Delacorte

Press, 1971. 165p. The speaker describes a man who never got past his high school fame as a basketball player.

6. Wolf, Virginia Euwer. **Make Lemonade**. New York: Henry Holt, 1993. 208p. $15.95. ISBN 0-8050-2288-7. The main character keeps her goal of going to college as she helps a single mother improve her own life and the lives of her children.

# MENTALLY

 Martinez, Victor. **Parrot in the Oven**. New York: Harper Trophy/ Joanna Cotler Books, 1996. 216p. $5.95pa. ISBN 0-06-447186-1.

### *Summary/Description*

Manny Hernandez, nicknamed Parrot by his father, wonders about his place in the world. His journey takes him through work, school, family, gang, and friendship until he decides his family is most important to him. Each chapter can be considered a short story about relationships. Together, these glimpses and reflections paint insightful portraits of the narrator and his father, mother, brother Nardo, and two sisters, Magda and Pedi. Martinez builds a good case for an imperfect family sticking together.

### *Booktalk*

Sometimes we want so much we can't decide. But our choices determine our life. Manny, the Parrot, is choosing whom to work with, date, respect, hang with, and accept. Should he trust the promises and blows of street friends, the good will of his lazy brother Nardo, the secrets of his beautiful sister Magda, the loyalty of his hardworking mother, the anger of his drinking father, or the innocence of his baby sister Pedi? He worries that he will be the "Parrot that complains how hot it is in the shade, while all along he's sitting inside an oven." He will not realize where he is and what's happening to him. In telling his story, he reminds us that each of us is a *Parrot in the Oven.*

## *Related Activities*

1. Define "barrio." According to *Parrot in the Oven*, what special problems does living in a barrio bring? What special pleasures does it bring? Compare the barrio that Martinez describes to your own neighborhood.

2. *Slam* and *Buried Onions* also describe life in "the neighborhood." Compare the descriptions of the neighborhoods in these novels to the description in *Parrot in the Oven.*

3. Explain a discovery Manny makes in each chapter. How does each realization lead to his final realization? Is Manny's journey a journey that only barrio boys make, or is it a journey that each of us must make?

4. Research gangs and gang warfare. You may wish to start with *Street Gangs* by Evan Stark, and *Gang Violence in America* narrated by Mike Wallace.

5. Manny wants to be a hero. After viewing *Heroes Hispanos*, write your own definition of a hero.

6. Manny explains his world through comparisons:

   Page 13 "He was right" introduces a description of the best field picker.

   Page 25 "But it was no use" begins his comparison of people to money.

   Page 81 "Grandma used to keep her face pretty" introduces the description of how his grandmother has aged.

   Page 92 "She was talking fast" begins the description of Manny's sister Magda.

   Page 140 "The day we took Magda to the hospital" begins the paragraph that sets the tone for the chapter. Using one of those passages as a model, describe a worker, classify people, describe a friend or family member, or set the tone for an event. Use one paragraph.

7. Now choose a scientific reaction, a historical event, or a machine. Explain it by using comparison. Make the comparison give new insight to the reader.

## *Related Works*

1. **Gang Violence in America**. Produced by A&E Television Networks, 1996. 50 min. Color. (20th Century with Mike Wallace). $19.95. AAE-21508. Videocassette. The program talks about how and why gangs form and some things being done to prevent gang violence.

2. **Heroes Hispanos**. Produced by A&E Television Networks, 1996. 150 min. Color. $29.95. AAE-40202. Videocassette. The program traces the participation of Spanish descendants in all the American wars.

3. Myers, Walter Dean. **Slam**. See booktalk above (p. 110). Slam must decide if he will adjust to his new school or live by the rules of his neighborhood.

4. Soto, Gary. **Buried Onions**. See booktalk below (p. 124). The main character decides to leave his neighborhood to be safe and successful.

5. Stark, Evan. **Street Gangs**. New York: The Rosen Publishing Group, 1995 rev. ed. 64p. (The Need to Know Library). $17.95. ISBN 0-8239-2121-2. The book explains the history of gangs, why people join them, and the difference between the good and bad ones.

 Bauer, Joan. **Rules of the Road**. New York: G. P. Putnam's Sons, 1998. 201p. $15.99. ISBN 0-399-23140-4.

## *Summary/Description*

Sixteen-year-old Jenna Boller sells shoes for Gladstone Shoes. Mrs. Gladstone recognizes Jenna's commitment to quality service and hires her for the summer. Jenna will drive Mrs. Gladstone to all the Gladstone stores and eventually to the hall where Mrs. Gladstone will make her retirement speech. During the journey, Mrs. Gladstone reunites with her friend, Alice Lovett, a former shoe model, and collaborates with her top salesman, Harry Bender. With the support of these three people, she decides to confront her son, Elden, who plans to sell out the stores and reduce their quality. Jenna's journey is just as important. She becomes a poised businesswoman who learns to speak her mind effectively and, in her private life, finally to confront her alcoholic father.

## *Booktalk*

Bring in headlines about buyouts, mergers, and company sales. Show the papers. Ask how many people a buyout, downsizing, or merger has affected.

Sixteen-year-old salesperson Jenna Boller has a quick tongue and a lot of "sole." She needs both to deal with her alcoholic father, her more beautiful, thinner sister, her schoolwork, and her job. Her boss, Mrs. Gladstone, makes her an offer. She will double Jenna's salary and add a bonus if Jenna will chauffeur Mrs. Gladstone to the company's yearly stockholders' meeting in Dallas. On the trip, Jenna becomes the spy, the nurse, the confidant, and the Girl Friday in a fight to save the company. When former shoe model, Alice Lovett, and the top salesman, Harry Bender, join her in the fight, she learns that quality business comes from quality people and that everybody has a family that is tougher to sell than their customers. Jenna is all business, and, in the *Rules of the Road*, good business is all about good people who sometimes win.

## *Related Actvities*

1. List Jenna Boller's three main career values. List the details from the book that lead you to your conclusions. You may want to refer to "What Do You Want Out of a Career?" by Janice Arenofsky.

2. List your career values. How do your academic courses and extra-curricular activities carry out these values? You may want to refer to "What Do You Want Out of a Career?" by Janice Arenofsky.

3. Research three jobs that do not require four years of college. Find out the education, training, and experience requirements, continuing education requirements, and salary. You may want to refer to "Careers Without College" by Mark Rowh.

4. Read "Hoisted Upon My Father's Shoulders" on pages 79–80 and "My Father: Mr. Pride, a Journal Entry" on pages 80–82 of *Ophelia Speaks*. These two essays describe relationships girls have with their fathers. Compare their concerns about their fathers with Jenna's concerns about hers. Write the father essay that you think Jenna might write.

5. In *Venus to the Hoop*, Sara Corbett describes the "classy" education that the 1996 Olympic team received, the effect it had on Lisa Leslie, and the class and strength Lisa Leslie brought to that education. Begin reading on page 58 with the words, "The uniform was neither . . ." to the break in text on page 64. The passage ends with the sentence beginning, "She had squared her shoulders . . .". Analyze the education Leslie receives and the strength she has. Then, analyze the education Jenna Boller receives and the strengths she has. Discuss the importance of working with new and challenging experiences.

## *Related Works*

1. Arenofsky, Janice. "What Do You Want Out of a Career?" **Career World**. (September 1998): 6 pages beginning on 6. The article helps the reader examine a variety of options when choosing a career.

2. Bauer, Joan. **Backwater**. See full booktalk in Chapter 1 (p. 28). The main character must face the disapproval of her entire family to enter the career of her choice.

3. Corbett, Sara. **Venus to the Hoop**. See full booktalk above (p. 99). Corbett records the games, struggles, and growth of the 1996 Women's Olympic basketball team.

4. McFarland, Rhoda. **Drugs and Your Parents**. New York: The Rosen Publishing Group, 1997 rev. ed. 64p. (The Drug Abuse Prevention Library). $17.95. ISBN 0-8239-2603-6. McFarland talks about the independence that children must develop in a drug abusing home. She includes a "Where to Go for Help" section.

5. Rowh, Mark. "Careers Without College." **Career World**. (April/May 1997): 4 pages beginning on 20. The article discusses skills and approaches needed to achieve a career without a four-year degree. It gives sources for more information, lists the "hot" careers, and gives ways for the person to identify interests.

6. Shandler, Sara. **Ophelia Speaks**. See full booktalk below (p. 126). The essays about girls' relationships with their fathers bring up some issues of need, distance, and independence.

Cooney, Caroline B. **Wanted!** New York: Scholastic, 1997. 230p. $4.99. ISBN 0-590-98849-2.

### *Summary/Description*

Alice's father calls her to bring him specific computer disks. As she's leaving, she hears an intruder. She flees but hears on the news that her father is dead and that she is the suspected killer. She starts to run, ditches the car, and secures disguises and computer access. Reading the tapes, she discovers her father was looking for his brother's killer. She sends out the information, goes to her mother to turn herself in, and finds that her mother's new boyfriend is the killer. The police arrive in time, and Alice discovers that no one, especially her mother, believed she was the killer. Caroline Cooney stresses that if Alice had trusted her friends, her mother, and the police, her flight and fear would have been brought to a quicker, safer conclusion.

### *Booktalk*

Alice's father is dead, and everyone, even Alice's mother, believes Alice is the killer. Where can she hide? How fast can she run? Someone killed her father for the disks he asked her to bring to him. The killer will still be after the disks and after her. Can she remember what she heard in her dad's condo that morning? Can she put the facts of her day together? Running away, hiding, and disguising herself brings her closer to the killer, but also brings the killer closer to her. She's sixteen, scared, and *Wanted!*

### *Related Activities*

1. Compare *Hush Little Baby*, *The Terrorist*, and *Wanted!* by Caroline Cooney. How does Ms. Cooney individualize her characters? What qualities distinguish a Caroline Cooney mystery?

2. Knowing whom to trust is a major factor in a successful life. Discuss how *Wanted!*, *A Door Near Here*, *Tenderness*, *The Pirate's Son*, *The Sacrifice*, *Bull Catcher*, *Buried Onions*, *The Terrorist*, *Hero*, *A Traitor Among Us*, and *The Smugglers* address that theme.

3. Alice makes a series of inferences in trying to straighten out her situation. Identify them. How accurate is Alice? What affects her accuracy?

4. Cooney chooses familiar words and phrases for her titles. Using newspaper, magazine, television, or song material, make up several titles for mysteries.

5. Using the suggestions from Chapters 3 and 4 in *What's Your Story? A Young Person's Guide to Writing Fiction*, develop characters for the titles from Activity 4.

## *Related Works*

1. Bauer, Marion Dane. **What's Your Story? A Young Person's Guide to Writing Fiction**. New York: Clarion Books, 1992. 134p. $6.95pa. ISBN 0-395-57780-2. The book provides suggestions for developing a complete work of fiction. Chapters 3 and 4 focus on character.

2. Carter, Alden. **Bull Catcher**. See full booktalk above (p. 96). The main character can't decide with whom he should live or love.

3. Cooney, Caroline. **Hush Little Baby**. See full booktalk in Chapter 3 (p. 168). The main character finds herself in charge of a baby being used in an illegal adoption scheme.

4. Cooney, Caroline. **The Terrorist**. See full booktalk in Chapter 3 (p. 135). The main character trusts a schoolmate who turns out to be part of an international terrorist ring.

5. Cormier, Robert. **Tenderness**. See full booktalk above (p. 64). The main character is released from prison and, with the help of a companion, starts to stalk more victims.

6. Matcheck, Diane. **The Sacrifice**. See full booktalk above (p. 89). The main character flees her own tribe to prove herself and finds that another tribe wants to sacrifice her.

7. McCaughrean, Geraldine. **The Pirate's Son**. See full booktalk above (p. 74). Three teenagers find themselves on a ship with a guardian willing to sell them.

8. Quarles, Heather. **A Door Near Here**. See full booktalk in Chapter 1 (p. 54). The main character tries to hide her mother's alcoholism from the authorities and endangers the family.

9. Rottman, S. L. **Hero**. See full booktalk in Chapter 4 (p. 223). The main character learns to trust and respect the man the court has assigned to him.

10. Soto, Gary. **Buried Onions**. See full booktalk below (p. 124). The main character decides that he must leave his neighborhood to stay alive.

11. Van Steenwyk. **A Traitor Among Us**. See full booktalk in Chapter 4 (p. 228). The main character must discover the informant for the German Army.

Hunter, Mollie. **The King's Swift Rider**. New York: HarperCollins, 1998. 241p. $16.95. ISBN 0-06-027186-8.

## *Summary/Description*

Sixteen-year-old Martin Crawford uses his wits and skill to rescue an outnumbered fugitive. Then he discovers he has rescued the King of the Scots, Robert The Bruce, who is fleeing from King Edward of England. The Bruce challenges Martin and Sean, Martin's older brother, to join him in the fight to free Scotland, Sean as a soldier and Martin as a page. Sean, the eager soldier, becomes an officer in The Bruce's triumphant army. Martin, the scholar and reluctant soldier, becomes a spy. But both come to know that each citizen, whether cleric, soldier, layman, or woman, must make a contribution to Robert The Bruce to save Scotland from English tyranny and cruelty. As Martin tells the story of his personal journey, he also tells the story of Robert The Bruce, who teaches by example as he puts "Duty before personal Ambition."

## *Booktalk*

What makes a good soldier? What makes a hero? Write down three roles a person can play in war. What qualities does each role demand?

Sixteen-year-old Martin Crawford wants to be a scholar, not a soldier. When he saves an outnumbered man hunted by hounds, he doesn't know he has saved his king. He doesn't know his king needs a scholar or that any army needs a scholar. Sean, Martin's older brother, has always been the soldier in the family. He will eagerly join Robert The Bruce. But it takes longer for Martin to realize that Scotland needs every man, woman, and child to claim its freedom and independence. Martin's ability to read and write and his knowledge of languages pull him unwillingly away from his family and scholarly pursuits to the center of dangerous secrets and masquerades. They become his new life and perhaps his death. He is *The King's Swift Rider*.

## *Related Activities*

1. Compare the roles of the spies in *The Journal of William Thomas Emerson*, *Come All You Brave Soldiers*, and *The King's Swift Rider.* Even though the tools are different, how are the jobs similar?

2. Martin Crawford is a thoughtful and reflective soldier. Write a poem you feel he would have written. He is the speaker. You might warm up by using the exercises with "Persona Poems" in *How to Write Poetry* by Paul B. Janeczko.

3. Research the reigns of Edward the First, Edward the Second, and Edward the Third. Explain how each king's reign affected Scotland.

4. After reading *The King's Swift Rider* and watching *The Medieval Foot Soldier*, write a definition of heroism in the time of Robert The Bruce.

5. Discuss *Hero* and *Megaboy* in terms of that definition. If the definition has changed, explain how and why.

## *Related Works*

1. **Braveheart**. Produced by Paramount Pictures Corporation, 1995. Two cassettes, each 177 min. Color. $19.99. PAR 331183. Videocassette. The R-rated film tells the story of the thirteenth-century hero William Wallace, whose life and death sparked the fight for the independence of Scotland. For the right audience, it would be a good motivating film for studying the period.

2. Cox, Clinton. **Come All You Brave Soldiers**. See full booktalk in Chapter 3 (p. 155). Cox tells how African American spies aided armies during the Revolutionary War.

3. Denenberg, Barry. **The Journal of William Thomas Emerson**. See full booktalk in Chapter 1 (p. 12). In his early teens, William Thomas Emerson finds himself a valuable spy for the American Revolution.

4. Janeczko, Paul B. **How to Write Poetry**. See full booktalk in Chapter 4 (p. 215). Janeczko includes exercises and suggestions for how a writer might adopt the voice of a character or object.

5. **The Medieval Soldier**. Produced by A&E Home Video, 1996. 50 min. Color. (Foot Soldier). $19.95. AAE-13912. Videocassette. With humor and some scenes for more mature audiences, *The Medieval Soldier* depicts the camp life of the common soldier and the expectations that his world placed on him.

6. Rottman, S. L. **Hero**. See full booktalk in Chapter 4 (p. 223). The main character comes to a definition of hero that is far different from the one believed in Robert The Bruce's time.

7. Walker, Virginia, and Katrina Roechelein. **Making Up Megaboy**. See full booktalk above (p. 82). The main character, confused by the ideal of the superhero, kills a storekeeper.

Mosier, Elizabeth. **My Life As a Girl**. New York: Random House, 1999. 193p. $17.00. ISBN 0-679-89035-1.

### *Summary/Description*

Jaime Cody is studying for finals at Bryn Mawr when Buddy, a boy from her previous summer, shows up. In this sleek, intellectual world, Buddy embarrasses her. She tries to hide him and get rid of him as soon as possible. When she returns home on break, however, Buddy again is tempting and desirable to her.

Jaime met Buddy when she was waitressing at Franklin's All-American Diner. The Diner was her day job. At night she worked at the Phoenix, an upscale resort. She was trying to replace the college nest egg her father took to cover his gambling debts. Buddy is always in trouble, never responsible for it, and adept at thinking of ways to get out of it. But Jamie succumbs to his charm and finally goes to bed with him. She discovers that Buddy is also sleeping with Diane, whose name he calls when Buddy and Jaime are making love.

Jaime's choices of that summer and her freshman year symbolize the choices she must make for her future. Her mother often talks about a boy in her own youth who took her out and then bragged about having sex with her. Although her mother then points to Jaime's father as the "good man" in her life, Jaime sees her mother cover for him time after time, even in the face of criminal charges. When her mother, aunts, and girlfriend encourage her to get away and go to school, they are encouraging her to declare her independence and get control of her life. Jaime must decide if she will continue to tackle the tough world of Bryn Mawr or return home, without an education, and let herself be victimized by men as her mother has been. In the final chapter, when Jamie threatens to leave Buddy in the desert with only his hat on, Jaime realizes her power to control her own life. The epilogue is a reflection of Jaime, now a successful medical student, who receives an unexpected gift from her father, the money from her "Future" fund.

## *Booktalk*

Girls have a tough life. They have to be pretty. They have to be brainy but hide the brains. They have to work hard and look like they're not working. Jaime Cody is a pretty and brainy girl who has to work harder than most girls, boys, men, or women. Her father has stolen her "Future" money, and she has one summer to earn enough for her freshman college year. She doesn't have time to worry about whether her father will go to jail. She doesn't have time to worry about whether her mother will be able to pay the bills. But when she meets Buddy, she has more than money on her mind. Then Jaime has to decide if she will spend her life in Arizona saving a wanna-be-big-time-charmer-cowboy or face the tough academic and social challenges at a college far from home and far from the familiar. In *My Life As a Girl*, Jaime sorts out her summer with Buddy and her choices. Now, she realizes that she must stop hiding her true self and start to think about her life as a woman.

## *Related Activities*

1. Compare Jaime in *My Life As a Girl* and LaVaughn in *Make Lemonade*. Both see education as a way out. What else do they have in common? How are their experiences different?

2. Compare the adjustment Cedric Jennings must make in *A Hope in the Unseen* and the adjustment Jaime must make in *My Life As a Girl*. Do you feel this adjustment is a universal experience? Is it restricted to just college?

3. *Life in the Fat Lane*, *Rules of the Road*, *The Spirit Window*, and *My Life As a Girl* all involve girls, coming of age, who must deal with problem fathers. Form four groups. Ask each group to choose one

novel, or ask each of four individuals within one group to choose a novel. Discuss how each girl matures and how the father/daughter relationship affects that process.

4. Read "Fathers" in *Ophelia Speaks*. What feelings are expressed? How do these expressions parallel the concerns expressed in the novels from Activity 3?

5. Read "Manipulated and Controlled" in *Ophelia Speaks*. Discuss how the poem and essay reflect Jaime's experience.

## *Related Works*

1. Bauer, Joan. **Rules of the Road**. See full booktalk above (p. 114). Running away from her family problems, the main character takes a summer job that makes her realize her power as a woman.

2. Bennett, Cherie. **Life in the Fat Lane**. See full booktalk in Chapter 1 (p. 1). A beauty queen deals with an uncontrollable weight problem and her parents' obsession with appearance as she is entering adulthood.

3. Shandler, Sara. **Ophelia Speaks**. See full booktalk below (p. 126). Shandler includes a collection of essays and poems that express the concerns of girls entering womanhood.

4. Suskind, Ron. **A Hope in the Unseen**. See full booktalk above (p. 94). In this nonfiction account, Suskind describes the adjustment of an inner-city youth to the Ivy League.

5. Sweeney, Joyce. **The Spirit Window**. See full booktalk in Chapter 1 (p. 19). The main character begins to realize her own love as her father struggles with the death of his first wife, his new marriage, and his relationship with his mother.

6. Wolf, Virginia Euwer. **Make Lemonade**. New York: Henry Holt, 1993. 208p. $15.95. ISBN 0-8050-2288-7. A fourteen-year-old girl takes a baby-sitting job to earn money for her college fund and discovers all the things that could keep her from going to college.

Soto, Gary. **Buried Onions**. New York: Harcourt Brace, 1997. 149p. $17.00. ISBN 0-15-201333-4.

### *Summary/Description*

At nineteen, Eddie has dropped out of college and is barely supporting himself doing odd jobs. His father, uncles, best friend, and cousin, Jesus, are all dead. Eddie sees the same thing happening to him. He lives in Fresno, home to gangs, thieves, and drug addicts. He sees his community's sorrow and bitterness caused by a huge buried onion that sends vapors through the ground to make the people cry and feed their unhappiness. Now his aunt and Angel, Jesus' best friend, want him to avenge his cousin's death. He tries to ignore their pleas. He bikes into the suburbs and finds a landscaping job with Mr. Stiles, who trusts him with his truck. When Eddie parks the truck in front of his own apartment for a few minutes, it is stolen. The head of the playground, Coach, talks to Mr. Stiles, who takes Eddie back but sets him up for arrest. José, Eddie's friend, is knifed trying to help Eddie recover the car. Eddie believes that Angel has stolen the car and murdered Jesus. He decides to fight him, and gets away with his life but realizes that Angel will come back and shoot him. With Coach's help, both Eddie and José decide to leave. José is in the Marines, and will never come home on leave again. Eddie will join the navy. *Buried Onions* is for mature readers. Eddie is a poetic and sensitive person who must survive in a violent and narrow world, but his own decisions contribute to his situation. His problem is how to break out of the cycle, and he must decide to give up almost everything he has known. The language is strong but appropriate.

### *Booktalk*

Sometimes we have to adjust a little to fit into a new environment. At other times we must change quite a bit. We must adapt. And sometimes, to survive, we have to conform. We have to find a whole new fit. But Eddie can't seem to conform. He dropped out of college. His gang days are behind him. His father, uncles, and cousin Jesus are all dead. So where does Eddie fit? His family and the street say that Eddie is supposed to avenge his cousin's death. But how can he be sure who was holding the knife, and how can he be sure he won't be next, or set up for the arrest? And then he has to get the stolen truck back, but is his friend the one who stole it? Fresno is the only home Eddie knows, but he wonders if its sorrow and bitterness, the *Buried Onions*, will overcome him. If he chooses to conform to Fresno, will his only home be a grave?

## *Related Activities*

1. On pages 4–5, Eddie compares himself to an ant. Read aloud Eddie's description of the ant and the advice Eddie gives himself. Discuss what the comparison and advice tell us about Eddie.

2. Choose an animal to compare to yourself. What do you learn from that animal that you can apply to your own life?

3. On page 2, Eddie explains his theory of the giant onion. On page 146, he realizes he is walking on "acres of buried onions." Read both onion passages out loud. Discuss what the onions represent to Eddie.

4. Compare Manny from *Parrot in the Oven* and Eddie from *Buried Onions*. One decides to stay in the neighborhood, and one decides to leave. Discuss how family and neighborhood influence each decision.

5. Research gangs. You may wish to start with *Street Gangs* by Evan Stark, and *Gang Violence in America* narrated by Mike Wallace.

6. Eddie's friend comes home on leave from the service and is knifed. He returns to the service and decides never to return to the neighborhood. Research the social and economic backgrounds of those men and women in the armed forces today. Research why military service is their career choice. Then explain how that information relates to the documentary *Heroes Hispanos.*

7. Compare the fictional situation described by Soto in *Buried Onions* to the real situation of Cedric Jennings in *A Hope in the Unseen.* What do they have in common? How are they different?

## *Related Works*

1. **Gang Violence in America**. Produced by A&E Television Networks, 1996. 50 min. Color. (20th Century with Mike Wallace). $19.95. AAE-21508. Videocassette. The program talks about how and why gangs form and some things being done to prevent gang violence.

2. **Heroes Hispanos**. Produced by A&E Television Networks, 1996. 150 min. Color. $29.95. AAE-40202. Videocassette. The program traces the participation of Spanish descendants in all the American wars.

3. Martinez, Victor. **Parrot in the Oven**. See full booktalk above (p. 112). A young man who lives in the barrio tries to find his place in his family and neighborhood.

4. Stark, Evan. **Street Gangs**. New York: The Rosen Publishing Group, 1995 rev. ed. 64p. (The Need to Know Library). $17.95. ISBN 0-8239-2121-2. The book explains the history of gangs, why people join them, and the difference between the good and bad ones.

5. Suskind, Ron. **A Hope in the Unseen**. See full booktalk above (p. 94). Cedric Jennings, growing up in Washington, DC, feels he must adjust to the Ivy League world to succeed.

## Shandler, Sara. **Ophelia Speaks**. New York: Harper Perennial, 1999. 285p. $12.95pa. ISBN 0-06-095297-0.

### *Summary/Description*

Seventeen-year-old Sara Shandler wrote *Ophelia Speaks* in reaction to Mary Pipher's *Reviving Ophelia*. Shandler has collected essays and poetry from teenage girls who have experienced the traumas of eating disorders, family conflict, friendship, love, and social pressure. These girls speak about problems, once considered adult, that are now part of the teenage world. Shandler introduces each section by relating her own experiences and then describing each author's perspective. The pieces are frank and often disturbing, but will provide strong starting points for discussion, writing, or research. All the works are short enough for read-aloud presentations, but the presenter should judge the maturity of the audience in relation to the selection.

### *Booktalk*

In *Ophelia Speaks*, teenage girls talk about their joys, problems, and sorrows. They worry about how they look, who they love, who will love them, and how successful they are going to be. These girls have the media, their teachers, their parents, their schools, their spiritual leaders, and their friends trying to give them life's answers, but they are still seeking answers on their own. Reading *Ophelia Speaks* may not give you any answers, but you'll certainly discover that many people are asking the same questions.

## *Related Activities*

1. Each day, read one selection aloud. Ask the audience to react in discussion or journal writing.

2. Choose media presentations that deal with the issues discussed in the five parts of *Ophelia Speaks*. Analyze the message and expectations that the media communicate. Try to determine how much of that message is related to selling a product.

3. In *Life in the Fat Lane*, Lara Ardeche makes some discoveries about beauty and friendship. Discuss "I Am Scared" from *Ophelia Speaks* in relation to Lara's journey.

4. Ask young men to write about the topics listed in *Ophelia Speaks*. Organize the responses in a collection of essays. Select an appropriate allusion for the title.

5. Identify your own sources of stress and compose an individual stress prevention handbook and schedule.

6. Read "The Academic Squeeze" essays in *Ophelia Speaks*. Discuss whether coping and study skill strategies might help the speakers. Refer to the techniques discussed in *Strategies for Studying: A Handbook of Study Skills*.

## *Related Works*

1. Ayer, Eleanor. **Choosing Sexual Abstinence**. New York: The Rosen Publishing Group, 1997. 64p. (The Need to Know Library). $17.95. ISBN 0-8239-2250-2. The author discusses the positive effects of sexual abstinence before marriage. "Why Is Teenage Sexual Activity on the Rise?" on page 15 suggests the media's role in encouraging sexual activity.

2. Bennett, Cherie. **Life in the Fat Lane**. See full booktalk in Chapter 1 (p. 1). The main character finds she no longer has control of her weight, but discovers that integrity and inner strength are more important than a number on a scale.

3. Carlson, Dale, and Hannah Carlson. **Girls Are Equal Too**. Madison, CT: 1998. 2d ed. 231p. $14.95. ISBN 1-884158-18-8. The book discusses the pressures of society and how to deal with them. It includes an extensive bibliography.

4. Curran, Christian. **Sexually Transmitted Diseases**. See full booktalk in Chapter 3 (p. 142). Curran talks about the myths surrounding sexually transmitted diseases and how ignorance has helped spread them.

5. DiSpezio, Michael A. **The Science, Spread, and Therapy of HIV Disease**. See full booktalk in Chapter 3 (p. 144). The question-and-answer format and extensive index make information easily accessible.

6. Packard, Gwen K. **Coping with Stress**. New York: The Rosen Publishing Group, 1997. 153p. (Coping: Overcoming Tough Situations). $17.95. ISBN 0-8239-2081-X. The book defines stress, identifies its causes, and gives suggestions on how to deal with it.

7. Silverstein, Alvin, Virginia Silverstein, and Laura Silverstein Nunn. **Depression**. See full booktalk in Chapter 3 (p. 150). This book defines depression and proposes ways to recognize and deal with it.

8. University of Victoria's Counseling Services. **Strategies for Studying: A Handbook of Study Skills**. Victoria, BC: Orca Book Publishers, 1996. 150p. $12.95pa. ISBN 1-55143-063-0. *Strategies for Studying* uses survey charts to help the reader determine strengths and weaknesses in studying. It provides explanations and exercises for various study techniques and a full reference list of books, tapes, and web sites. The "Coping with Stress" section helps the student deal with the anxieties and pressures of school. Although it often refers to the adult learner, the text is an important tool for any student with a complicated and demanding schedule.

## Trembath, Don. **A Fly Named Alfred**. Victoria, BC: Orca Book Publishers, 1997. 138p. $6.95pa. ISBN 1-22143-083-5.

### *Summary/Description*

Harper Winslow, from *The Tuesday Cafe*, is now reporting for his school newspaper. Inspired by his writing teacher, Josh Simpson, and his friend, Billy, Harper develops a column, "Fly on the Wall." He watches people and writes about what he sees. Because what he sees is sometimes funny but not flattering, he uses the pseudonym Alfred. With the power of the pen, Harper can get to some people he wouldn't dare touch with his fists. Unfortunately, one of the bullies he makes fun of wants to find out Alfred's identity. Also unfortunately, the curious bully puts pressure on another bully (one who likes to push Harper around) to get the information.

In his struggle to hide his identity, Harper finds out that he hasn't seen himself or his subjects clearly.

## *Booktalk*

Harper Winslow is taking writing seriously. He reports for the school paper and decides to write his own "Fly on the Wall" column under the pseudonym Alfred. He watches people, writes about what he sees, and finds that people are pretty funny. But everybody doesn't have a sense of humor, especially the bullies, so Harper finds himself dodging a bully's investigator with only Billie, from the Tuesday Cafe class, to help him. And Billie gets his advice from Mickey Spillane novels. In *The Tuesday Cafe*, writing helped Harper straighten out his life. In *A Fly Named Alfred*, Harper uses his words to catch some powerful people in some sticky situations. But Harper gets caught in a web of his own words and finds out that there are plenty of angry spiders around who are willing to finish him off.

## *Related Activities*

1. On pages 18–19, Harper describes the class writing assignment, his choice of subject, the class reaction, Billie's suggestion for a column, and Josh's reservations about the column. Read the passage aloud. Discuss the value of the assignment, the context in which Billie wishes to place it, and Josh's reservations about it. Read some of Alfred's columns. Does he follow the assignment guidelines? Where does he depart from what he knows for sure?

2. Ask students to write a short observation of someone or something. Tell them that they must only report what can be verified. Ask them to read the reports in class. Ask other members of the class to listen for non-report statements.

3. Choose some columns from the local newspaper or ask students to bring them in. Read the columns aloud. Determine the purpose and audience of each column. Identify reports, inferences, and judgments in the columns.

4. Ask students to rewrite the short observation from Activity 2. Tell them to add reports, inferences, and judgments. Ask them to read their columns aloud. Ask the rest of the class to identify the column's audience and purpose. Discuss whether the writer agrees, and why.

5. Harper also predicts reactions. See italics on pages 78–85 and 109–10 in *A Fly Named Alfred.* Ask students to imagine themselves in a situation and write the dialogue that they think would occur. Then ask for volunteers to act out some of the dialogue scenes. Discuss how each character is developed.

6. Compare Harper Winslow from *A Fly Named Alfred* and Paulie Roy Lockwood in *Safe at Second.* What are their strengths and weaknesses as writers? What are their strengths and weaknesses as people? How is their writing affected by their personalities? How does writing help them to grow?

7. *A Fly Named Alfred*, *Parrot in the Oven*, *Holes*, and *Buried Onions* all involve standing up to bullies. Ask four people or four groups to read the books. Each person or group should choose a book. Then compare the bullies the main characters must face and how each character reacts to those bullies.

## *Related Works*

1. Johnson, Scott. **Safe at Second**. See full booktalk above (p. 101). Scott finds that athletics, writing, academics, and life involve risk and hard work.

2. Martinez, Victor. **Parrot in the Oven**. See full booktalk above (p. 112). The main character finds there is more reward in being a strong family man than a strong street man.

3. Sachar, Louis. **Holes**. See full booktalk in Chapter 1 (p. 35). The main character finds he must stand up against bullies and his own bad luck.

4. Soto, Gary. **Buried Onions**. See full booktalk above (p. 124). The main character finds he must leave his violent and gang-ruled neighborhood to build a healthy life.

5. Trembath, Don. **A Beautiful Place on Yonge Street**. See full booktalk in Chapter 3 (p. 166). Harper falls in love. This book follows *A Fly Named Alfred.*

6. Trembath, Don. **The Tuesday Cafe**. See full booktalk in Chapter 1 (p. 23). Sentenced by the court to write an essay, Harper Winslow finds that writing can help shape his life. This book precedes *A Fly Named Alfred.*

# 3

# Forces Try to Confound Us

## GOOD VERSUS EVIL

 Kerven, Rosalind. **King Arthur**. New York: DK Publishing, 1998. 63p. (Eyewitness Classics). $14.95. ISBN 0-7894-2887-3.

### *Summary/Description*

*King Arthur* clearly tells the Arthurian legend. Large, full-page pictures illustrate the story, and sidebars give appropriate background information. The sidebars explain issues such as the significance of the sword, the foreign invaders who created the need for an Arthur, and the differences in the magic of Merlin and Morgan le Fay. Chapters 1, 3, and 8 include supplementary sections. These sections explain the concept of magic, the Knights of the Round Table, the drive to verify Arthur's existence, and the continuing power of the Camelot story.

## Booktalk

King Arthur is a hero and an ideal in which we wish to believe. He lived in a time of magic and mystery. The knights were gallant; the ladies were beautiful; and Arthur struck a perfect balance between the good and evil of the world. But somewhere along the way, Hollywood, Disney, and Broadway took control of the story. Now, Rosalind Kerven tells the original legend in modern language. She explains Arthur's times and why he has kept one foot in reality and the other foot in myth. *King Arthur* is three books in one. Read the story, look at the pictures, and learn how Arthur's people believed and lived.

## Related Activities

1. Prepare a performance of "The Homecoming of Beorhtnoth Beorhthelm's Son." Discuss the ideas that Tolkien presents and how these ideas agree and/or disagree with those ideals expressed in the story of King Arthur.
2. Discuss how Gwendolyn Brooks uses the Villain, Prince, and Happiness-Ever-After clichés in her poem "A Bronzeville Mother Loiters in Mississippi. Meanwhile, a Mississippi Mother Burns Bacon" (in *Shimmy Shimmy Shimmy Like My Sister Kate: Looking at the Harlem Renaissance Through Poems*). Discuss how the poem is related to the legend of Arthur.
3. Discuss how George Ella Lyon uses the legends of Arthur and Galahad in "What Began at the Post Office" (in *Where I'm From: Where Poems Come From*).
4. On pages 62–63 of *King Arthur*, several versions and references to Arthur's legend are listed. Choose one of the works and explain how the legend is told or used.
5. After viewing *Dragonheart*, explain the use of the Arthurian legend in the movie.

## Related Works

1. Brooks, Gwendolyn. "A Bronzeville Mother Loiters in Mississippi. Meanwhile, a Mississippi Mother Burns Bacon." In **Shimmy Shimmy Shimmy Like My Sister Kate: Looking at the Harlem Renaissance Through Poems**. See full booktalk in Chapter 4 (p. 236). The romantic pursuit of a so-called violator is really a cover for prejudice.

2. **Dragonheart**. Produced by MCA Home Video, 1996. 103 min. Color. $14.99. Videocassette. A freelance knight fights an evil monarch he once trained, but in trying to kill the monarch, he must kill a good and wise dragon as well.

3. **King Arthur: His Life and Legend**. Produced by A&E Television Networks, 1995. 50 min. Color. (Biography). $14.95. AAE-14040. Videocassette. The film tells the total story of Arthur through the eyes of each of the authors who wrote about him.

4. Lyon, George Ella. "What Began at the Post Office." In **Where I'm From: Where Poems Come From**. See full booktalk in Chapter 4 (p. 217). The speaker describes a strange encounter in her home with Sir Galahad.

5. Tolkien, J. R. R. "The Homecoming of Beorhtnoth Beorhthelm's Son." In **Poems and Stories**. New York: Houghton Mifflin, 1994. 342p. ISBN 0-395-68999-6. Two men are looking for the body of their dead leader on the battlefield. Their conversation criticizes the poets who glorify war and the hero. The two essays "Beorhtnogh's Death" and "Offermod" explain the context of the conversation in relation to *The Battle of Maldon*, *Beowulf*, and *Sir Gawain.* In a footnote, Tolkien suggests how the piece may be performed. Although *Poems and Stories* was published in 1994, it is currently out of print.

Kraft, Betsy Harvey. **Sensational Trials of the 20th Century**. New York: Scholastic, 1998. 216p. $16.95. ISBN 0-590-37205-X.

### *Summary/Description*

*Sensational Trials of the 20th Century* includes eight trials: Sacco-Vanzetti, Scopes, Lindbergh, Rosenbergs, *Brown v. Board of Education*, Watergate, Hinckley, and O. J. Simpson. Each chapter explains the details, historical context, and social implications of a particular trial. The Sacco-Vanzetti trial was influenced by the immigration and anarchy scare fueled by the Russian Revolution. The Scopes "Monkey" trial began as a town promotion. The Lindbergh trial, because it involved both tragedy and a national hero, was the social event of the year. The Rosenberg trial revealed the fear of Communists. *Brown v. Board of Education* established that separate is not equal. Watergate revealed the dark side of a presidency. The John Hinckley trial showed celebrity creating the vulnerability of both a screen star and a president. The Simpson trial revealed that the United States was still split along racial lines. At the end of the book, Kraft includes a bibliography for each trial and an index for the entire book.

## Booktalk

Freedom of speech, freedom to learn, prejudice, privilege, abuse of power, and insanity are all on trial in *Sensational Trials of the 20th Century*. Betsy Harvey Kraft gives the details surrounding eight major trials, ranging from the Lindbergh kidnapping to the O. J. Simpson trial. Some trials seem to need a ringmaster instead of a judge and produce more publicity than common sense. One was staged to improve a town's business; another was considered the "social event of the decade." With public opinion fueled by ambitious media, can the law treat everyone equally? You be the judge.

## Related Activities

1. Research the trials in the last fifty years that have ruled on student rights. Discuss which trial you feel has been most important.
2. Invite a lawyer to speak to the group about how juries are selected.
3. Research the trial of Timothy McVeigh. Discuss how public opinion influenced the outcome. Discuss the press coverage rules.
4. After reading *Sensational Trials of the 20th Century* and viewing *The Monkey Trial* and *True Story of Sacco and Vanzetti*, discuss the media's role in determining a trial's significance.
5. Read "A Newspaper" by Stephen Crane. Describe the speaker. Describe the speaker's attitude about newspapers. How might the speaker's remarks be applied to other elements of the media?

## Related Works

1. Blatner, David. **The Joy of Pi**. See full booktalk in Chapter 4 (p. 232). Pages 80–81 show the transcript from the Simpson trial, in which an FBI agent reveals that he did not make the correct calculation because he did not understand the use of Pi.
2. Crane, Stephen. "A Newspaper." In **The Mentor Book of Major American Poets** edited by Oscar Williams and Edwin Honig. New York: New American Library, 1962. Crane's poem berates the newspaper as an irresponsible voice pandering to an ignorant public.

3. **The Monkey Trial**. Produced by A&E Television Networks, 1997. Black and White. (In Search of History). $19.95. AAE-40219. Videocassette. The film corroborates Kraft's analysis and provides original pictures of the town and trial.

4. Nadeau, Elaine. "The Circus Comes to Town." *Canada & the World Backgrounder* (December 1995): 3 pages beginning on 13. The article discusses the effect of media coverage on justice. It includes two suggested activities for research and discussion.

5. Stein, M. L. "Less of a Circus." *Editor & Publisher* (June 7, 1997): 2 pages beginning on 12. The article compares the security of the O. J. Simpson trial with that of the Timothy McVeigh trial.

6. **True Story of Sacco and Vanzetti**. Produced by A&E Television Networks, 1998. Black and White. (In Search of History). $19.95. AAE-42280. Videocassette. The film expands on the argument that the trial was unfair and fueled by the fear and prejudice of the time.

Cooney, Caroline B. **The Terrorist**. New York: Scholastic, 1997. 198p. $15.95. ISBN 0-590-22853-6.

## *Summary/Description*

The Williams family is living in London for a year. Laura and Billy attend the London International Academy, where they meet students from all over the world. Neither Billy nor Laura is aware of political movements and motivations, but most of the other students in the school are actually connected to the political pressures. Billy, moving freely and fearlessly through the city, is killed by a terrorist bomb. Laura, in her grief and rage, tries to figure out who was responsible and why it happened. In doing so, she moves farther from friends who would help her and closer to the actual killer.

Jehran, Laura's classmate, persuades Laura to give her Billy's passport. Jehran explains she has been betrothed to a fifty-four-year-old man who will take her money and keep her in virtual slavery. If Laura escorts her, Jehran can pass as Billy, and flee to the United States. Laura cooperates with the plan until they get to the airport. Noting Jehran's behavior, Laura figures out that Jehran is Billy's killer. Laura is able to thwart Jehran's plan with the help of the police, who have been tipped off by Laura's loyal and concerned classmates. Throughout the novel Cooney emphasizes that American teenagers need to be more aware of international issues and more trusting of the adults they know.

## *Booktalk*

Hold up a newspaper headline or several headlines about a terrorist attack. Read a few details about where these attacks happened (e.g., an airport, a day-care center, a newsstand).

Ask how the students would define a terrorist. Ask how many feel they are in danger of being harmed by a terrorist. Discuss their definitions and reactions.

Laura and Billy Williams live in London. They move through the city unafraid. Even though their international school has bomb drills, they are having one of the best, most exciting years of their lives—until *The Terrorist* kills Billy. Suddenly, Laura sees the world as threatening and uncaring. She sees terrorists everywhere. Everyone in her international school could have a motive. Every worker her father fires could have a motive. Everyone Billy asked questions of or made lists about could have a motive. But no one can find the terrorist who killed Billy, and no one (the police, her teachers, or her friends) seems to care enough. So Laura will do all the searching and caring. She, alone, will make Billy's death mean something; but Laura, alone, may be the next victim.

## *Related Activities*

1. Read "If You Think" by Lotte Moos, aloud. Write a sentence that expresses the idea in each section. Compare your own statements with other statements in the group. Then discuss the following questions:

   Why does the speaker mention Ireland and Pakistan?

   Why does the speaker include "needles" as well as "bullets?"

   The last section answers the question "so what?" How is that question answered?

2. *Starplace*, *The Singing Mountain*, and *The Terrorist* all involve young people whose view of the world changes as they begin to pay attention to events outside the United States. Compare the journeys and the realizations of the characters.

3. Read the interviews with *Teenage Refugees from Bosnia-Herzegovina*. Discuss their concerns. How are their concerns similar to your own? How are they different? Do any of the interviews express ideas similar to those expressed in *The Terrorist*?

4. Read the interviews in *No More Strangers Now: Young Voices from a New South Africa.* Discuss the youths' concerns. How are their concerns similar to your own? How are they different? Do any of the interviews express ideas similar to those expressed in *The Terrorist*?

5. Interview some American teenagers. In the interviews, explore how the teenagers' personal concerns connect with national and international concerns. Compare the American responses with those from *No More Strangers Now: Young Voices from a New South Africa* and *Teenage Refugees from Bosnia-Herzegovina.*

6. Using the titles and characters you have developed from *Wanted!*, Activity 5 (see full booktalk and activities in Chapter 2), develop a focus and plot for a mystery. You may wish to refer to Chapters 5 and 6 in *What's Your Story? A Young Person's Guide to Writing Fiction*.

## *Related Works*

1. Bauer, Marion Dane. **What's Your Story? A Young Person's Guide to Writing Fiction**. New York: Clarion Books, 1992. 134p. $6.95pa. ISBN 0-395-57780-2. Chapters 5 and 6 build on the work students already may have completed in Activity 5 for *Wanted!*

2. Cooney, Caroline B. **Wanted!** See full booktalk in Chapter 2 (p. 117). A young girl flees the scene of her father's murder and thinks she is the suspected killer.

3. Grove, Vicki. **The Starplace**. See full booktalk in Chapter 1 (p. 4). The main character becomes more aware of national events when personal conflicts enter her family's life.

4. Leviten, Sonia. **The Singing Mountain**. See full booktalk in Chapter 1 (p. 86). The main character travels to Israel and finds his spiritual life influenced by its history of struggle.

5. McKee, Tim, and Anne Blackshaw. **No More Strangers Now: Young Voices from a New South Africa**. See full booktalk in Chapter 2 (p. 77). Interviews explain how the young people are trying to work together to build their country.

6. Moos, Lotte. "If You Think." In **Life Doesn't Frighten Me at All** edited by John Agard. New York: Henry Holt, 1989. The poem talks about how the violence and addictions of others will affect us.

7. Tekavec, Valerie. **Teenage Refugees from Bosnia-Herzegovina Speak Out**. New York: The Rosen Publishing Group, 1997 rev. ed. 64p. (In Their Own Voices). $17.95. ISBN 0-8239-2560-9. The introduction explains the breakup of Yugoslavia. The teenagers interviewed are Muslim, Serb, or Croat. They explain their reactions to the conflict and their new American culture.

Reynolds, David West. **Star Wars: Episode I, Incredible Cross-Sections, The Definitive Guide to the Craft of *Star Wars*: Episode 1**. New York: DK Publishing, 1999. 32p. $19.95. ISBN 0-7894-3962-X.

Reynolds, David West. **Star Wars: Incredible Cross-Sections, The Ultimate Guide to Star Wars Vehicles and Spacecraft**. New York: DK Publishing, 1998. 32p. $19.95. ISBN 0-7894-3480-6.

### *Summary/Description*

These two volumes explain the *Star Wars* aircraft in terms of history, technology, and purpose. The author is an archeologist. He considers Star Wars to be a real place and time. The cross-sections contain incredible detail and become extensions of the people who invent and pilot them. Some of the aircraft are characters themselves. The illustrations suggest interesting relationships between reality and myth as well as humans and technology.

### *Booktalk*

Show the following foldouts: "Death Star" in the 1998 volume and/or "Droid Control Ship" in the 1999 volume. The interest should be incredibly high.

### *Related Activities*

1. After reading *King Arthur* and the Star Wars books, identify parallel ideals and evils that exist in the two time periods.
2. Research the equipment, clothes, homes, and symbols of Arthur's time. What do those artifacts tell us about the time? How are they similar to and different from those in the Star Wars stories?

3. Draw your own cross-section of a room or public building. Show how the room or building reveals the character of the inhabitants or builders.

4. After reading about the world of Harry Potter, begin to draw a guide to Harry's world. You might wish to include cross-sections of buildings and illustrations of equipment and characters.

5. Both Harry Potter and Luke Skywalker live in larger-than-life worlds. Harry's world is magical, and Luke's is technological. Discuss the processes, tools, and limits of each system. Compare the goals of each system.

## *Related Works*

1. **The Empire Strikes Back**. Produced by Lucas Films, 1980. 127 min. Color. $19.99. 6098. Videocassette. The battle between good and evil continues. Luke searches for Yoda. This is the second in the series.

2. Gray, Paul. "Wild About Harry." *Time* (September 20, 1999): 67–70. The article includes an illustrated guide to the Wizard World.

3. Hamilton, Jake. **Special Effects in Film and Television**. See full booktalk in Chapter 4 (p. 210). The book explains and illustrates how the special effects are carried out.

4. Kerven, Rosalind. **King Arthur**. See full booktalk above (p. 131). The book explains the story of Arthur, which contains many of the ideals present in *Star Wars*. It includes pictures and illustrations that depict the period.

5. **The Return of the Jedi**. Produced by Lucas Films, 1983. 135 min. Color. $19.99. 6099. Videocassette. Luke rescues Solo and Princess Leia from Jabba the Hutt. Then Luke returns to complete his Jedi training with Yoda. This is the third in the series.

6. Reynolds, David West. **Star Wars: The Visual Dictionary, the Ultimate Guide to Star Wars Characters and Creatures**. See full booktalk below (p. 140). The characters, creatures, and equipment are defined and illustrated in extensive detail.

7. Rowling, J. K. **The Harry Potter Series**. See full booktalks below (pp. 181–87). Harry Potter's world seems to be a rich source for an artist's imagination.

8. **Star Wars**. Produced by Lucas Films, 1977. 125 min. Color. $19.99. 6097. Videocassette. Luke Skywalker confronts evil. This is the first of the series.

 Reynolds, David West. **Star Wars: The Visual Dictionary, the Ultimate Guide to Star Wars Characters and Creatures**. New York: DK Publishing, 1998. 64p. $19.95. ISBN 0-7894-3481-4.

### *Summary/Description*

In this *Star Wars* volume, Reynolds has defined the characters, creatures, and equipment of *Star Wars* in extensive detail. As in his cross-section books, Reynolds has treated Star Wars as a real place and time. Again, the equipment is part of the character, and the line between human and non-human is blurry.

### *Booktalk*

Give a *Star Wars* quiz:

1. Define carbon-freezing and explain its uses. (p. 15)
2. How many masters has C-3PO had? (Data File, p. 18)
3. Who are the Tauntauns? (p. 28)
4. How is Darth Vader able to dress himself? (p. 30)
5. What is a gimer stick? (p. 25)

Show the pages as the students check the answers. The student with the most right answers will get to see the book first.

### *Related Activities*

1. Using the *Star Wars: The Visual Dictionary* as a model, choose a person who takes on a public role in society (e.g., a teacher, a doctor, a judge, a police officer). Illustrate elements such as their equipment, home, and clothing. Explain how it reveals their function and character.

2. Identify the grotesque characters listed in the dictionary. Explain their function in the *Star Wars* saga.

3. Identify the beautiful characters listed in the dictionary. Explain their function in the *Star Wars* saga.

4. Examining both grotesque and beautiful groups, discuss whether a pattern emerges.

5. Using the *Star Wars* encyclopedia and cross-sections guides, write questions for a *Star Wars* trivia contest.

## *Related Works*

1. **The Empire Strikes Back**. Produced by Lucas Films, 1980. 127 min. Color. $19.99. 6098. Videocassette. The battle of good and evil continues. Luke searches for Yoda. This is the second in the series.

2. **The Return of the Jedi**. Produced by Lucas Films, 1983. 135 min. Color. $19.99. 6099. Videocassette. Luke rescues Solo and Princess Leia from Jabba the Hutt. Luke completes Jedi training from Yoda. This is the third in the series.

3. **Star Wars**. Produced by Lucas Films, 1977. 125 min. Color. $19.99. 6097. Videocassette. Luke Skywalker begins his confrontation with evil. This is the first in the series.

4. Reynolds, David West. **Star Wars: Episode I, Incredible Cross-Sections: The Definitive Guide to the Craft of *Star Wars*: Episode 1**. See full booktalk above (p. 138). In this book, Reynolds depicts and analyzes the craft into which the characters fit.

5. Reynolds, David West. **Star Wars: Incredible Cross-Sections: The Ultimate Guide to Star Wars Vehicles and Spacecraft**. See full booktalk above (p. 138). In this book, Reynolds depicts and analyzes the craft into which the characters fit.

6. Stern, Jerome. "Grotesque." In **Making Shapely Fiction**. New York: A Laurel Book, 1991. 283p. $6.50. ISBN 0-440-21221-9. Stern talks about the many uses of the grotesque in story construction.

# DISEASE

 Curran, Christian Perdan. **Sexually Transmitted Diseases**. Berkeley Heights, NJ: Enslow Publishers, 1998. 128p. (Diseases and People). $18.95. ISBN 0-7660-1050-3.

### *Summary/Description*

*Sexually Transmitted Diseases* begins with a what, who, and how profile of STDs. Chapter 1 explains the ease of transmission and difficulty in tracking these diseases. Chapter 2 gives the history of each disease and how it has escalated with improved transportation. Then the authors distinguish the different types of STDs and describe their treatments. Finally, they talk about the myths and fears that spread the diseases and methods that will prevent contracting them. Like the other books in the Enslow Diseases and People Series, this book includes a timeline; lists of organizations and hotlines; endnotes; a glossary; lists of books, pamphlets, articles, and Internet sources; and an index.

### *Booktalk*

STDs are the diseases we talk about when other people have them. We think we know how to protect ourselves. But maybe we don't. Teens are one of the highest-risk groups. *Sexually Transmitted Diseases* explains STDs, ranging from the deadly HIV to Trichomonas, a disease so common that it can be transmitted on sheets and bath towels. Learn how to really protect yourself. If you need even more information, the book lists books, Internet sources, and hotlines. It's a strong source of research, help, and protection.

### *Related Activities*

1. Make a chart of sexually transmitted diseases. Include the name of each disease, its effects, its transmission, and methods of prevention.
2. Using the bibliography at the end of the book, pursue additional sources and add sources of your own.

3. Curran includes a list of names, addresses, and phone numbers for more information and help. Make a similar list of local resources.

4. Using the format employed by Michael DiSpezio, the author of *The Science, Spread, and Therapy of HIV Disease*, make up a question-and-answer pamphlet about sexually transmitted diseases.

5. Ask a doctor to speak to the group about sexually transmitted diseases and the problems he or she has observed.

## *Related Works*

1. Ayer, Eleanor. **Choosing Sexual Abstinence**. New York: The Rosen Publishing Group, 1997. 64p. (The Need to Know Library). $17.95. ISBN 0-8239-2250-2. This book makes the case for choosing sexual abstinence rather than giving in to peer and media pressure.

2. DiSpezio, Michael A. **The Science, Spread, and Therapy of HIV Disease**. See full booktalk below (p. 144). DiSpezio uses a question-and-answer format to give information on HIV. He also includes references to print and Internet resources.

3. Farrell, Jeanette. **Invisible Enemies**. See full booktalk below (p. 146). Farrell explains AIDS in the context of plagues that have been spread through ignorance.

4. **Love & Death in America: Sexual Revolution/Aids**. Produced by A&E Television Networks, 1996. 50 min. Color. (20th Century with Mike Wallace). $19.95. AAE-50038. Videocassette. Mike Wallace traces the sexual revolution and how its attitudes have helped to spread AIDS. He also points out that AIDS has been a surprise epidemic since its discovery.

5. **Outbreak! The New Plagues**. Produced by A&E Television Networks, 1996. 50 min. Color. (20th Century with Mike Wallace). $19.95. AAE-21532. Videocassette. The film presents the new plagues that are resistant to antibiotics. AIDS is one of the diseases discussed.

DiSpezio, Michael A. **The Science, Spread, and Therapy of HIV Disease**. Shrewsbury, MA: ATL Press, 1998. 142p. $13.95pa. ISBN 1-882360-19-2.

### *Summary/Description*

*The Science, Spread, and Therapy of HIV Disease* is written in a question-and-answer format. DiSpezio describes the history of the outbreak and the basic biological principles necessary to understand the workings of the disease. He then describes the virus structure, HIV transmission, and HIV disease. Finally, he tells how the disease is monitored and how it is being combated. The question-and-answer format and several diagrams allow a gradual buildup of information so that the reader can understand the terms and principles involved in the disease. Each section ends with a three-question self-test or review, and the index allows the reader to quickly access information. DiSpezio's explanations are detailed and carefully worded. He includes a bibliography of print and Internet resources, a dedicated web site, and a description of DiSpezio's curriculum package on HIV.

### *Booktalk*

At random, select questions from the text. See how accurately students can answer them.

HIV and AIDS are frightening words. The more we know about them, the more we can protect our loved ones and ourselves. *The Science, Spread, and Therapy of HIV Disease* can answer hundreds of questions about HIV and AIDS, and to accommodate the pool of information growing daily, the book has its own dedicated web site. In addition, it has a bibliography and a list of Internet resources. It's a serious source of information. You can quickly access specific information or read the entire book.

### *Related Activities*

1. Read the poem "AIDS" by May Sarton. Discuss the following questions: Who is the speaker? What is the situation? Does the change the speaker describes apply only to AIDS patients?

2. Read "Elegy for John, My Student Dead of AIDS" by Robert Cording. Discuss the following questions: Who is the speaker? What does he reveal about his student? What does he reveal about himself?

3. *Ophelia Speaks* talks about "Media-Fed" images of the body. Examine the media. Describe the "Media-Fed" images of sex that the media present.

4. *Ophelia Speaks* talks about several aspects of sex, but not STDs. Discuss the possible reasons for this omission. Write your own essay about the topic.

5. In *My Life As a Girl*, the main character makes love to a boy she knows for only a brief time. She realizes he has other partners and leaves him. Write another chapter for *My Life As a Girl.*

## *Related Works*

1. Ayer, Eleanor. **It's Okay to Say No: Choosing Sexual Abstinence**. New York: The Rosen Publishing Group, 1998. 64p. (The Teen Pregnancy Prevention Library). $16.95. ISBN 0-8239-2777-6. The book points out that much of the pressure to have sex before marriage comes from the media.

2. Curran, Christian Perdan. **Sexually Transmitted Diseases**. See full booktalk above (p. 142). AIDS is included in the sexually transmitted diseases discussed.

3. Farrell, Jeanette. **Invisible Enemies**. See full booktalk below (p. 146). Farrell talks about AIDS in the context of the prejudice surrounding it.

4. Gordon, Ruth, ed. **Pierced by a Ray of the Sun: Poems About the Times We Feel Alone**. New York: HarperCollins, 1995. 105p. $15.89. ISBN 0-06-023613-2. "AIDS" by Mary Sarton describes the deep love found in reaching out and caring for AIDS patients. "Elegy for John, My Student Dead of AIDS" by Robert Cording reflects on a brilliant student who never had the opportunity to express who he really was.

5. **Love & Death in America: Sexual Revolution/AIDS**. Produced by A&E Television Networks, 1996. 50 min. Color. (20th Century with Mike Wallace). $19.95. AAE-50038. Videocassette. Mike Wallace traces the sexual revolution and how its attitudes have helped to spread AIDS. He also points out that AIDS has been a surprise epidemic since its discovery.

6. Mosier, Elizabeth. **My Life As a Girl**. See full booktalk in Chapter 2 (p. 121). The main character, in figuring out where she fits in the world, has a sexual relationship with a young man whom she knows little about.

7. **Outbreak! The New Plagues**. Produced by A&E Television Networks, 1996. 50 min. Color. (20th Century with Mike Wallace). $19.95. AAE-21532. Videocassette. The film presents the new plagues resistant to antibiotics. AIDS is discussed extensively.

8. Shandler, Sara. **Ophelia Speaks**. See full booktalk in Chapter 2 (p. 126). This anthology by teenage authors addresses several teen problems and concerns.

9. Shire, Amy. **Being HIV-Positive**. New York: The Rosen Publishing Group, 1999 rev. ed. 96p. (The Need to Know Library). $17.95. ISBN 0-8239-2614-1. The book explains the new decisions a person must make when living with HIV.

 Farrell, Jeanette. **Invisible Enemies**. New York: Farrar, Straus & Giroux, 1998. 224p. $17.00. ISBN 0-374-33637-7.

## *Summary/Description*

*Invisible Enemies* tells the stories of smallpox, leprosy, plague, tuberculosis, malaria, cholera, and AIDS. The author includes the outbreaks, the battles, the rare cures, and the psychological implications of the diseases. From her stories emerge patterns of mistakes, bravery, and possible victories in which the germs' strongest allies are prejudice, fear, and misconception. Farrell includes a glossary of unfamiliar terms, annotated recommendations for further reading, and a selected bibliography of sources discussing each disease.

## *Booktalk*

Ask the following questions: What do you do when you have a sore throat? Why do you do it? George Washington is said to have died of a sore throat, but he really died from ignorance, not his own but his doctors'. At that time, doctors bled a patient to cure a sore throat, and Washington was literally bled to death.

As people move around in the world, they bring change. Often that change awakens diseases living in remote areas and transports them to huge populations. Often the move itself creates huge populations ready to be infected. But sometimes, the change brings medicine men and healers with natural cures. Jeanette Farrell writes about the *Invisible Enemies* that came to the New World and held off the British and others in their march for colonization. She also tells about the researchers brave enough and inventive enough to focus on the germ instead of the fear surrounding it. One such researcher swallowed a fresh cholera sample taken from a dying patient's feces. Another discovered that the armadillo is the only animal besides humans that can develop leprosy. As she moves from smallpox to AIDS, Farrell confirms that the humans' best defense against disease is mind over emotion.

## *Related Activities*

1. Make a timeline for each disease discussed in *Invisible Enemies* and *Outbreak! The New Plagues.* What are the overlaps among the diseases? What historic events does each affect?

2. Read "The Pardoner's Tale" from Chaucer's *The Canterbury Tales.* The three men are surrounded by the Plague, meet an old man who cannot die, and then cause their own deaths. Discuss Chaucer's message about death.

3. Discuss how the Plague influences the events of *Fire Bed and Bone.*

4. In Chapter 16 of *Huckleberry Finn* ("The Rattlesnake Skin Does Its Work"), Huck throws off men seeking runaway slaves. He lets them imagine one of their greatest fears and then plays to that fear. Begin reading on page 310, "One of them says . . ." and read over to page 312 up to the phrase "make some money by it." Discuss what the passage tells you about the men, Huck, and the time period.

5. Using the annotated bibliography in *Invisible Enemies*, choose one of the diseases and continue your research. Find additional resources also.

6. Farrell uses the words "scourge" and "pandemic." Find the meaning of these words and explain why they are appropriate within their contexts.

## *Related Works*

1. Branford, Henrietta. **Fire Bed and Bone**. See full booktalk in Chapter 2 (p. 68). The book is set in the period of the Plague and the Peasant's Revolt, two closely related historical events.

2. Chaucer, Geoffrey. "The Pardoner's Tale." In **The Canterbury Tales**. Translated by Nevill Coghill. New York: Penguin Books, 1951. Three young men meet death through their own greed rather than from the Plague that surrounds them.

3. Curran, Christian Perdan. **Sexually Transmitted Diseases**. See full booktalk above (p. 142). The book includes a section on AIDS as well as explanations about the prevention of and research into sexually transmitted diseases. It also contains sources for more help and information.

4. DiSpezio, Michael A. **The Science, Spread, and Therapy of HIV Disease**. See full booktalk above (p. 144). This book gives clear information about HIV in a question-and-answer format.

5. **Love & Death in America: Sexual Revolution/AIDS**. Produced by A&E Television Networks, 1996. 50 min. Color. (20th Century with Mike Wallace). $19.95. AAE-50038. Videocassette. Mike Wallace explains the relationship between AIDS and the sexual revolution.

6. **Outbreak! The New Plagues**. Produced by A&E Television Networks, 1996. 50 min. Color. (20th Century with Mike Wallace). $19.95. AAE-21532. Videocassette. The film traces plagues that have emerged in the twentieth century, speculates about their causes, and predicts more problems.

7. Shire, Amy. **Being HIV-Positive**. New York: The Rosen Publishing Group, 1999 rev. ed. 96p. (The Need to Know Library). $17.95. ISBN 0-8239-2614-1. The book explains how to cope when living with HIV.

8. Twain, Mark. "The Rattlesnake-Skin Does Its Work." In **The Adventures of Huckleberry Finn, in The Portable Mark Twain** edited by Bernard DeVoto. pp. 291–316. New York: The Viking Press, 1946. The chapter shows the prejudice, superstition, and fear of the times.

Hesser, Terry Spencer. **Kissing Doorknobs**. New York: Delacorte Press, 1998. 149p. $15.95. ISBN 0-385-32329-8.

### *Summary/Description*

Tara Sullivan is nicknamed "Count" because of her obsessive-compulsive disorder (OCD). She feels compelled to count every crack in the sidewalk and finally to kiss doorknobs and count the number of times she does it. *Kissing Doorknobs* tells about the voices Tara can't control, the misdiagnoses she undergoes, and the conflict she creates with friends and family. By the end of the novel, she finds a friend who shares her disease and a therapist who can help her. When her friend suffers a relapse, Tara must help him. The Afterword by A. J. Allen, M.D., Ph.D. explains OCD, its history, and its treatment. Following the "Afterword" is an annotated list of resources.

## *Booktalk*

When does double-checking turn into a disease? When does counting become a compulsion? When does pain become relief? Tara Sullivan knows the answers. To friends and family, Tara Sullivan seems too bright and maybe a little weird. She has to have everything just so, even the rice on her plate. She can't tell anyone about her voices. Who would believe her? But her voices are getting louder and more demanding. Her family can't get through a meal without the voices ruining it. Tara can't open the door without kissing the doorknob a certain number of times. Her mother can't stop hitting Tara, and her father is breaking into tears. The evil voices of obsessive-compulsive disorder seem to be destroying Tara and driving away everybody she loves.

## *Related Activities*

1. *Kissing Doorknobs*, *Ethan Between Us*, and *When She Was Good* all deal with mental illness. Describe how the mental illness or illnesses in each novel affect those around the mentally ill character.

2. *Drugs and Your Parents*, *Coping with ADD/ADHD*, *Depression*, *Coping with Compulsive Eating*, and *Coping with Stress* all emphasize techniques to deal with the problems they describe. Compare the techniques suggested. Identify those techniques suggested by more than one author. Make up a core of coping techniques and behaviors that would help a person develop a healthy emotional lifestyle.

3. Discuss how obsessive-compulsive behavior might be confused with ADD/ADHD.

4. Both Tara Sullivan and her friend Kristin have eating disorders. Try to describe each girl's relationship with food by using metaphors. Is the food a monster, a possession, a friend, a toy, medicine? Then describe your own or a friend's relationship with food. Use the same technique.

5. Using the annotated list of resources at the end of the book, continue to research obsessive-compulsive behavior. Then present a report to the group that expands and supports what you have learned by reading *Kissing Doorknobs*.

## *Related Works*

1. Mazer, Norma Fox. **When She Was Good**. See full booktalk below (p. 176). The main character is the victim of a violent, mentally ill sister.
2. McFarland, Rhoda. **Drugs and Your Parents**. New York: The Rosen Publishing Group, 1997 rev. ed. 64p. (The Drug Abuse Prevention Library). $17.95. ISBN 0-8239-2603-6. The book explains how to recognize chemical dependence, how to deal with your chemically dependent parent, and how to deal with your own feelings about your dependent parent.
3. Morrison, Jaydene. **Coping with ADD/ADHD**. New York: The Rosen Publishing Group, 1996. 96p. (Coping). $17.95. ISBN 0-8239-2070-4. The book defines and makes suggestions about how to overcome ADD/ADHD.
4. Myers, Anna. **Ethan Between Us**. See full booktalk in Chapter 4 (p. 221). The main character befriends a young man driven by voices.
5. Packard, Gwen. **Coping with Stress**. New York: The Rosen Publishing Group, 1997. 153p. (Coping). $17.95. ISBN 0-8239-2081-X. The book defines stress, identifies its causes, and gives suggestions on how to deal with it positively.
6. Silverstein, Alvin, Virginia Silverstein, and Laura Silverstein Nunn. **Depression**. See full booktalk below (p. 150). The book defines depression, distinguishes it from less serious conditions, explains how to recognize and battle the disease, talks about its history, and projects its future.
7. Simpson, Carolyn. **Coping with Compulsive Eating**. New York: The Rosen Publishing Group, 1997. 89p. (Coping). $17.95. ISBN 0-8239-2516-1. The book defines compulsive eating, explores its causes, and suggests ways to deal with it.

Silverstein, Alvin; Virginia Silverstein; and Laura Silverstein Nunn. **Depression**. Springfield, NJ: Enslow Publishers, 1997. 128p. (Diseases and People). $18.95. ISBN 0-89490-713-1.

## *Summary/Description*

*Depression* begins with a who, what, and how profile. The opening chapters explain the disease and its history and acknowledge the roles of genetics, medication, and stress in producing depression. Chapter 2 provides the history and specific examples from history to explain the disease's severity and significance. The definition chapter provides a checklist for determining when a person needs professional help with depression, and finally there are suggestions for treatment and stress management. Like the other books in Enslow's Diseases and People Series, *Depression* includes a time line; lists of organizations and hotlines; endnotes; a glossary; a bibliography of books, pamphlets, and articles; a list of Internet sources; and an index.

## *Booktalk*

Read the list of symptoms on pages 34–35.

If these symptoms are familiar to you, you may know or be someone who is clinically depressed. *Depression* explains how to recognize the disease, how to understand it, and how to get help with it. Depression can happen to anyone at anytime. The Bible talked about it. Shakespeare wrote about it, and Lincoln suffered from it. Today, however, there are many more sources of help and understanding. *Depression* includes lists of organizations, hotlines, books, pamphlets, articles, and Internet sources. It's a good source for information and help.

## *Related Activities*

1. Choose one of the topics discussed in *Depression.* Refer to the sources listed on pages 120–25. Find as much information as possible on that particular topic. Report your findings to the class.

2. If you are worried about an exam, follow the steps suggested in "Coping with Stress" from *Strategies for Studying*. Then rewrite the suggestions to apply to another situation that might be stressful. How much did you have to rewrite?

3. Think of one way to reduce stress each week. You might refer to the "Prevention" chapter of *Depression*. Explain what you did and the results of your action.

4. Find as much information as possible about the Elizabethan concept of melancholy. Discuss how this concept agrees with and differs from a modern definition of depression.

5. When Hamlet appears at the court in his "inky cloak," he shows himself to be mourning his father's death. Claudius, however, sees this appearance much differently. Read Claudius's reaction to Hamlet's words and dress (Act 1, Scene 2, lines 87–117). Discuss Claudius's reaction.

6. After finding information about the Elizabethan concept of melancholy, identify evidence throughout the play that would indicate that Hamlet is melancholy. Then find evidence that would indicate that he is not.

## *Related Works*

1. **Abraham Lincoln: Preserving the Union**. Produced by A&E Home Video, 1996. 100 min. Color. (American Presidents). $14.95. AAE 14175. Videocassette. This biography covers the depression Lincoln lived with and fought all his life.

2. Packard, Gwen. **Coping with Stress**. New York: The Rosen Publishing Group, 1997. 153p. (Coping). $17.95. ISBN 0-8239-2081-X. The book defines stress, identifies its causes, and gives suggestions on how to use and deal with it.

3. Shakespeare, William. **Hamlet** edited by G. L. Kittredge. New York: Ginn, 1939. Hamlet seems to be plagued by melancholy.

4. University of Victoria's Counseling Services. **Strategies for Studying: A Handbook of Study Skills**. Victoria, BC: Orca Book Publishers, 1996. 150p. $12.95pa. ISBN 1-55143-063-0. The entire book gives advice on how to handle a complicated academic workload, but "Coping with Stress" deals specifically with emotional issues in studying and taking tests.

5. Wilson, Dover. **What Happens in Hamlet**. London: Cambridge at the University Press, 1964. Wilson discusses the Elizabethan concept of melancholy in relation to *Hamlet.*

# HATE AND PREJUDICE

 Baer, Edith. **Walk the Dark Streets**. New York: Farrar, Straus & Giroux/Frances Foster Books, 1998. 280p. $18.00. ISBN 0-374-38229-8.

### *Summary/Description*

*Walk the Dark Streets* tells Germany's story and Eva Bentheim's story during the Nazi rise to power. The novel opens in 1933 when Hitler is appointed chancellor and ends in 1940 when Eva leaves Germany for America. The Nazis slowly strangle the Jews by restricting health care, education, and even food. Eva's extended family slowly dwindles as relatives sicken, die, and emigrate. Baer illustrates that the path to the Final Solution was made up of thousands of small compromises and denials.

Eva, in her teens, experiences the betrayal of friends, the discovery of love, and the necessity of self-sacrifice. Finally, she must emigrate to America alone, knowing that she may never see her family and friends again.

### *Booktalk*

If one day you came to school and the teacher told you that you could come to class only two days a week, because you weren't good enough or pure enough, what would you do? If your classmates then said they were coming to get you, what would you do? For Eva Bentheim, these questions are realities, not "ifs." She is a Jew in Nazi Germany. Her father fought for Germany in the First World War. Her family has a business there. She does well in school, and her family gathers together to show their love and celebration, but suddenly they are not Germans. They are animals. They are criminals. They are Jews. What would you do? *Walk the Dark Streets* gives many possible answers, but no answer that could stop the terrible hate that the Bentheims and other "undesirables" had to face.

## *Related Activities*

1. Research the Third Reich's signs and slogans. List the methods used to encourage hate. Discuss whether any of those methods are employed today in the media. Collect examples of modern propaganda. Group them by technique.
2. Define "coalition party." Research the coalition parties' role in Hitler's rise to power. Speculate how coalition parties would affect our modern-day government.
3. Define Zionism. Trace its development in Jewish history.
4. Hitler's Germany was based on a two-valued orientation. Show how it was used in Nazi Germany. Find examples of its use in our society today. You may wish to refer to *Language in Thought and Action* by S. I. Hayakawa.
5. Research the 1936 Olympics. What was Jesse Owen's role, and why was he so hated by the Nazi regime?
6. Read "The Children's Exodus," from *War and the Pity of War*, aloud. Why is the poem difficult to read aloud? Describe the speaker and his feelings about his situation. Discuss why the author chose to eliminate punctuation. Do you feel that decision helped or hindered the poem's impact?
7. *The Hidden Children of the Holocaust*, *The Lost Children of Berlin*, and *Tomi: A Childhood Under the Nazis* are all nonfiction accounts. What details in these accounts corroborate the fictional account *Walk the Dark Streets?*

## *Related Works*

1. Gershon, Karen. "The Children's Exodus." In **War and the Pity of War** edited by Neil Philip and illustrated by Michael McCurdy. See full booktalk in Chapter 1 (p. 44). The poem describes the feelings of a young Jewish refugee "saved" in a children's transport train to England.
2. Hayakawa, S. I., and Alan R. Hayakawa. "The Two-Valued Orientation." In **Language in Thought and Action**, 5th ed. New York: Harcourt Brace Jovanovich, 1990. 287p. $42.50. ISBN 0-15-550120-8. The chapter defines two-valued orientation and illustrates it with several examples from Nazi propaganda.

3. Kustanowitz, Esther. **The Hidden Children of the Holocaust**. See full booktalk below (p. 158). Jewish children describe their experiences hiding from the Nazis.

4. Levitin, Sonia. **The Singing Mountain**. See full booktalk in Chapter 2 (p. 86). The novel describes a young man's discovery of his Jewish faith and the history of Israel.

5. Lobel, Anita. **No Pretty Pictures: A Child of War**. See full booktalk in Chapter 1 (p. 31). This nonfiction account describes the lives of two small children who are hiding during the Nazi regime.

6. **The Lost Children of Berlin**. Produced by A&E Television Networks, 1997. 50 min. Color. $19.95. AAE-16117. Videocassette. Students from the same Jewish school reunite and tell their stories.

7. Ungerer, Tomi. **Tomi: A Childhood Under the Nazis**. See full booktalk below (p. 164). In this nonfiction account, a man recalls his life and indoctrination under the German occupation of Alsace.

Cox, Clinton. **Come All You Brave Soldiers**. New York: Scholastic, 1999. 182p. $15.95. ISBN 0-590-47576-2.

## *Summary/Description*

*Come All You Brave Soldiers* describes the contribution that black soldiers made to both sides of the Revolutionary War. Slaves and indentured servants had more reason to believe in liberty and the pursuit of happiness than their masters did. But they could not tell which side would allow them these rights. Crispus Attucks exemplifies the bitter irony of their participation. He is considered by many to be the first man to die in the Revolution. Yet, when he died, he was a fugitive slave. Although some states proposed freedom for slaves who would fight for the Revolution, others sent slaves in place of their masters, or gave slaves as an enlistment bonus to white soldiers. Although some states and patriots awarded loyal black soldiers with freedom and homes, others sent their most loyal fighters back to slavery. Although many patriots spoke against slavery, their voices were not strong enough to guarantee freedom for all. Cox provides numerous examples of brave contributions, broken promises, and the hopes and fears that motivated them. An extensive bibliography of books and journals suggests additional sources, and an index makes information easily accessible within the book.

## *Booktalk*

Black people did not win their freedom in the Revolutionary War, but they fought for it, on both sides. The British and the Colonists had cooperated in enslaving them. Who could they trust? Who would finally agree that they had a right to be free? Some fought and spied for the British. Some fought and spied for the Continental army. Slaves could show the British the slave escape routes and attack routes that they had used to fool their own masters. Slaves could easily slip in and out of British camps as spies. Which side would see their value as human beings and free them? Which side would use their talents and continue to enslave them? Many black soldiers chose the American side and were rewarded, but many were betrayed. Clearly, *Come All You Brave Soldiers* shows us that the Civil War had its roots in the Revolutionary War, and that thousands of black soldiers like Peter Salem, Lemuel Haynes, and James Armistead planted the seeds.

## *Related Activities*

1. Read "Dark Symphony" by Melvin Tolson (in *Shimmy Shimmy Shimmy Like My Sister Kate: Looking at the Harlem Renaissance Through Poems*). Identify and explain the allusions in "Dark Symphony." Then explain how these allusions aid the author's purpose.

2. Read "Checking Out Me History" by John Agard (in *Life Doesn't Frighten Me at All*). Discuss the following: Who is the speaker? Why does he or she speak? What does the speaker do to make the point?

3. Compare "Dark Symphony" and "Checking Out Me History." How are they alike? How are they different?

4. Read "Crispus Attucks" by Jay Wright. Describe the speaker. "Crispus Attucks" was published in 1971. Why does the speaker reflect on Crispus Attucks, a revolutionary war hero, in the 1970s?

5. Using the extensive bibliography at the end of *Come All You Brave Soldiers*, choose one aspect of Cox's research, gather more information about it, and share it with other members in the group.

## *Related Works*

1. **Abraham Lincoln: Preserving the Union**. Produced by A&E Home Video, 1996. 100 min. Color. (American Presidents). $14.95. AAE 14175. Videocassette. Although Lincoln guided the nation through the Civil War, his true opposition to slavery and support of equal rights came only after his experience with black soldiers challenged his own prejudices.

2. Agard, John. "Checking Out Me History." In **Life Doesn't Frighten Me at All** compiled by John Agard. New York: Henry Holt, 1989. The speaker compares the facts given about white history and those left out about black history.

3. **America's Black Warriors: Two Wars to Win**. Produced by A&E Television Networks, 1998. 50 min. Color. (Special Presentation). $19.95. AAE-40352. Videocassette. The film records the prejudice against the black soldier that has dated from the Revolutionary War, and the growing acceptance and respect afforded that soldier today. Colin Powell speaks in the film.

4. Severance, John B. **Thomas Jefferson: Architect of Democracy**. See full booktalk in Chapter 4 (p. 245). Severance explores Jefferson's relationship to slavery and the Declaration of Independence.

5. Tolson, Melvin. "Dark Symphony." In **Shimmy Shimmy Shimmy Like My Sister Kate: Looking at the Harlem Renaissance Through Poems** edited by Nikki Giovanni. See full booktalk in Chapter 4 (p. 236). The speaker tells how the black race has been blocked from its history. The poet uses musical terms to direct the changing tones of the verses.

6. Wright, Jay. "Crispus Attucks." In **Literature As Experience: An Anthology** edited by Irving Howe, John Hollander, and David Bromwich. New York: Harcourt Brace Jovanovich, 1979. The editors provide additional study questions for the poem.

Kustanowitz, Esther. **The Hidden Children of the Holocaust: Teens Who Hid from the Nazis**. The Rosen Publishing Group, 1999. 63p. (Teen Witnesses to the Holocaust). $17.95. ISBN 0-8239-2562-5.

## *Summary/Description*

Chapter 1 provides historical background. Chapters 2 through 6 give six personal narratives of teenagers who hid either through false identities or in actual hideouts. Anne Frank's plight and the network that supported these children are also described. The conclusion tells what happened to these people after the war. A map at the beginning shows some of the towns where the children lived and were hidden. At the end of the book, a timeline explains the progression of the war and Jewish persecution; a glossary explains German and military terms; and a source list includes books (basic and advanced), videos, and web sites for additional information. The book also includes a name and subject index and biographical information about the author and series editor. Pictures accompany each of the narratives. *The Hidden Children of the Holocaust* is one of eight books in the Teen Witnesses to the Holocaust series.

## *Booktalk*

Anne Frank is probably the most famous hidden child of World War II. Her experience was repeated throughout the war. Jewish children had to hide in basements, in forests, behind false names, and under false religions. While they lived in uneasy safety, they knew their relatives were also being hunted and killed. In *The Hidden Children of the Holocaust*, teenagers who managed to hide throughout the war tell their stories. Some were betrayed by people they trusted. Some were helped by people they thought were their enemies. Even though they were lucky to escape the concentration camps, they never overcame their haunting fear. Even today, they realize that they will never fully explain that fear to the friends and relatives who did not experience it. But, here, in their own words, they try.

## *Related Activities*

1. Read "Don't Be Afraid" by David Vogel. Who is the speaker? What is the situation? What images does the speaker use in the poem? Why is the use of these images ironic? How does the poet employ dramatic irony?

2. Read "War Has Been Given a Bad Name" by Bertolt Brecht. Who is the speaker? Why does he speak? What is the tone of the poem? What is the purpose? How does the poet employ understatement to accomplish his purpose?

3. *A Traitor Among Us* recounts the journey of a twelve-year-old boy when he becomes part of the Dutch Resistance. Compare the details of that story to Yvonne Kray Sokolow's account in Chapter 6 of *The Hidden Children of the Holocaust.*

4. Anita Lobel was a small child, not a teenager, when she was hidden from the Nazis. What details of Lobel's hiding in *No Pretty Pictures: A Child of War* match the accounts of *The Hidden Children of the Holocaust*?

5. Choose one aspect of the flight and hiding of Jewish children and teenagers. Using the bibliography at the end of *The Hidden Children of the Holocaust*, pursue that topic and share with the group the information that you find.

## *Related Works*

1. Baer, Edith. **Walk the Dark Streets**. See full booktalk above (p. 153). A Jewish teenage girl's story begins with Hitler's bid for power and ends with her emigration to America.

2. Lobel, Anita. **No Pretty Pictures: A Child of War**. See full booktalk in Chapter 1 (p. 39). Lobel describes her own ordeal in hiding, as a small child, from the Nazis.

3. **The Lost Children of Berlin**. Produced by A&E Television Networks, 1997. 50 min. Color. $19.95. AAE-16117. Videocassette. Students from the same Jewish school recall how they hid and fled from the Nazis.

4. Philip, Neil, ed., and Michael McCurdy (illus). **War and the Pity of War**. See full booktalk in Chapter 1 (p. 44). "Don't Be Afraid" by David Vogel is a mother's comforting speech to her child. "War Has Been Given a Bad Name" by Bertolt Brecht is a detached report about why World War II has received such a bad name.

5. Tito, Tina E. **Liberation: Teens in the Concentration Camps and the Teen Soldiers Who Liberated Them**. See full booktalk in Chapter 4 (p. 225). Both teenage prisoners and soldiers tell the stories of the teenagers not able to get out or hide. This book is also part of the Teen Witnesses to the Holocaust series.

6. Van Steenwyk, Elizabeth. **A Traitor Among Us**. See full booktalk in Chapter 4 (p. 228). A young boy must dodge the town spy while serving as a member of the Dutch Resistance.

Lindquist, Susan Hart. **Summer Soldiers**. New York: Delacorte Press, 1999. 178p. $14.95. ISBN 0-385-32641-6.

## *Summary/Description*

Twelve-year-old Joe Farrington must become the "man of the house" when his father decides to serve in World War I. Left without their fathers to protect them, Joe and his three friends must fight their own war against the Thorton brothers, who regularly bully and humiliate the boys. This war intensifies because Mr. Morgon, the father of one of Joe's friends, has chosen not to join the service. The town unites in hatred against Morgon. They even refuse to take Morgon's sheep to market. When Joe's father is reported missing in action, Joe starts to feel this same resentment. Then Mr. Morgon dies a hero while trying to save horses from a sinking ship. The owner of the horses offers to buy the Morgons' sheep if someone will deliver them to market. Despite a disastrous performance on a previous drive, the four young friends take on the drive, deliver the sheep, and face off the Thorton brothers on their return. Although Joe still does not know if his father is alive, because of his own success, he now has hope that his father will return.

## *Booktalk*

Nobody can ignore a bully, whether that bully is a country or a next-door neighbor. When Joe Farrington is twelve, his father and most of his friends' fathers go to fight the Kaiser, Europe's bully. Then Joe and his friends must fight the Thorton brothers, the town bullies, alone. But suddenly, people who were friends now seem to be enemies, and heroes aren't always the ones with the toughest talk or the biggest fists. Joe and his friends must stick together and become men, good men and tough men, like their fathers. When the boys become *Summer Soldiers* they find out that what their fathers made look simple is pretty complicated after all.

## *Related Activities*

1. Research the songs, slogans, and posters used in World War I. Report on the images, words, and national mood that motivated men to sign up for the war.
2. Research World War I. Try to determine what separated this war from previous wars.
3. Read "Wars" by Carl Sandburg. How does Sandburg communicate the difference and sameness of World War I in comparison with other wars?
4. In *No Man's Land* and *The Journal of James Edmond Pease*, the main characters who go to war are not too much older than Joe Farrington in *Summer Soldiers*. Compare the realizations they have about people and Joe's realizations about people.
5. *Holes*, *Hero*, and *Summer Soldiers* explore the topics of conflict, heroism, and integrity. Discuss the statement that each work makes about each of the topics.

## *Related Works*

1. Bartoletti, Susan. **No Man's Land**. See full booktalk in Chapter 1 (p. 37). The main character signs up for service in the Civil War and discovers a completely new definition of heroism.
2. Murphy, Jim. **The Journal of James Edmond Pease**. See full booktalk in Chapter 1 (p. 42). The main character discovers that the small decisions in wars create the heroes.
3. Philip, Neil, ed., and Michael McCurdy (illus). **War and the Pity of War**. See full booktalk in Chapter 1 (p. 44). This poetry collection contains "Wars" by Carl Sandburg, and many other World War I poems.
4. Rottman, S. L. **Hero**. See full booktalk in Chapter 4 (p. 223). The main character defines the word *hero* for himself.
5. Sachar, Louis. **Holes**. See full booktalk in Chapter 1 (p. 35). The main character becomes stronger as he deals with the problems that he feels his family has given him.

Miklowitz, Gloria D. **Masada: The Last Fortress**. Grand Rapids, MI: Eerdmans Books, 1998. 188p. $16.00. ISBN 0-8028-5165-7.

### *Summary/Description*

*Masada: The Last Fortress* is a novel, based on fact, about the small band of Jewish Zealots who defended themselves against an overwhelming Roman army. Simon, seventeen-year-old son of Zealot leader Eleazar ben Yá ir, tells his own and the Zealot's story through a daily journal. The Zealots hold the fortress for seven months against the Romans. During that time they plan for the future through study and celebration, even a wedding. Their world is spiritual and intellectual. But when their situation becomes hopeless, even though they have their entire lives and plans ahead of them, they agree to mass suicide rather than submission to the Roman government, a submission that they would consider slavery.

Flavius Silva, commander-in-chief of the Roman Tenth Legion, tells the Roman story of military domination and personal ambition. From his materialistic point of view, the Zealots are madmen who threaten to destroy the powerful Roman government. His plans center on punishment, destruction, and torture. He does not understand or predict the Zealots' level of self-sacrifice. The chapters by both Simon and Flavius show the powerful resolve and unyielding stands that produced the sacrifice of Masada.

### *Booktalk*

Discuss the following statement and question: The winner of the wars has the privilege of telling the stories about the wars. Why does telling any story of war matter?

Simon, John, Debra, Adam, and Sara have just started their own life stories. They are all in their teens and beginning the love and work of their lives. But they live in *Masada: The Last Fortress*, the last home of the Jewish Zealots. Now, with their fellow Zealots, they must face the overwhelming Roman army that has marched through the desert to defeat and enslave them. They must decide to become part of a corrupt society or give up life completely. Simon, the son of the Zealot leader, writes their story. Flavius Silva, the Roman general, writes his. After the Zealots and the Romans meet at Masada, you decide whose story the world will remember and admire.

## *Related Activities*

1. Using a word finder or synonym guide, look up the word *zealot* and its synonyms. What connotations distinguish this word from its synonyms? What do these connotations suggest about any zealot movement?

2. Others in history have also fought and died for their beliefs. John Brown fought what he perceived as a corrupt, materialistic government that supported slavery. After reading *Mine Eyes Have Seen*, try to classify Brown and his followers by referring to the definitions in Activity 1.

3. Research the mass suicide of Masada. Report your findings to the class.

4. Both *The Singing Mountain* and *Masada* deal with the spiritual versus the material worlds. Both are written from more than one point of view. *The Singing Mountain* alludes to Masada. Discuss how the visions of the main characters in each novel are related.

5. In Act 4, Scene 4, of *Hamlet*, Hamlet ponders the action of Fortinbras, who leads an army to defend a land valued only for what it symbolizes. In Act 5, Scene 2, however, Hamlet asks Horatio to live and tell Hamlet's story. Hamlet, himself, then becomes a symbol. Discuss the reasons for Hamlet's request. Compare Horatio's role to the role of the Masada survivors.

6. Read "Roman Wall Blues" by W. H. Auden. Who is the speaker? What is the situation? What are his concerns? Is this soldier the voice of this particular campaign only or of all professional soldiers?

## *Related Works*

1. Auden, W. H. "Roman Wall Blues." In **War and the Pity of War** edited by Neil Philip and illustrated by Michael McCurdy. See full booktalk in Chapter 1 (p. 44). Although the historical setting of the poem is far later than Masada, the soldier ponders a military assignment in which he has no emotional investment and a religion that would ask him to move from his own world-centered views.

2. Hayakawa, S. I. **Choose the Right Word: A Modern Guide to Synonyms**. New York: Harper & Row, 1968. (Perennial Library). This reference volume distinguishes differences in meaning among synonyms, with explanations and illustrations.

3. Levitin, Sonia. **The Singing Mountain**. See full booktalk in Chapter 2 (p. 86). The main character is seeking his spiritual life in the roots of Jewish tradition.

4. Rinaldi, Ann. **Mine Eyes Have Seen**. See full booktalk in Chapter 4 (p. 243). The main character tells the story of John Brown through a daughter's eyes.

5. Shakespeare, William. **Hamlet** edited by G. L. Kittredge. New York: Ginn, 1939. Throughout the play, Hamlet ponders the qualities of the hero and leader.

Ungerer, Tomi. **Tomi: A Childhood Under the Nazis**. Niwot, CO: The Roberts Rinehart Publishing Group, 1998. 175p. $29.95. ISBN 1-57098-163-9.

### *Summary/Description*

Tomi Ungerer explains his Alsatian childhood under Nazi rule. He is seven when the Second World War begins. He is fourteen when it ends. Tomi is the youngest of four children and only three years old when his father dies. He lives through the German occupation and French domination. He uses his own childhood drawings, family pictures, poems, old copybooks, and examples of both French and German propaganda to explain how the Germans and the French attempted to control the minds and fate of this small community. His family's reaction to these attempts, especially his mother's, illustrates how people, with humor and wit, can maintain their own national character and integrity. On pages ix–x, Ungerer describes and characterizes Alsace for the reader.

### *Booktalk*

Show a map of Germany, France, and Alsace. Discuss Alsace's resources and the desirability of controlling it. Discuss the following questions with the group: What would happen if another state or city tried to annex your city? What might that city have to do to make the citizens become like the citizens of the dominating country (e.g., required clothes, slang, food, families)? What would the reaction be in the town?

Tomi is seven when World War II begins. He is fourteen when it ends. He lives through the German occupation and French domination. He has saved his copybooks, report cards, family pictures, drawings and mementos. Sorting them and organizing them in this book, he shows us not only his own history but also his country's history. The French want him to be French. The Germans want him to be German, but he is Alsatian. Before the German invasion, he rightfully questions the French soldier's preference for drinking and romance over fighting. During the German occupation he learns to distrust a man who can talk about the glory of his son's death, hanging Jews, and his wife's carrot cake recipe in the same conversation. He wonders about his mother's prejudices and marvels at her shrewdness. In his world of swastikas and soldiers, even Donald Duck, Mickey Mouse, and Superman would be candidates for the concentration camps.

## *Related Activities*

1. After reading *Tomi*, read *1984*. What parallels can you find between the world Tomi Ungerer describes in his nonfiction account and the world George Orwell describes in his novel?

2. Begin a scrapbook of your pictures, poems, programs, and memorabilia. After six months, write a journal entry about what trends in culture your scrapbook reveals. Compare your journal entry with journal entries by other people in the group who have completed the same project. What trends repeat?

3. Research censorship during the Third Reich. Be sure to include cartoon characters in your research.

4. *No Pretty Pictures: A Child of War*, *Walk the Dark Streets*, *A Traitor Among Us*, *The Hidden Children of the Holocaust: Teens Who Hid from the Nazis*, *The Lost Children of Berlin*, and *Tomi* all deal with children living during World War II. Ask five individuals or five groups to each choose one of the books. Ask them to read the book, determine whether it is fiction or nonfiction, and then share the experiences about which they have read. Discuss the patterns as well as the unique elements.

5. Read "From a German War Primer" by Bertolt Brecht. Who is the speaker? Why does he choose to speak? How does the poem relate to *Tomi*?

### *Related Works*

1. Baer, Edith. **Walk the Dark Streets**. See full booktalk above (p. 153). A teenage Jewish girl must flee Germany under Nazi rule.
2. Brecht, Bertolt. "From a German War Primer." In **War and the Pity of War** edited by Neil Philip and illustrated by Michael McCurdy. The speaker notes how a politician's statement really means something quite different.
3. Kustanowitz, Esther. **The Hidden Children of the Holocaust: Teens Who Hid from the Nazis**. See full booktalk above (p. 158). First-hand accounts tell how families and friends protected Jewish children.
4. Lobel, Anita. **No Pretty Pictures: A Child of War**. See full booktalk in Chapter 1 (p. 39). A young girl and her brother hide from the Nazis.
5. **The Lost Children of Berlin**. Produced by A&E Television Networks, 1997. 50 min. Color. $19.95. AAE-16117. Students from the same Jewish school tell about their war-time experiences.
6. Orwell, George. **1984**. New York: New American Library, 1949. (Signet Classic). The world of *1984* uses many of the same propaganda tactics that Nazi Germany used.
7. Van Steenwyk, Elizabeth. **A Traitor Among Us**. See full booktalk in Chapter 4 (p. 228). A young boy participates in the Dutch Resistance.

## FAMILY CONFLICTS

Trembath, Don. **A Beautiful Place on Yonge Street**. Victoria, BC: Orca Book Publishers, 1998. 190p. $6.95pa. ISBN 1-55143-121-1.

### *Summary/Description*

Harper Winslow's parents send him to writing camp. There he meets twins Mickey and Sunny Taylor. He makes friends with Mickey and falls in love with Sunny. Everything about Sunny fascinates him. She is interested in his writing, gives him pictures she has painted, and thinks to bring his mother presents. He becomes involved with her family and sees how much they contrast with his own. He admires their interest in literature and their joy in being with each other. But Sunny is an independent lady, and when she decides to move to Toronto to go to art school, Harper has his first lesson in letting go.

## *Booktalk*

Remember Harper Winslow? Now he's eighteen and falling in love. Sunny, his girlfriend, does not seem to fit in Harper's family or even his neighborhood. And Harper's timing hasn't improved. He can't find a good time to introduce her to his friends or even to kiss her. But in addition, Sunny is independent, smart, and sophisticated. Harper doesn't know if he can handle all of that. She wants to be an artist as much as Harper wants to be a writer. Can Harper and Sunny find happiness in *A Beautiful Place on Yonge Street*?

## *Related Activities*

1. Ask the students to complete Harper's first writing assignment. Ask them to write about a color, and tell them that they cannot use an essay form.

2. Ask some of the students in the class to illustrate their writing or ask another student to illustrate it.

3. Read "That Kiss" in *Just People & Paper/Pen/Poem: A Young Writer's Way to Begin*. Complete Appelt's writing invitation on page 85.

4. Compare Harper Winslow in *A Beautiful Place on Yonge Street* to the Harper Winslow in *Tuesday Cafe* and *A Fly Named Alfred.* Using the discussion and questions about character on pages 28–33 in Chapter 4 of *What's Your Story? A Young Person's Guide to Writing Fiction*, describe Harper Winslow.

5. After completing Activity 4, create the next situation that you think Harper will encounter. Then describe how he will react.

6. In *Bull Catcher*, Bull is also dealing with his love life. Compare and contrast the two situations. What conflicts and questions do the two characters share? How is each character's experience unique?

## *Related Works*

1. Appelt, Kathi (text), and Kenneth Appelt (photographs). **Just People & Paper/Pen/Poem: A Young Writer's Way to Begin**. See full booktalk in Chapter 4 (p. 195). In the poem, a young man steals a kiss on the school stairs and tries to figure out what happened.
2. Bauer, Marion Dane. **What's Your Story? A Young Person's Guide to Writing Fiction**. New York: Clarion Books, 1992. 134p. $6.95pa. ISBN 0-395-57780-2. Bauer's guidance in how to build a character helps to analyze a character also.
3. Carter, Alden R. **Bull Catcher**. See full booktalk in Chapter 2 (p. 96). The main character tries to figure out his feelings for very different types of girls.
4. Trembath, Don. **A Fly Named Alfred**. See full booktalk in Chapter 2 (p. 128). Harper Winslow decides to become an anonymous columnist for the school paper. This is the second book in the series.
5. Trembath, Don. **The Tuesday Cafe**. See full booktalk in Chapter 1 (p. 23). Harper Winslow signs up for a night writing class when a judge sentences him to write an essay. This is the first book in the series.

Cooney, Caroline B. **Hush Little Baby**. New York: Scholastic, 1999. 258p. $4.99pa. ISBN 0-590-81974-7.

## *Summary/Description*

Kit Innes lives with her mother and stepfather in New Jersey. Her stepfather, who lives in California, has a furnished house nearby for his visits. When Kit stops by the house to pick up a sweatshirt, Dusty, her ex-stepmother comes to the house, leaves a newborn baby, and drives away. Kit is then caught up in a baby sale scheme financed by an ATM fraud. Instead of calling her mother for advice, Kit decides to make the decisions herself and involves her acquaintances and their families. Dusty and three of her equally self-centered and unstable cousins try to retrieve the baby as Kit, Rowen, and nine-year-old Muffin try to protect him. Kit, Rowen, and Muffin save themselves and the baby. The police catch the baby traders (ATM robbers). Kit and her now good friends have a new appreciation for their own families.

## Booktalk

Ask the following questions:

1. Has anyone here had to baby-sit?

2. Have the parents ever come home later than they promised?

3. What have their reasons been? How did you feel about the reasons?

Kit Innes doesn't even know she is going to baby-sit until her ex-stepmother, Dusty, arrives with a baby and then drives away. As Kit waits for her to return, the day gets more complicated. The boy who would like to date her comes to pick her up and brings his nine-year-old sister. A sinister man in an old Cadillac drives across her flowerbed when she refuses to give him the baby. A frantic woman calls and says she has adopted the baby. And finally, Dusty returns and wants the baby. What should the baby-sitter do? Is Dusty reliable? Is the lady on the phone believable? Is the man in the Cadillac too frightening to ignore? The decisions Kit makes throws herself and her friends into a world of abuse, hideouts, kidnapping, and robbery. *Hush Little Baby* begins as a regular day that builds into a journey of love and fear.

## Related Activities

1. In *Hush Little Baby*, *The Terrorist*, and *Wanted!*, Cooney stresses the importance of trusting and relying on the adults we know. Discuss this advice.

2. *Tenderness*, also a mystery, has a much more sinister tone than any of the Cooney mysteries listed in Activity 1. Discuss how the events, details, and characters account for that difference in tone.

3. *Coping in a Blended Family* cautions us about believing in myths about what families should be rather than communicating to build a family. Discuss how the advice applies or does not apply to *Hush Little Baby*.

4. Compare the blended family situations of *A Door Near Here*, *The Spirit Window*, and *Hush Little Baby*. What conflicts in each novel stem from the difficulty in blending families?

5. Using the material developed from Activity 6 of *The Terrorist* booktalk and Activity 5 of the *Wanted!* booktalk, decide on focus and plot. You may wish to refer to *What's Your Story?* Chapters 5 and 6.

## *Related Works*

1. Bauer, Marion Dane. **What's Your Story? A Young Person's Guide to Writing Fiction**. New York: Clarion Books, 1992. 134p. $6.95pa. ISBN 0-395-57780-2. Bauer explains how to use and direct details to a final focus.
2. Cooney, Caroline B. **The Terrorist**. See full booktalk above (p. 135). The writing exercise in the activities is related to *Wanted!* and *Hush Little Baby.*
3. Cooney, Caroline B. **Wanted!** See full booktalk in Chapter 2 (p. 117). The writing exercise in the activities is related to *The Terrorist* and *Hush Little Baby.*
4. Cormier, Rob. **Tenderness**. See full booktalk in Chapter 2 (p. 64). A serial killer is released from prison and continues to stalk victims.
5. Hurwitz, Jane. **Coping in a Blended Family**. See full booktalk below (p. 170). The book explains how to develop skills that will help separate families merge into one.
6. Quarles, Heather. **A Door Near Here**. See full booktalk in Chapter 1 (p. 54). The oldest daughter in a broken family feels she must hide her mother's alcoholism.
7. Sweeney, Joyce. **The Spirit Window**. See full booktalk in Chapter 1 (p. 19). The main character must deal with the tensions of her extended and step-families.

 Hurwitz, Jane. **Coping in a Blended Family**. New York: The Rosen Publishing Group, 1997. 102p. $17.95. ISBN 0-8239-2077-1.

## *Summary/Description*

*Coping in a Blended Family* speaks to the fact that divorce, remarriage, and cohabitation have changed the "traditional" American family. Indeed, *Blended Family* works on the premise that any group of people who decide to live and work together can eventually become a strong family unit. The book deals with the skills needed to build realistic communication, trust, and independence, and maintains that the "perfect family" that the media models creates more problems than solutions. It gives several situation examples for each concept and practical suggestions for dealing with those situations. Family cooperation and communication are discussed within the context of marriage, divorce, death, remarriage, or cohabitation. The book includes addresses and resources, a bibliography, and a topic index.

## *Booktalk*

Discuss the following questions with the group: What is a traditional family? What is a non-traditional family? List some traditional families on television. Are they realistic? List some non-traditional families on television. Are they realistic? What feelings do the words "traditional" and "non-traditional" suggest to you?

Instead of using the word "non-traditional," Jane Hurwitz uses the word "blended." Fifty percent of Americans have a step-relative. Many blended families are happy, healthy, communicating units. But some blended families are not so well adjusted—especially when they first come together. If your family or your friend's family doesn't look like the *Brady Bunch*, you might want to read *Coping in a Blended Family*. It lists the myths or expectations that can get a family in trouble before it even really starts becoming a family. Then it gives suggestions and resources to deal with or prevent that trouble.

## *Related Activities*

1. After reading *Coping in a Blended Family*, list and discuss the behaviors that would help any family become a better blend.

2. Using the listed resources, continue research on the blended family, group communication, and cooperation.

3. Watch television shows that depict family life. List the expectations these shows communicate. Discuss whether you agree with Hurwitz that these shows are unrealistic pictures that produce dangerous myths.

4. Watch television shows that depict groups of people living together who are not necessarily related. List the expectations these shows communicate. Discuss whether these shows produce dangerous myths about communication and cooperation.

5. Read any of the fiction selections from the Related Works section. Analyze the communication problems the books present and decide how the situations might have been improved. Discuss how many of the problems are related to poor family blending.

## *Related Works*

1. Cooney, Caroline B. **Hush Little Baby**. See full booktalk above (p. 168). Divorce, remarriage, and adoption problems cause mystery, danger, and excitement.
2. McCaughrean, Geraldine. **The Pirate's Son**. See full booktalk in Chapter 2 (p. 74). Three young people form their own family when death, remarriage, and poor custody arrangements leave them to face hostility and danger on their own.
3. Quarles, Heather. **A Door Near Here**. See full booktalk in Chapter 1 (p. 54). Divorce, remarriage, and a baby with an unknown father cause four children to form a unit of protection against the world.
4. Sweeney, Joyce. **The Spirit Window**. See full booktalk in Chapter 1 (p. 19). Death, divorce, remarriage, reconciliation, and young love test an entire family's communication skills.
5. Walker, Virginia, and Katrina Roechelein. **Making Up Megaboy**. See full booktalk in Chapter 2 (p. 82). A young boy from a traditional family murders a shopkeeper. Interviews with family and friends show poor communication skills and poor social development.
6. Wynne-Jones, Tim. **Stephen Fair**. See full booktalk in Chapter 1 (p. 56). Kidnapping of a child, a father's desertion, and a brother's search bring out family secrets and feelings.

Danziger, Paula, and Ann M. Martin. **P.S. Longer Letter Later**. New York: Scholastic, Apple Paperbacks, 1998. 234p. $4.99pa. ISBN 0-590-21311-3.

## *Summary/Description*

Elizabeth and Tara★Starr are best friends. The year they are to enter seventh grade, Elizabeth's parents move. Their letters throughout that seventh-grade year make up the book.

Elizabeth's family buys things rather than talking to each other. Her father has a high-paying job and sees his role as the gift giver. When he loses his job, Elizabeth finds out that they have been spending much more than they have. Eventually, the mother takes control of the finances and gets her own job. Elizabeth discovers that she is strong enough to make friends in her new school and take on the added responsibility in her family. Elizabeth's father leaves the family without really telling them goodbye.

Tara★Starr's parents married when they were seventeen. Tara★Starr was always the adult in the family. Now Tara★Starr finds her parents setting more rules, paying more attention to saving money, getting better jobs, going to school, and having a baby. Her anger comes from a fear that she will either be pushed out or again be expected to be the responsible one in the group. By the end of the book, both girls have faced up to the changes in their families and themselves. Their summer reunion will include two older and wiser young ladies.

### *Booktalk*

Friends are hard to find. When Elizabeth discovers that her father is transferred, she, and her best friend Tara★Starr, decide to hang on to their friendship. They will stay friends through letters. But seventh grade brings big changes in family and school. Elizabeth's family isn't as wealthy and as happy as she thought. Suddenly, Tara★Star's parents decide they need to grow up and change their own lives. Writing is not as good as talking on the phone or seeing each other everyday. Soon, both girls find the anger from home spilling over into their letters. They start to wonder if anything, including their friendship, can last.

Danziger, Paula, and Ann M. Martin. **Snail Mail No More**. New York: Scholastic, 2000. 336p. $16.95. ISBN 0-439-06335-3.

### *Summary/Description*

Elizabeth and Tara★Starr have e-mail. In eighth grade, they continue to correspond as they try to talk out problems and maintain their friendship. Tara★Starr focuses on the arrival of her new baby sister. She is both jealous and anxious. She knows that she will have to share her room and her time. Because Elizabeth has helped to take care of her own little sister, Emma, for five years, she reassures Tara★Starr that the baby will be a joy as well as a responsibility. The family continues their *Gone with the Wind* theme and names the baby Scarlett. Tara★Starr discovers that her parents find Scarlett changing their lives as well as hers. They feel the need to go out on dates with each other again, and her mother worries about returning to work. Tara★Starr is beginning to see herself as part of the team that will work through these problems.

Elizabeth still worries about and fears her alcoholic father. Each time he arrives or calls, he upsets the family. Both Elizabeth and Tara★Starr want him to disappear completely. Elizabeth's mother is dating again, and Elizabeth is interested in the man's son. When her father dies in an automobile accident, however, Elizabeth discovers that she, her sister, and her mother still love him although they have tried to rebuild their lives without him.

The girls continue to compare notes on their boyfriends, new friends, families, classes, clothes, and hobbies. Elizabeth now edits the school poetry magazine. Tara★Starr is trying to start a reading club and act in the school plays. Both girls make new friends, and Tara★Starr is testing limits with partying and underage drinking. As they find themselves and their relationship changing, much of their correspondence deals with their fear of losing their close friendship, which they still work very hard to maintain.

## *Booktalk*

Elizabeth and Tara★Starr from *P.S. Longer Letter Later* are back and writing again, but *Snail Mail No More*. Now it's all about e-mail. They can share news about dates, groundings, siblings, and parents almost as it's happening. Is that good? They're not sure. The words, kind or cruel, come faster, and some events, after they think about them, aren't even worth talking about. But Tara★Starr, the dramatic, and Elizabeth, the responsible, are still trying to hang on to their friendship long distance, find some new friends, help their parents grow up, and figure out life, and no one has figured out a faster or easier way to do any of those things.

## *Related Activities for* **P.S. Longer Letter Later** *and* **Snail Mail No More**

1. Read "Lunch" by Kathi Appelt in *Just People & Paper/Pen/Poem: A Young Writer's Way to Begin*. Complete the invitations on page 76.

2. Starting with the "Where to Go for Help" section of *When a Parent Is out of Work*, research how to prepare for a job, how to get a job,

how to change jobs, and how to change careers. Make a summary chart of the information you find that shows the most important requirements for each task.

3. Compare the parents described in *P.S. Longer Letter Later*, *Snail Mail No More*, *Armageddon Summer*, and *Stephen Fair*. What do the parents do to complicate their children's lives? How do these complications strengthen their children?

4. Compare how Lucy Rising in *The Great Eye* and Elizabeth and Tara★Starr in *P.S. Longer Letter Later* and *Snail Mail No More* use writing to help them work through their problems and develop self-confidence and self-respect.

5. What letters will Elizabeth and Tara★Starr exchange in fifteen years? Discuss what issues they might include. Choose a partner. One person will take the role of Elizabeth, and one will take the role of Tara★Starr. Write three letters each.

6. Write down the issues that you feel should be included in the next Tara★Starr/Elizabeth saga. Exchange your list with another person who has read the book. Compare the lists, then discuss how each issue might be resolved.

7. Both Elizabeth and Tara★Starr use dress to express themselves. Create a character you might want to write about and describe the clothes he or she might choose.

## *Related Works for* P.S. Longer Letter Later *and* Snail Mail No More

1. Appelt, Kathi. "Lunch." In **Just People & Paper/Pen/Poem: A Young Writer's Way to Begin**. p. 21. See full booktalk in Chapter 4 (p. 195). At lunch in the school cafeteria, a young student realizes how lonely the fresh start in a new school can be.

2. Bauer, Marion Dane. **What's Your Story? A Young Person's Guide to Writing Fiction**. New York: Clarion Books, 1992. 134p. $6.95pa. ISBN 0-395-57780-2. Chapters 3 and 4 will help the writer to analyze as well as develop a character.

3. Bridgers, Jay. **Having an Addictive Personality**. New York: The Rosen Publishing Group, 1998. 64p. (The Need to Know Library). $17.95. ISBN 0-8239-2777-6. Pages 24–29 present an example of teenage alcoholism and discuss the results of alcoholism in general.

4. McFarland, Rhoda. **Drugs and Your Parents**. New York: The Rosen Publishing Group, 1997 rev. ed. 64p. (The Drug Abuse Prevention Library). $17.95. ISBN 0-8239-2603-6. McFarland explains how a child, having a dependent parent, must develop love and respect for both the parent and himself or herself.

5. Shalant, Phyllis. **The Great Eye**. New York: Puffin Books, 1996. 150p. $4.99pa. ISBN 0-14-130072-8. The main character must deal with her father moving to Australia, her mother starting a new job and a new life, and her sister coming home with a new boyfriend.

6. St. Pierre, Stephanie. **When a Parent Is out of Work**. New York: The Rosen Publishing Group, 1997 rev. ed. 64p. (The Need to Know Library). $17.95. ISBN 0-8239-2608-7. The book tells about the reasons for losing a job, the resulting problems, and the way families can work together to get through a crisis.

7. Wynne-Jones, Tim. **Stephen Fair**. See full booktalk in Chapter 1 (p. 56). The novel presents situations that show how parents' immaturity complicates their children's lives.

8. Yolen, Jane, and Bruce Coville. **Armageddon Summer**. See full booktalk in Chapter 1 (p. 50). The two main characters are drawn into the world of a cult by their parents.

Mazer, Norma Fox. **When She Was Good**. New York: Arthur A. Levine Books, 1997. 228p. $16.95. ISBN 0-590-13506-6.

### *Summary/Description*

*When She Was Good* is the Em Thurkill story. She is born to a chronically depressed mother and an alcoholic, abusive father. Her older sister, Pamela, emotionally disturbed, abuses Em physically and emotionally just as their father has abused their mother. When Em is thirteen her mother dies. Soon, her father remarries. Because of the new wife's attitude toward them, both Pam and Em decide to live on their own. Em is the main financial support, but Pam is the tyrant who dictates their life. When Pamela dies of a stroke at age twenty-one, Em must deal with her new freedom. Although haunted by Pam's abusive voice, she finds employment and friends. The book tells about a person trapped by abuse, abandonment, mental illness, and promiscuity, but because of the portrayal of Em's personal strength, it concludes with a positive promise for the future.

## *Booktalk*

Pamela Thurkill dies of a stroke at age twenty-one. Em, her eighteen-year-old sister, doesn't know if she should just drop Pam's body in the ground or buy a locked casket. She doesn't have the money for the lock but fears that strong, bullying Pam will escape, will scream and beat her again. Will Em be free or will that jeering voice always belittle her, threaten her, and drive away her friends? Will the memories of beatings and bruises ever go away? Will she ever learn the right things to do?

Em wants to find what her magic words promise, a "happy home." Now she struggles with the search. It's hard to know what to expect or what to give because Em was blamed and punished even *When She Was Good.*

## *Related Activities*

1. Em remarks that her name can be reduced to M. That name helps us to understand how reduced and insignificant she feels. In Chapters 3 and 4 of *What's Your Story? A Young Person's Guide to Writing Fiction*, Marion Dane Bauer suggests how an author constructs and places a character in motion. Using her suggestions, discuss the construction of the characters in *When She Was Good.*

2. Em writes in her journal for English class and discovers poetic thoughts that her sister destroys. In *How to Write Poetry*, Paul B. Janeczko talks about how to construct a journal and how important it is to protect its individuality. Read the chapter aloud in the group and then discuss Janeczko's advice. Then locate and read one of the books Janeczko suggests on page 13.

3. In "Voices" in *Where I'm From: Where Poems Come From*, George Ella Lyon writes poems by listening to voices from her past. After reading the exercises and poems on pages 73–83, write a poem for Pamela's voice or Em's voice.

4. On pages 44–45, Em listens to and reflects on "Bridge Over Troubled Water" sung by Paul Simon and Art Garfunkel. Read the lyrics of the song. Discuss which words and phrases speak specifically to Em's situation.

5. *Ethan Between Us* and *Kissing Doorknobs* also deal with mental illness. Compare the choice of narrator in each novel. Discuss how that choice affects the reader's view of the illness and the mentally ill character. Rewrite one paragraph of *When She Was Good* from a

different point of view. You may wish to start by reading Chapters 3 and 4 in *What's Your Story? A Young Person's Guide to Writing Fiction.*

6. Read Chapter 5 in *Family Violence* by Evan Stark. Discuss how the chapter relates to Pamela and Em in *When She Was Good.*

## *Related Works*

1. Bauer, Marion. **What's Your Story? A Young Person's Guide to Writing Fiction**. New York: Clarion Books, 1992. 134p. $6.95pa. ISBN 0-395-57780-2. Chapters 3 and 4 give suggestions for building characters.

2. Hesser, Terry Spencer. **Kissing Doorknobs**. See full booktalk above (p. 148). The main character struggles to control her obsessive-compulsive condition, which threatens to destroy her and her family.

3. Janeczko, Paul B. **How to Write Poetry**. See full booktalk in Chapter 4 (p. 215). Chapter 1 suggests guidelines for starting a resource journal.

4. Lyon, George Ella. "Voices." In **Where I'm From: Where Poems Come From**. pp. 73–83. See full booktalk in Chapter 4 (p. 217). The exercises and poems suggest how one might create a poem by constructing or recalling a voice.

5. Myers, Anna. **Ethan Between Us**. See full booktalk in Chapter 4 (p. 221). The book centers on a friendship with a mentally ill boy whose voices throw him into a frenzy of musical composition.

6. Simon, Paul. "Bridge Over Troubled Water." In **Bridge Over Troubled Water** by Paul Simon, Arthur Garfunkel, and Roy Halee. New York: Columbia Records. KCS 9914. The song depicts Em's situation and hopes. It would be excellent background music for the booktalks about *When She Was Good, Ethan Between Us*, and *Kissing Doorknobs.*

7. Stark, Evan. **Family Violence**. New York: The Rosen Publishing Group, 1997 rev. ed. 64p. (The Need to Know Library). $17.95. ISBN 0-8239-2296-6. Stark distinguishes between abuse and argument, explains how violence can be prevented, and provides sources for help.

# THE SUPERNATURAL

Lally, Soinbhe. **A Hive for the Honeybee**. New York: Arthur A. Levine Books, 1996. 226p. $16.95. ISBN 0-590-51038-X.

### *Summary/Description*

In her allegory of the hive, Soinbhe Lally portrays the lives of honeybees as they develop as much individualism as possible within the constraints of fate. Thora, a worker bee who dares to dream; Bell, a worker whose sharp tongue vents her angers and frustrations; Alfred, the poetic drone; Mo, the questioning rebel drone; Guy, the macho drone; the Grand Drone, who makes the laws of the hive and the universe; and the Queen, who decides the physical life of the hive, all must follow their bee instincts and sacrifice to the larger life of the hive and species. Giving the bees human characteristics, Soinbhe Lally poses questions about the productivity of political, spiritual, and aesthetic activities. She asks whether any actions truly change lives or just carry bees and people along on a vain, ignorant wave of busyness to an inevitable destiny.

### *Booktalk*

Sweet and stinging: What kinds of things in your life would you describe as sweet? What kinds of things in your life would you describe as stinging? Can an event be both sweet and stinging? Do you feel you control this pleasure and pain?

In *A Hive for the Honeybee*, Soinbhe Lally describes the sweet and stinging life of the hive. Her bees are like people. Some work too hard. Some work very little. Some think all the time. Some can't think or don't have time to think. Some make rules for the Earth, and some translate the rules of a higher being. What happens to all of them makes us question what happens to us. The hive is both charming and chilling. It holds Belle and Thora, the unwilling and willing workers; Mo and Alfred, the political and spiritual thinkers; Guy, the hulk; Daisy, the intuitive bee; and even the lovely Queen supported by her Grand Spiritual and Temporal Leader. In the lovely world of flowers, pollen, nectar, and nature dances, a very sinister force could be making the real and inescapable rules.

## *Related Activities*

1. Read "Design" by Robert Frost. Divide the poem into sections. Describe the purpose of each section. Who is the speaker? Why does he reflect on what he sees? Is the title appropriate? Why? How is the speaker's view related to *The Hive and the Honeybee*?

2. Read "Leaf by Niggle" by J. R. R. Tolkien. Discuss who or what Niggle and Parish represent. State the purpose of the story. What techniques do Tolkien and Lally share?

3. Read *Who Moved My Cheese?* by Spencer Johnson, M.D. This story about mice illustrates how humans should act if they wish to be successful. How is it similar to and different from *A Hive for the Honeybee*?

4. Observe an animal or insect in nature. Then write your own story or poem that communicates a message to the human race.

5. Read "Beehive" by Jean Toomer. Who is the speaker? What is the speaker's world like? How does the speaker feel about his world? Does the speaker have a choice of worlds? How does the speaker's view agree or disagree with Lally's?

6. Read "Departmental" by Robert Frost. How does Frost's description of the ant colony parallel Lally's description of the hive? How does it differ? What comment is Frost making about humans?

## *Related Works*

1. Frost, Robert. **Robert Frost's Poems** edited by Louis Untermeyer. New York: Washington Square Press, 1946. "Design" paints a sinister picture in nature and then asks what power created the situation. "Departmental" uses a description of an ant colony to suggest the coldness of an over-organized society.

2. Johnson, Spencer, M.D. **Who Moved My Cheese?** New York: G. P. Putnam's Sons, 1998. 94p. $19.95. ISBN 0-399-14446-3. This allegory about mice teaches people how to deal with change in their lives. Unlike *A Hive for the Honeybee*, it suggests that people do have control over their lives and should use it.

3. Toomer, Jean. "Beehive." In **I, Too, Sing America** by Catherine Clinton (text) and Stephen Alsorn (illus). See full booktalk in Chapter 4 (p. 219). A drone, relaxing and eating at night in the hive, reflects on the freedom of the farmyard.

4. Tolkien, J. R. R. "Leaf by Niggle." In **Poems and Stories**. New York: Houghton Mifflin, 1994. 342p. Unfortunately, *Poems and Stories* is out of print. "Leaf by Niggle" is a parable or allegory about Niggle and Parish. One cultivates nature and the other paints it. Throughout the story, they grow to appreciate each other's contributions to beauty.

Rowling, J. K. **Harry Potter and the Sorcerer's Stone**. New York: 1997. 509p. $17.95. ISBN 0-590-35340-3.

### *Summary/Description*

Orphaned Harry Potter is left on the Dursleys' doorstep with a letter explaining his wizard blood. The Dursleys are horrified and hide the truth from Harry and their own pampered son, Dudley. The Dursleys—Harry's aunt, uncle, and cousin—are Muggles (non-wizard people) who work to change Harry into an ordinary person by giving him a Cinderella-type existence. On Harry's tenth birthday, Harry begins to receive magical mail, which his uncle tries to hide or destroy, but the Hogwarts School of Witchcraft and Wizardry persists until his uncle is forced to allow Harry to meet his fate. At Hogwarts, Harry meets the huge, loving Weasley family and super-intelligent Hermione Granger. He discovers that he has inherited exceptional powers and wealth, and beyond being the best Quidditch player, he is also the best wizard in the battle of good and evil. By the end of the book, he is a friend of Ron Weasley and Hermione Granger, and together, they foil Voldemort, the personification of evil, who killed Harry's parents. Harry leaves for his summer vacation knowing that he has made progress in learning witchcraft, finding family, and making friends.

### *Booktalk*

Happy Birthday Harry Potter! It's no more spider-filled closets under the stairs and no more secondhand school uniforms. Today, Harry Potter will become a wizard. He'll have his own owl, his own magic wand, and his own invisibility cloak. No matter how hard the Dursleys, his adopted Muggle family, try to prevent it, Harry will find his family's fortune and accept his place as a hero in the battle of good and evil. No trolls, three-headed dogs, ghosts, or jealous classmates can stop him either. Harry Potter is on his way to seek his destiny at the Hogwarts School of Witchcraft and Wizardry. Look out evil, here comes Harry!

Rowling, J. K. **Harry Potter and the Chamber of Secrets**. New York: Arthur A. Levine Books, 1998. 341p. $17.95. ISBN 0-439-06486-4.

### *Summary/Description*

When Harry, the Weasleys, and their friend, Hermione Granger, return to Hogwarts, they face great danger from the darker powers. The jealous Draco Malfoy and his father plot to destroy Harry and his friends, the Weasleys. Mr. Malfoy gives a dark power diary to Ginny Weasley. The diary brings Ginny under the power of the evil Lord Voldemort. Harry must eventually descend into the Chamber of Secrets so that he can confront Voldemort and save Hermione, Ginny, and himself. After Harry's triumph, Professor Dumbledore points out that Harry's choices, more than his abilities, have allied him with the good cosmic powers and have demonstrated to the world who Harry Potter really is.

### *Booktalk*

Welcome back to the wizard's world. If you get in trouble, your mother will probably send you a Howler. If you can speak Parselmouth, you probably are related to Slytherin, and if you have never heard of Aragog, you probably are a Muggle. But knowing all this technical jargon doesn't make the clash between good and evil any easier for Harry Potter. Being an admired student at the Hogwarts School of Witchcraft and Wizardry sets Harry against the forces of evil. Harry and his friends must break some Hogwart rules to figure out who is trying to destroy them and the school. When they do, Harry must descend into *The Chamber of Secrets* and again prove that good can triumph over evil.

Rowling, J. K. **Harry Potter and the Prisoner of Azkaban.** New York: Arthur A. Levine Books, 1999. 431p. $19.95. ISBN 0-439-13635-0.

### *Summary/Description*

Harry Potter, third-year student, is the target of the evil Sirius Black. Black, supposedly Voldemort's servant, has been in Azkaban for the murders of Peter Pettigrew and the innocent bystanders surrounding him. Harry discovers that Peter Pettigrew, now Ron's pet rat, is the real murderer and servant of Voldemort. Harry, Ron, and Hermione also discover that Sirius Black, Harry's father, and Peter Pettigrew were all friends of Professor Lupine, a werewolf. To help him during his transformations, they became Animagi so that they might keep him company and stay out of danger themselves. Learning these transformations, Peter betrayed Harry's parents, framed Black for his own crime, and then escaped as a rat. Sirius Black finally escaped prison as a dog.

Professor Snapes still holds a schoolboy grudge against Sirius Black, Harry's father, and Lupine. He refuses to listen to Black's explanation. He wants to turn him over to the dementors, the prison guards, who control men by destroying their positive thoughts and eventually sucking out their souls. By now, Harry has learned that Black is his godfather and his parents' best friend. Black offers Harry a home with him, and Harry is determined to help him. Through time travel, Harry and Hermione rescue Black and Hagrid's doomed pet, Buckbeak. After Harry and Hermione save Buckbeak from execution, Black uses Buckbeak to escape and pledges his eternal support to Harry. In this battle, Harry discovers that he has the power to defeat the dementors. He experiences a vision of his father's animal form, realizes that his father will always be with him, and learns that his own strength and magnanimity are stronger than the negatives of the world.

### *Booktalk*

Harry's in trouble now! Sirius Black, feared by both wizards and Muggles, wants to kill him. The dementors who guard the prisoners of Azkaban may succeed in sucking out Harry's soul. Malfoy is determined to defeat him in Quidditch, and Harry might not be able to pass Snape's class. Can Harry pass his class, save the trophy, and defeat all the evil in the world? Well, he's a third-year student, now, and, with the help of Ron and Hermione, he's willing to give it a try.

Rowling, J. K. **Harry Potter and the Goblet of Fire**. New York: Arthur A. Levine Books, 2000. 734p. $25.95. ISBN 0-439-13959-7.

### *Summary/Description*

As Lord Voldemort plots his return, Harry Potter sees the scene in a dream and experiences the painful burning of his scar. Previously, Voldemort and Wormtail (Peter Pettigrew) captured, questioned, and killed Bertha Jorkins, a worker in the Ministry of Magic. During the questioning, they discovered that Hogwarts is hosting two other schools in a wizard competition that occurs every 100 years. With that information, Voldemort plots Harry's death. Voldemort directs his most loyal Death Eater, disguised as Mad-Eye Moody, a retired "Auror" or "Dark Wizard Catcher," to place Harry's name in the "Goblet of Fire" so that Harry will participate in the competition and then be captured and killed by Voldemort. Throughout the tasks, Harry perceives the impostor as a friend who gives advice and protection, but this help keeps Harry safe only for Voldemort's final purpose.

As Harry meets his life-threatening challenges, he continues to learn more about himself. He feels reassured by the direction and support of his godfather, Sirius Black. Because he becomes jealous over Cho Chang, a girl he wishes to date, he almost ignores important advice from the rival for her affection. Harry also realizes that he has overlooked the intelligent Hermione's beauty and recognizes it only when a rival star Quidditch player appreciates it first. Harry is more concerned for his teammates and opponents than winning, and he can lose patience with even his closest friends.

Harry continues to learn that the perceived world is not always the real world. He finds that the press can be his enemy when the unethical reporter, Rita Skeeter, literally bugs Hogwarts and then slants and distorts information about Harry and his friends. Snapes again proves to him that a person can be both hostile and loyal. The softhearted Professor Dumbledore demonstrates that he is a strong and tenacious defender of right. The "kindly" Cornelius Fudge focuses more on comfort and status quo than right and wrong. The upright Mr. Crouch, considered a guardian of morality, promises his dying wife to control and protect their evil son, the Death Eater who tries to deliver Harry to Voldemort. Living with such a contradiction, Crouch destroys himself. The jovial Mr. Bagman is really a petty opportunist who can't pay his gambling debts. Also, all giants are not as kind as Hagrid. As in the other Potter books, Harry learns that both magic and insight require time and practice.

## *Booktalk*

"Potter stinks." That's what the flashing buttons at Hogwarts are saying. Harry isn't going to be the star Quidditch player this year. In fact, he might not be the star anything. Harry might die. Voldemort's sign, the skull, has reappeared after thirteen years and is glowing in the night. Rita Skeeter, the all-too-roving reporter, is writing about how crazy Harry is. His friends are starting to get tired of Harry grabbing all the glory. These are hard times for Harry, but he loves a challenge, and the threat of death just gives his life a little edge. Harry learns about new spells, new monsters, and a lot more about human and superhuman nature. He has to stay alive and save the world from evil again, but this time he has to do it on a whole new playing field in *Harry Potter and the Goblet of Fire.*

## *Related Activities for the Harry Potter Series*

1. Read *King Arthur.* Compare the use of magic in the legend and the use of magic in any of the Harry Potter adventures. Then compare the moral messages in each world. Discuss the similarities you find and the reason for the continued popularity of both the magic methods and the morality messages.

2. Read *Star Wars: Incredible Cross-Sections*, *Star Wars, Episode I: Incredible Cross-Sections*, and *Star Wars: The Visual Dictionary.* These books describe a fantasy world rooted in technology rather than magic. The war between good and evil is just as strong, however. Identify the forces of good and evil in the *Star Wars* movies and the Harry Potter novels. Compare the definitions of good and evil presented in each series.

3. Following the pattern of *Star Wars: Incredible Cross-Sections*, *Star Wars, Episode I: Incredible Cross-Sections*, and *Star Wars: The Visual Dictionary*, create a cross-section book and/or visual dictionary for Harry Potter's World.

4. Read "Wild About Harry" in the September 20, 1999 issue of *Time* magazine. Refer to "The Charms of Fantasy Worlds." Choose a selection listed there that you have already read or read a selection with which you are unfamiliar. Then research information about the author and the time period. Share your information with the group. Listen to the information each person has found. What comparisons and contrasts do you find? Do any patterns emerge? You might want to use a chart format like that used by Paul Gray, the article's author.

5. In *Making Up Megaboy*, Robbie Jones creates a fictional hero who pulls him into a fantasy world. The result is disastrous. In *A Door Near Here*, a little girl is almost seriously harmed because she pursues the world of Narnia. Discuss the pros and cons of fantasy literature.

6. In *Love Among the Walnuts*, the good guys and the bad guys are easily identified. What does this story share with the Harry Potter stories?

7. The Harry Potter stories use a great deal of personification to accomplish their purpose. Identify where Rowling has used personification. Explain how she has used it and for what purpose. What does her use of personification communicate about problems in real life?

## *Related Works for the Harry Potter Series*

1. Ferris, Jean. **Love Among the Walnuts**. See full booktalk in Chapter 2 (p. 70). In a comic tone, the novel tells a story of good triumphing over evil.

2. Gormley, Beatrice. **C. S Lewis: Christian and Storyteller**. See full booktalk in Chapter 2 (p. 84). Gormley tells about the man and his motivation in creating the world of Narnia.

3. Gray, Paul. "Wild About Harry." *Time* (September, 20, 1999): 67–72. Gray explains the series content and success. He includes a chart that compares it to other fantasies. He introduces us to the author, J. K. Rowling, and describes what the future promises for Harry Potter.

4. Kerven, Rosalind. **King Arthur**. See full booktalk above (p. 131). Kerven clearly explains the Arthurian legend and the magical battle between good and evil.

5. Quarles, Heather. **A Door Near Here**. See full booktalk in Chapter 1 (p. 54). The youngest child in a dysfunctional family seeks safety in Narnia.

6. Reynolds, David West. **Star Wars, Episode I: Incredible Cross-Sections**. See full booktalk above (p. 138). The book parallels *Star Wars: Incredible Cross-Sections.*

7. Reynolds, David West. **Star Wars: Incredible Cross-Sections**. See full booktalk above (p. 138). The book's detailed cross-sections are extensions of the characters that use them.

8. Reynolds, David West. **Star Wars: The Visual Dictionary**. See full booktalk above (p. 140). The dictionary shows and defines the use and history of all *Star Wars* equipment.

9. Walker, Virginia, and Katrina Roechelein. **Making Up Megaboy**. See full booktalk in Chapter 2 (p. 82). A young boy creates a hero cartoon character, believes his fantasy, and kills a man.

## Naylor, Phyllis Reynolds. **Sang Spell**. New York: Atheneum Books, 1998. 176p. $16.00. ISBN 0-689-82007-0.

### *Summary/Description*

After his mother dies in a car accident, Joshua Vardy decides to ignore his plane ticket and get to his Aunt Carol's, his new home, on his own. His decision throws him into an Appalachian ghost world of moving towns and indeterminable time called Canara. It is the land of the Melungeons, a group of people from a settlement founded by Captain Juan Pardo and the Moorish and Turkish galley slaves of Sir Francis Drake. The community represents the individuals and races who have lost their way and are now healing. They live on their ginseng crop, which the leaders trade at The Edge. In Canara, Josh encounters three elders: Pardo, a mainstay of the community who helps him heal physically; Old Sly, who constantly searches but cannot figure out how to leave; and Isobel, the old wise one, who tells him that to go forward he must go back. He also encounters Kasper, a Penn State student, who was drawn into the community two years earlier. Kasper is willing to plot murder to escape. He even talks about killing Josh. Because of his willingness to turn against others, he is sentenced to isolation in the schoolhouse that appears once a year on the equinox. In contrast, Josh reacts to the village people with compassion, even though he wants to leave. Finally, he decides that he is committed to a new life with his aunt, and like the citizens of Canara, he finds an emotional or spiritual rebirth based on his past experiences.

### *Booktalk*

Joshua Vardy pleads to leave "a village held hostage" by time and space. He hears dogs no one else hears, sees buildings that disappear, and a road that leads into but not out of Canara, his new home. He can't tell how old the people are who call themselves the Melungeons. He can't even tell if he is one of them, and he can't understand the advice from the strange old Isobel who is pushed in a buggy by the mute Leone. And then there is Kasper, who wants to kill him, and Old Sly, who has spent his whole life looking for the road out. It all seems beyond his understanding. He knows only that in one moment, his mother is dead, and in another moment, by the "merest chance," they have pulled him into the *Sang Spell.*

## *Related Activities*

1. Define "ginseng." Find a picture of the plant and list its properties.
2. Naylor provides a bibliography of works about the Melungeons. Continue to read about them. On a map of the Appalachian Mountains, mark where Canara might possibly be.
3. List the inhabitants of Canara. Note the characteristics of each. Discuss the stage of life each character might represent.
4. In *Sang Spell*, *The Transall Saga*, *The Boxes*, *Holes*, *Harry Potter and the Chamber of Secrets*, *No Man's Land*, *Armageddon Summer*, *The Pirate's Son*, *The Sacrifice*, and *I Rode a Horse of Milk White Jade*, the main characters find themselves pulled into new worlds that change them. Some of the worlds are realistic, and others are magical or fantastic. Ask individuals or groups to choose one of the books. They should read the book and describe the following: the character and the character's world at the beginning of the novel, the new world the character encounters and the problems it presents, and the ways the character has changed by the end of the novel. Discuss the similarities and differences among the novels and how and why the changes occur.
5. The world of *Sang Spell* might also be considered a transition world between lives. In that sense it compares to the transitional world described in *The Heavenly Village.* Discuss how each author has constructed the world and used it to carry out her purpose.

## *Related Works*

1. Bartoletti, Susan. **No Man's Land**. See full booktalk in Chapter 1 (p. 37). A young man leaves home to prove his bravery and finds that bravery means something much different than he expected.
2. Matcheck, Diane. **The Sacrifice**. See full booktalk in Chapter 2 (p. 89). The main character leaves her village to discover her true identity.

2. Matcheck, Diane. **The Sacrifice**. See full booktalk in Chapter 2 (p. 89). The main character leaves her village to discover her true identity.

3. McCaughrean, Geraldine. **The Pirate's Son**. See full booktalk in Chapter 2 (p. 74). When three young people leave England, they discover worlds that change them.

4. Paulsen, Gary. **The Transall Saga**. See full booktalk below (p. 192). The main character is transported to a mysterious jungle, where he must figure out how to survive.

5. Rowling, J. K. **The Harry Potter Series**. See full booktalks above (pp. 181–87). The main character increases his strength and self-understanding as he confronts evil.

6. Rylant, Cynthia. **The Heavenly Village**. See full booktalk in Chapter 1 (p. 52). People with unfinished business on Earth work, rest, and reflect before moving to heaven.

7. Sachar, Louis. **Holes**. See full booktalk in Chapter 1 (p. 35). The main character is sentenced to a detention camp and must save his friend.

8. Sleator, William. **The Boxes**. See full booktalk below (p. 189). The main character becomes responsible for a world of telepathic bugs and saves her own world from evil land developers.

9. Wilson, Diane Lee. **I Rode a Horse of Milk White Jade**. See full booktalk in Chapter 1 (p. 8). The main character rides a magical horse to carry out the fate her grandmother has predicted.

10. Yolen, Jane, and Bruce Coville. **Armageddon Summer**. See full booktalk in Chapter 1 (p. 50). The two main characters define their own beliefs and values when they are drawn into a cult community by their parents.

Sleator, William. **The Boxes**. New York: Dutton, 1998. 196p. $15.99. ISBN 0-525-46012-8.

### *Summary/Description*

Annie Levi lives with her mysterious, magical Uncle Marco and her bitter, begrudging Aunt Ruth. Her Uncle Marco leaves and places Annie in charge of boxes she is not to open. Her Aunt Ruth, who spends her time complaining about her responsibilities, tells Annie never to listen to Uncle

Marco. Annie's curiosity, not her aunt's warning, drives her to open one box, in which she finds telepathic bugs who rapidly multiply and build intricate cities. When she opens the second, she discovers their god, a clock that slows time, and she is drawn into a supernatural world. She becomes the nervous system in a three-part relationship, and with her friend, Henry, takes responsibility for the consequences of her seemingly irresponsible act. Her new power and daring help her save her own world from evil land developers. Eventually, she finds out that Uncle Marco, whom her aunt calls irresponsible, wanted her to use her curiosity and learn from the consequences. The decisions she must make transform her from a child into an adult.

## *Booktalk*

Ask the group if they know the story of Pandora. Let someone tell her story and its significance. Then discuss whether Pandora's curiosity was a bad thing.

Pandora's story raises some questions for all of us. How important is it to follow orders? Should we always do what we are told? Uncle Marco leaves Annie with orders not to open two huge, heavy boxes he places in her care. Aunt Ruth tells her never to listen to Uncle Marco. Meanwhile, a land developer tells them all that they should sell the family house and land and move away. In each case, Annie wonders "what if" and "why." Like the mythical Pandora, Annie makes her own decision, opens *The Boxes*, and plunges herself into a battle between good and evil that tests her brain and heart. She lets each of us see our Pandora within.

## *Related Activities*

1. Choose a mythological figure. Discuss what the figure is supposed to represent and if that quality is an evil part of mankind or a natural part with which each of us must cope.

2. Write a synonym poem for the mythological figure you have chosen. You may wish to refer to Chapter 3 of *How to Write Poetry* by Paul B. Janeczko. Share your poem with others in the group.

3. Uncle Marco is absent throughout most of the novel, and yet he has a major influence. Explain his function.

4. Discuss what the boxes symbolize.

5. Questioning authority sometimes means we must take charge. Discuss how this theme is carried out in the following novels: *Boxes*,

*Cowboy Ghost*, *Out of the Dust*, *Holes*, *No Man's Land*, *Cast Two Shadows*, *The Fated Sky*, *Armageddon Summer*, *A Door Near Here*, *The Pirate's Son*, *The Sacrifice*, and *The Terrorist.*

## *Related Works*

1. Bartoletti, Susan. **No Man's Land**. See full booktalk in Chapter 1 (p. 37). The main character decides to challenge his father's authority by proving himself on the battlefield.

2. Branford, Henrietta. **The Fated Sky**. See full booktalk in Chapter 1 (p. 48). The main character must defy the will of the gods to build her own life.

3. Cooney, Caroline B. **The Terrorist**. See full booktalk above (p. 135). The main character ignores the help of friends and parents when she tries to help a terrorist.

4. Hesse, Karen. **Out of the Dust**. See full booktalk in Chapter 1 (p. 30). The main character decides she must make a life for herself in the face of the tragedy of her mother's death and the Depression.

5. Janeczko, Paul B. **How to Write Poetry**. See full booktalk in Chapter 4 (p. 215). Chapter 3 of *How to Write Poetry* tells how to write two-line synonym poems. The chapter also includes examples and supplementary exercises.

6. Matcheck, Diane. **The Sacrifice**. See full booktalk in Chapter 2 (p. 89). The main character completes a journey to clarify her destiny.

7. McCaughrean, Geraldine. **The Pirate's Son**. See full booktalk in Chapter 2 (p. 74). Three teenagers embark on a sea voyage and independent life.

8. Peck, Robert Newton. **Cowboy Ghost**. See full booktalk in Chapter 1 (p. 15). The main character proves his manhood by taking over a cattle drive.

9. Quarles, Heather. **A Door Near Here**. See full booktalk in Chapter 1 (p. 54). The main character hides her family's problems and finds that the secret threatens to destroy them.

10. Rinaldi, Ann. **Cast Two Shadows**. See full booktalk in Chapter 1 (p. 46). The main character finds out that her white family has sold her black mother.

11. Sachar, Louis. **Holes**. See full booktalk in Chapter 1 (p. 35). The main character runs away from a detention camp to save a friend.

12. Yolen, Jane, and Bruce Coville. **Armageddon Summer**. See full booktalk in Chapter 1 (p. 50). The main characters must go against their parents' wishes when they are forced into a cult community.

 Paulsen, Gary. **The Transall Saga**. New York: Delacorte Press, 1998. 248p. $15.95. ISBN 0-385-32196-1.

### *Summary/Description*

A blue light transports thirteen-year-old Mark Harrison to another world in another time. He starts backpacking along the Magruder Missile Range and arrives in Transall. Here he meets Willie, the bear monkey, and discovers possible danger from The Howling Thing. An arrow tells him he is not alone. When he saves Leeta from The Howling Thing, he joins the arrow people. Then he is swept up in the war between the arrow people and the Tsook tribe. In Transall, he grows into a man who must provide for himself and protect his loved ones. Finally, while confronting the evil of his first and second worlds, he is transported back to his own place and time. In the epilogue, he has become a successful scientist who wishes to return to Transall and help the girl he had to leave behind. When Mark descends into the world of the unknown and danger, he prepares himself for the heroic battles and triumphs of his adult life.

### *Booktalk*

Mark Harrison believes he can survive in the wilderness. He has read the manuals, camped out, and hiked. But the blue light transports him to a new world one of bear monkeys, Howling Things, quicksand, firebugs, and warring tribes. He must confront evil, survive, and find the blue light, his path back home. But through his search, Mark, now known by the mythical name Kakon, discovers strength, loyalty, love, and a new home. *The Transall Saga* tells of both a boy and a world transformed.

### *Related Activities*

1. Mark becomes a hero in the land of Transall. Trace his development.

2. Discuss what each of the characters in the story represents and the qualities that the story promotes.

3. Discuss what *The Transall Saga* has in common with *Star Wars* and *Harry Potter and the Chamber of Secrets.*

4. *Hero* by S. L. Rottman, has a much different definition of a hero. Read Sean Parker's essay, "My hero is. . . ." How does the essay contradict the hero Mark represents?

5. *Hatchet* by Gary Paulsen, and *Between a Rock and a Hard Place* by Alden R. Carter, are also survival stories. Compare the heroes and obstacles.

## *Related Works*

1. Carter, Alden R. **Between a Rock and a Hard Place**. New York: Scholastic, 1995. 213p. $4.99pa. ISBN 0-590-37486-9. Cousins who have little respect for each other or themselves embark on a traditional family survival trip that goes wrong.

2. Paulsen, Gary. **Hatchet**. New York: Puffin Books, 1987. 195p. $4.95pa. ISBN 0-14-032724-X. Left in the wilderness by an airplane crash, a young boy confronts nature and survives.

3. Rottman, S. L. **Hero**. See full booktalk in Chapter 4 (p. 223). A young man decides that the common, everyday man has enough to face to earn him heroism.

4. Rowling, J. K. **The Harry Potter Series**. See full booktalks above (pp. 181–87). In each Harry Potter book, the main character confronts a new aspect of evil and must discover a new strength in himself to combat it.

5. **Star Wars**. Produced by Lucas Films, 1977. 125 min. Color. $19.99. 6097. Videocassette. A young boy leaves the farm to join the battle between good and evil.

# 4

# *We Struggle and Give*

## ENTERTAIN AND CREATE

Appelt, Kathi (text), and Kenneth Appelt (photographs). **Just People & Paper/Pen/Poem: A Young Writer's Way to Begin**. Spring, TX: Absey & Company, 1997. 91p. (Writers & Young Writers Series #1). $11.95pa. ISBN 1-888842-07-5.

### *Summary/Description*

*Just People & Paper/Pen/Poem* combines the original poems of Kathi Appelt and the photographs of Kenneth Appelt. It is the first book of the Writers & Young Writers Series by Absey Press. At the back of the book, Appelt matches each poem with an explanation and an invitation. The explanation tells how the poem connects to her experience, and the invitation suggests how the reader might write about the experience that he or she remembers. At the beginning of this section is a suggestion that the reader/writer keep all the poems or responses in a book or journal. The invitations will encourage a writer to build journal responses, full-blown poems, essays, and short stories. It is a useful source for the independent writer and the writing teacher.

## Booktalk

Kathi Appelt is a poet. Her husband is a professional photographer. They have joined forces to create *Just People & Paper/Pen/Poem: A Young Writer's Way to Begin.* At the end of the book, Kathi Appelt asks some questions that invite you to write poems of your own. If you like to write, this small volume will keep the creative juices flowing. If you have problems writing, this book offers you many ways to get started. In fact their method is an almost guaranteed anti-writer's block. You don't have to be a poet to enjoy it.

## Related Activities

1. Each week, read one of Appelt's poems and respond to a matching invitation.
2. Within a group of writers, decide on one invitation response to share.
3. Appelt's book is the first in a series called Writers & Young Writers Series by Absey & Company. *Where I'm From: Where Poems Come From* is the second in that series. Compare the plans of both books. Write down your suggestions for a third book. Send these suggestions to Absey & Company.
4. Harper Winslow and Sean Parker are both writers who express their thoughts in essays. Read their essays. Convert part of one of the essays into a poem. Then convert one of your poems into an essay. Illustrate each finished work with drawings or pictures.
5. Choose one response to an invitation that outlines a story or describes a character. Using that material and Marion Dane Bauer's *What's Your Story? A Young Person's Guide to Writing Fiction*, complete a short story or character description.

## Related Works

1. Bauer, Marion Dane. **What's Your Story? A Young Person's Guide to Writing Fiction**. New York: Clarion Books, 1992. 134p. $6.95pa. ISBN 0-395-57780-2. Bauer talks about what questions to ask about character and plot. Those questions help the beginning writer build a complete story.

2. Lyon, George Ella (text), and Robert Hoskins (photographs). **Where I'm From: Where Poems Come From**. See full booktalk below (p. 217). Lyon, using poems and pictures, suggests ways that writers may structure their own thoughts and experiences.

3. Rottman, S. L. **Hero**. See full booktalk below (p. 223). At the end of the novel, Rottman includes Sean Parker's essay that gives Sean's definition of a hero.

4. Trembath, Don. **A Beautiful Place on Yonge Street**. See full booktalk in Chapter 3 (p. 166). This is the third in the series. Harper Winslow completes writing assignments while falling in love during a writer's camp.

5. Trembath, Don. **A Fly Named Alfred**. See full booktalk in Chapter 2 (p. 128). This is the second in the series. Harper gets in trouble as an anonymous columnist.

6. Trembath, Don. **The Tuesday Cafe**. See full booktalk in Chapter 1 (p. 23). This is the first in the series. Harper enrolls in writing school when a judge orders him to write an essay about what he will do with his life.

 Carlson, Laurie. **Boss of the Plains: The Hat That Won the West**. New York: DK Ink, 1998. 31p. $16.95. ISBN 0-7894-2479-7.

### *Summary/Description*

Twelve-year-old John Batterson Stetson made hats in Philadelphia, but he dreamed of making his fortune in the West. When sickness drove him there, he found that the tents and hats were no match for the rugged Western climate. First he built a felt tent, and then made his own felt hat. When his gold rush dreams went bust and he returned to Philadelphia, he brought many ideas for hats, but they didn't sell. Then he remembered his felt hat that a fellow prospector had bought for $5.00. He made samples and sent them West. The response meant his success and the birth of the signature Western hat. *Boss of the Plains* is a large picture book with a readable text appropriate for middle school and above. At the end of the story, the authors include a picture and short biography of John B. Stetson. Stetson's story illustrates how practical considerations and an appreciation for quality influenced Stetson's journey and the American way of life.

## *Booktalk*

John Stetson started his hat career when he was twelve years old. He lived in Philadelphia, not Texas, and he wanted to discover gold, not make hats. Lured by the promise of fabulous gold strikes, he headed West to make his fortune. But he discovered that his own skill and ingenuity were more valuable than what he could find in the ground. He went out West to find gold, listened, learned, and came back with a twenty-four-karat idea. The result was the *Boss of the Plains: The Hat That Won the West.*

## *Related Activities*

1. Stetson's idea made his name and product a part of American history. After viewing *Milton Hershey: The Chocolate King* and *P. T. Barnum: American Dreamer*, discuss how Milton Hershey, P. T. Barnum, and John Stetson made their names and ideas part of American history. Also discuss what quality and respect contributed to each man's success.

2. *Rules of the Road* is the story of Jenna Boller's commitment to quality and her journey to self-confidence. After reading *Boss of the Plains: The Hat That Won the West* and *Rules of the Road*, discuss the relationship between product and personality.

3. Research the cowboys' clothes. Report what they considered practical and necessary, and why. Compare the information that you find with the wardrobe choices for Hollywood cowboys.

4. Read "Cowboys: One, Two, Three" by Rod McKuen. What type of cowboy is depicted? Why would the Stetson be an important part of that cowboy's wardrobe and life?

5. Stetson lived from 1830 to 1906. Research Western expansion at that time, particularly expansion due to gold rushes.

## *Related Works*

1. Bauer, Joan. **Rules of the Road**. See full booktalk in Chapter 2 (p. 114). The main character finds that trust in herself and a commitment to quality are her greatest assets in the business world.

2. McKuen, Rod. "Cowboys: One, Two, Three." In **Mindscapes: Poems for the Real World** edited by Richard Peck. New York: Delacorte Press, 1971. The three poems depict the world of the cowboy, including the all-important Levi jeans and Stetson hats.

3. **Milton Hershey: The Chocolate King**. Produced by Loureda Productions, 1995. 50 min. Color. (Biography). $14.95. AAE-10478. Videocassette. Like Stetson, Hershey used his career knowledge to give Americans a quality product bearing his own name.

4. **P. T. Barnum: American Dreamer**. Produced by A&E Television Networks, 1994. Color. (Biography). $14.95. AAE-10477. Videocassette. This documentary tells how Barnum used his talent as a showman to contribute to the American heritage.

5. Peck, Robert Newton. **Cowboy Ghost**. See full booktalk in Chapter 1 (p. 15). In Florida, rather than the West, this cattle drive proves to the main character that he has become a man.

Dyer, Daniel. **Jack London: A Biography**. New York: Polaris, Scholastic, 1997. 221p. $5.99. ISBN 0-590-22217-1.

### *Summary/Description*

*Jack London: A Biography* tells about the tumultuous, against-the-odds life of Jack London. One of the most popular authors in the world, Jack London lived less than forty-one years. In that time he completed a ninth-grade education, served time in the penitentiary, married twice, had two children, supported his mother and nephew, prospected for gold, traveled the road as a vagrant, built an ill-fated boat and house, tried to found an artists' colony, and wrote so well and fast that his advance publications lasted three years after his death. Daniel Dyer includes a seven-page bibliography of works by and about London as well as a short general reference bibliography. The index provides easy access to the people, places, and ideas in London's life.

### *Booktalk*

Jack London had many jobs in his lifetime: newspaper boy, pinsetter, oyster pirate, fish patrolman, deep-sea sailor, and prospector. He even spent some time as a "road-kid" and a convict. For most people, these experiences would add up to failure. For London, they added up to stories. He added the phrase "call of the wild" to our language, and is still popular worldwide more than eighty years after his death. He taught himself how to write by trial, error, and persistence. Although he completed only the ninth grade, he spoke at Harvard. He not only broke the rules but also made up some of his own. Like so many of his characters, London took the big risks and found both disaster and success.

## *Related Activities*

1. Jack London, C. S. Lewis, and R. L. Stine are very different writers from very different backgrounds, and yet each occupies an important place in modern culture. Research each writer and describe how he has influenced us.

2. Read the stories in *House of Pride.* Discuss how these stories are similar to and different from London's stories about animals.

3. Read one of London's most famous short stories, "To Build a Fire." Here, London takes a simple task and makes it life threatening. Discuss how he gives the operation suspense.

4. Read *Call of the Wild* and *White Fang*. Here London gives animals human perceptions and characteristics. Compare his characterizations of humans to his characterizations of animals.

5. *Martin Eden* is a novel that is supposed to draw from London's own life and writing career. Compare some of the details to the information in *Jack London: A Biography.*

6. In each of London's works listed in Related Works, London includes the theme of pride, power, and dominance. Discuss what he reveals about these issues in the works you have read.

7. Choose a simple task. Describe it in such a way that it becomes dangerous, suspenseful, or embarrassing.

8. Tell a story about yourself, a friend, or a family member from your dog or cat's point of view.

## *Related Works*

1. Gormley, Beatrice. **C. S. Lewis: Christian and Storyteller**. See full booktalk in Chapter 2 (p. 84). Gormley describes Lewis's life as a scholar and writer.

2. London, Jack. "Call of the Wild." In **Jack London**. New York: Amaranth Press, 1984. (Masters Library). A half-dog, half-wolf pup learns to live with and love a man.

3. London, Jack. **House of Pride**. New York: Macmillan, 1912. These short stories about Hawaii reveal London's feelings about the exploitation of Hawaii by Americans and Europeans. They also reveal his feelings about the treatment of lepers.

4. London, Jack. **Martin Eden**. New York: Macmillan, 1928. This novel is supposed to be largely biographical.

5. London, Jack. "To Build A Fire." In **Adventures in American Literature** edited by Edmund Fuller and B. Jo Kinnick. New York: Harcourt, Brace & World, 1963. A simple task, building a fire, becomes overwhelming when a man underestimates the forces of nature.

6. London, Jack. "White Fang." In **Jack London**. New York: Amaranth Press, 1984. (Masters Library). A dog is stolen and sent to the wild, where he learns to survive.

7. Steger, Will, and Jon Bowermaster. **Over the Top of the World: Explorer Will Steger's Trek Across the Arctic**. See full booktalk in Chapter 1 (p. 32). One of the explorers in the Arctic team has been inspired by the Jack London stories.

8. Stine, R. L. **It Came from Ohio! My Life As a Writer**, as told to Joe Arthur. New York: Scholastic Inc./Parachute Press, 1997. 140p. $3.99pa. ISBN 0-590-93944-0. Stine describes how he became a successful writer and the not-so-glamorous jobs he held along the way.

 Elmer, Howard. **Blues: Its Birth and Growth**. New York: The Rosen Publishing Group, 1999. 64p. (The Library of African American Arts and Culture). $17.95. ISBN 0-8239-1853-X.

### *Summary/Description*

*Blues: Its Birth and Growth* traces the development of the blues from its African roots to its worldwide explosion in the second half of the twentieth century. Elmer describes the basic construction of the original field songs and spirituals and then details how historical events and individual artists shaped them into the many facets of blues today. Folk blues, classic blues, and Chicago blues made rock, Motown, and the British Invasion possible. *Blues* includes a discography, a bibliography, and a name and topic index. The music and selections it mentions and discusses would provide background music for presentations about almost any period of American history.

## *Booktalk*

Ask how many people have heard of Nirvana's MTV *Unplugged* album. Then ask how many people have heard of Huddie Leadbetter.

Huddie Leadbetter is better known as "Leadbelly," and he originally recorded "Where Did You Sleep Last Night," the last song on the *Unplugged* album. But the blues go back farther than Leadbelly. The blues landed on this continent with the first slaves in 1619. Since then, this music has helped the world express its frustration and sorrow, and it has also helped people send forbidden messages and inspire others to freedom and faith. The blues pull people, countries, and continents together, combining happy and sad all at the same time. Whenever we listen to any music, we'll probably be a little blue.

## *Related Activities*

1. Read "Dark Symphony" by Melvin B. Tolson (in *Shimmy Shimmy Shimmy Like My Sister Kate: Looking at the Harlem Renaissance Through Poems*). Describe the speaker. What is his purpose? What techniques, especially musical techniques, allow him to accomplish his purpose?

2. Read "Notes on the Broadway Theatre" (in *Shimmy Shimmy Shimmy Like My Sister Kate: Looking at the Harlem Renaissance Through Poems*). Describe the speaker. Describe the audience. Describe the occasion. What is the author's purpose? What techniques does the author use to communicate his purpose?

3. Read "Dream Variations" (in *Shimmy Shimmy Shimmy Like My Sister Kate: Looking at the Harlem Renaissance Through Poems*). Describe the speaker. Describe the audience. What is the poet's purpose? How does the speaker carry out that purpose?

4. Make a list of musical and rhythmic devices in language. Find an example of each to illustrate the device's definition and use. You may want to consult "Poetcraft: Sound" in Chapter 2 and "Writing Poems That Rhyme," Chapter 3 in *How to Write Poetry* by Paul B. Janeczko. You might also want to consult Chapter 11, "Musical Devices," Chapter 12, "Rhythm and Meter," and Chapter 13, "Sound and Meaning," in *Sound and Sense* by Laurence Perrine.

5. Choose a topic. Write phrases or sentences about that topic. Now try to add sound and rhythm elements to the phrases and sentences. Be sure these musical elements reinforce the meaning and tone of the phrases and sentences.

## *Related Works*

1. Giovanni, Nikki. **Shimmy Shimmy Shimmy Like My Sister Kate: Looking at the Harlem Renaissance Through Poems**. See full booktalk below (p. 236). Read the following poems selected by Giovanni and follow the suggestions in Related Activities: "Dark Symphony," "Dream Boogie," "Dream Boogie: Variation," "Same in Blues," "Dream Variations," and "Notes on the Broadway Theatre."

2. Hacker, Carlotta. **Great African Americans in Jazz**. New York: Crabtree Publishing, 1997. 64p. (Outstanding African Americans). $8.95pa. ISBN 0-86505-818-0. The book describes the childhoods of, contributions of, and obstacles faced by performers such as Louis Armstrong, Bessie Smith, and Wynton Marsalis.

3. Janeczko, Paul. **How to Write Poetry**. See full booktalk below (p. 215). The book provides definitions, examples, and process suggestions for writing poetry.

4. Myers, Walter Dean (text), and Christopher Myers (illus). **Harlem**. See full booktalk below (p. 241). Walter Dean Myers talks about the blues as intertwined with the life of Harlem and echoes the blues rhythms and sounds in his poem.

5. Perrine, Laurence. **Sound and Sense: An Introduction to Poetry, 7th ed**. New York: Harcourt Brace Jovanovich, 1987. Chapters 11, 12, and 13 deal with how sound and rhythm support an author's purpose. The entire book is dedicated to a thorough analysis of poetry.

Freedman, Russell. **Martha Graham: A Dancer's Life**. New York: Clarion Books, 1998. 175p. $18.00. ISBN 0-395-74655-8.

## *Summary/Description*

*Martha Graham: A Dancer's Life* chronicles the seventy-year dance career of a leader and innovator in contemporary dance. Graham believed that dance should express story and emotion and that it should carry message over entertainment. When Graham began to dance at twenty-one, her instructors told her she was too old, too short, and too fat. When she proved them wrong and became financially successful, she left the world of popular dance and dedicated herself to discovering her own style of expression. That search led to the creation of her own dance company, her own school, and international acclaim. She saw even breathing, walking, and falling as dancing, and she saw dancing as a way to express what words and music could not. Her dance reflected her own controversial life, a life that counted Eleanor Roosevelt and Helen Keller as friends and the Nazis as her enemies. Martha Graham believed that dancers were the "acrobats of God," and dedicated her life to protecting that sacred trust. Russell Freedman includes notes for each chapter; a four-page bibliography of books, articles, and films; and a name and topic index. The photographs communicate the tone and power of Graham's life and times.

## *Booktalk*

Martha Graham wanted to dance. Her teachers said her timing and her body were wrong. Her father disapproved of what she wanted to do, and society disapproved of how she wanted to do it. But she did it anyway, for seventy years. She became one of the most controversial and influential figures in the dance world. She rebelled way before Woodstock, hippies, or flower power. For Martha Graham, dance was communication, and the audience often did not like what or how she communicated. But she did it her way anyway.

## *Related Activities*

1. On pages 46–47, Freedman talks about the transition from classical to modern dance. He lists several names of dancers and choreographers in both the classical and modern fields of study. Other dancers are listed in *Visual and Performing Artists* by Shaun Hunter, and *Great African Americans in the Arts* by Carlotta Hacker. Define both classical and modern dance. Then choose a choreographer or dancer from either modern or classical dance. Research his or her career and contributions to dance.

2. *The Singing Mountain* and *Backwater* both deal with young people who, like Graham, make career decisions that are unpopular with their families. Discuss how that resistance might contribute to the soundness of the final decision.

3. Read "Spanish Dancer" by Rainer Maria Rilke (Stephen Mitchell translation). What is the situation? What comparisons and images does the speaker use to describe the experience? Discuss how the poet's use of line length and punctuation enhances her purpose.

4. Read "Break Dance" from *Life Doesn't Frighten Me at All.* Discuss how the line length, word choice, and punctuation communicate the style and rhythm of the dance.

5. Using the advice from the "Poetcraft" sections of *How to Write Poetry*, write a poem about your favorite dance or dancer. Describe the dance using words, line lengths, and punctuation that you feel mimic the rhythm, sound, and movement of the dance.

## *Related Works*

1. Bauer, Joan. **Backwater**. See full booktalk in Chapter 1 (p. 28). The main character pursues a writing career in spite of her entire family's pressure to choose a law career.

2. Hacker, Carlotta. **Great African Americans in the Arts**. New York: Crabtree Publishing, 1997. 64p. (Outstanding African Americans). $8.95pa. ISBN 0-86505-821-0. The profiles include Alvin Ailey, Debbie Allen, and Katherine Dunham, all African Americans who have made significant contributions to dance.

3. Hunter, Shaun. **Visual and Performing Artists**. New York: Crabtree Publishing, 1999. 48p. (Women in Profile). $8.95. ISBN 0-7787-0035-6. The book includes a full profile of Natalie Makarova, who came to the United States so that she might find freedom of artistic expression. It also includes a brief profile of British dancer Margot Fonteyn.

4. Janeczko, Paul B. **How to Write Poetry**. See full booktalk below (p. 215). The Poetcraft sections focus on individual skills involved in writing poetry.

5. Leviten, Sonia. **The Singing Mountain**. See full booktalk in Chapter 2 (p. 86). Against his parents' wishes, a young man pursues a spiritual life. His example inspires his family to rethink their own lives.

6. Nichols, Grace. "Break Dance." In **Life Doesn't Frighten Me at All** edited by John Agard. New York: Henry Holt, 1989. The speaker describes how she will break dance in a poem of celebration.

7. Rilke, Rainer Maria. "Spanish Dancer." Translated by Stephen Mitchell. In **Literature: Reading Fiction, Poetry, Drama, and the Essay** by Robert DiYanni. New York: Random House, 1986. The speaker describes the dance igniting the dancer and the room.

Granfield, Linda. **Circus: An Album**. New York: DK Ink, 1998. 96p. $19.95. ISBN 0-7894-2453-3.

### *Summary/Description*

*Circus: An Album* tells about the history and operation of the circus. The story begins in ancient Egypt and concludes with Cirque du Soleil and the other international circuses now leading a worldwide revival. Packed with pictures and illustrations, *Circus* explains how the circus is announced, how circus performers live, and how a circus is organized. It even includes movies, art, language, and lifestyles inspired by the circus. A detailed index provides easy access to the families, traditions, and pioneers of circus life.

### *Booktalk*

Have you ever hung around with "lot lice?" Do you think you'll have some "cherry pie" this week? Have you ever listened to a "windjammer?" If you can answer those questions, you've spent some time in the circus. If you can't answer those questions, *Circus: An Album* will catch you up on the language, the sights, the people, and the history of an old and ever-changing way of life, thrills, and laughter. If you read *Circus*, maybe you will want to go to clown school, invent a signature act no one else has attempted, or just see one of the new and glamorous circuses like Cirque du Soleil. But no matter what you decide to do, you will understand why a Roman writer in A.D. 50 said that all the people want is bread and circuses.

### *Related Activities*

1. In "The End of the World" by Archibald MacLeish, the speaker explains the end of the world through a comparison to the circus. Discuss why MacLeish chose this comparison.

2. In "Constantly Risking Absurdity" by Lawrence Ferlinghetti, the speaker compares the poet to an acrobat. Discuss the extent and appropriateness of the comparison.

3. *P. T. Barnum: American Dreamer* shows how Barnum used language to promote his acts and entertain the public. Title and describe some acts, like the "man eating chicken," that depend more on the language than the actual act for entertainment.

4. *The Circus Train* presents the train as a major part of the circus experience. Research train transportation as entertainment.

5. In *Huckleberry Finn*, Chapter 22, Huck goes to the circus. What does Huck's reaction reveal about the circus and about Huck? Discuss whether Huck is a typical member of the audience.

6. Compare Huck's description of the circus and Dan Rice's song, "One-Horse Show, or Magic, Matrimony and Multiplication." What does the song tell about Rice's audience? Also read Dan Rice's song, "Things That I Like to See!" What does the song reveal about the audience, the time period, and Dan Rice himself? Compare Huck's and Rice's views. Write a "Things That I Like to See!" song from Huck Finn's point of view.

7. After viewing *P. T. Barnum* and *P. T. Barnum: American Dreamer*, discuss the meaning of the phrase, "based on fact."

## *Related Works*

1. **The Circus Train**. Produced by A&E Television Networks, 1998. 50 min. Color. (Trains Unlimited). $19.95. AAE-40407. This documentary describes how the circus traveling on the train evolved from a liability to an asset.

2. Ferlinghetti, Lawrence. "Constantly Risking Absurdity." In **Sound and Sense: An Introduction to Poetry** edited by Laurence Perrine. New York: Harcourt Brace Jovanovich, 1982, 6th ed. The speaker compares the poet to an acrobat. Analysis questions help the reader pay attention to word choice, images, line placement, theme, figures of speech, and tone.

3. Juleus, Nels, ed. **The Annotated Dan Rice: Dan Rice's Great Song Book of 1866**. York, PA: Nels Juleus, 1977 (photocopy). Dan Rice's speeches reveal a very simplistic view of politics and life. You may receive a copy by sending a letter of request and $5.00 to Dr. Nels Juleus, 74 Eisenhower Drive, York, PA 17402.

4. MacLeish, Archibald. "The End of the World." In **Voices**, vol. 4 edited by Geoffrey Summerfield. Chicago: Rand McNally & Company, 1969. In the first eight lines of the Italian sonnet the circus acts perform and then the explosion occurs. The last six lines focus on the audience's reaction to the disaster.

5. **P. T. Barnum**. Produced by A&E Television Networks, 1999. 4 hrs. Color. $29.95. AAE 14379. Videocassette. This fictional presentation dramatizes much of the information presented in the documentary in number 6.

6. **P. T. Barnum: American Dreamer**. Produced by A&E Television Networks, 1994. Color. (Biography). $14.95. AAE-10477. Videocassette. This documentary depicts Barnum as a driving entrepreneur who learned from his own mistakes and the tricks others played on him.

7. Twain, Mark. **The Portable Mark Twain** edited by Bernard DeVoto. New York: Viking Press, 1946. Like the rest of the crowd, Huckleberry Finn is amazed and fooled by the glamour and excitement of the circus.

Greenburg, Jan, and Sandra Jordon. **Chuck Close Up Close**. New York: DK Publishing, 1998. 48p. $19.95. ISBN 0-7894-2486-X.

### *Summary/Description*

*Chuck Close Up Close* describes Chuck Close as an artist and human being. Close faced many obstacles. He was awkward and clumsy in sports. His teachers labeled him "dumb" and "lazy." His father died when Close was eleven. His poor grades offered him only an open admissions acceptance at a junior college. But Close was finally accepted at the Yale University School of Art, and because of the personal discipline his learning disabilities taught him, he went on to become a famous artist who would overcome a sudden paralysis as well. The book includes a glossary of terms, many examples of Chuck Close's work, and an essay that explains the history of portraits and Chuck Close's place in that history.

### *Booktalk*

Do your teachers give you a hard time? Do you have trouble concentrating in class? Are there personal problems at home? Maybe all those difficulties are the good news. In *Chuck Close Up Close,* Chuck Close explains how his personal and physical challenges translated into self-discipline and a powerful art form. When he was a kid, he was at the bottom of the list and chosen last. Today, he is a world-renowned artist who gives us an entirely new way to look at ourselves.

## *Related Activities*

1. Read "On Education" in *Pierced by a Ray of the Sun*. Discuss the following: What happens to the boy in the poem? What do you think his picture stands for? How does the speaker perceive schools?

2. Read "Lies" by Yevgeny Yevtushenko in *Pierced by a Ray of the Sun*. Discuss how this poem might apply to the life of Chuck Close. Does it share the author's purpose in "On Education"?

3. Read one or all of the poems from the "Poems and Paintings" in *Literature: Reading Fiction, Poetry, Drama, and the Essay*. Also examine the picture or the artist's work to which each is related. Discuss the relationships that you find between the two art forms.

4. Research the lives of each of the poets and artists whose work you examine. Try to determine if there are any relationships between the poets' and artists' times and their work. Report your findings to the group.

5. After examining Chuck Close's work, write a poem in reaction to one of his faces or to his work as a whole. You may wish to refer to Paul Janeczko's *How to Write Poetry*.

## *Related Works*

1. Bouchard, Dave (text), and Robb Terrence Dunfield (paintings). **If Sarah Will Take Me**. Victoria, BC: Orca Book Publishers, 1997. 30p. $16.95. ISBN 1-55143-081-9. Robb Terrence Dunfield is paralyzed from the waist down and ventilator-dependent. David Bouchard wrote the poems that accompany the paintings. In dealing with his handicaps and talents, Dunfield has become an internationally known artist, a motivational speaker, and a philanthropist.

2. DiYanni, Robert. **Literature: Reading Fiction, Poetry, Drama, and the Essay**. New York: Random House, 1986. This anthology includes a section titled "Poems and Paintings." Some of the poems and works of art included are the following:

   "The Starry Night" by Robert Fagles and "The Starry Night" by Vincent van Gogh

   "In Goya's Greatest Scenes We Seem to See" by Lawrence Ferlinghetti

"I Am Goya" by Andrey Voznesensky (trans. Stanley Kunitz) and "The Third of May, 1808: The Execution of the Defenders of Madrid"

"Landscape with the Fall of Icarus" by William Carlos Williams

"Musée des Beaux Arts" by W. H. Auden and "Landscape with the Fall of Icarus" by Pieter Breughel the Elder

"Hunters in the Snow: Breughel" by Joseph Langland

"Winter Landscape," by John Berryman and "Hunters in the Snow" by Pieter Breughel the Elder

3. Gordon, Ruth, ed. **Pierced by a Ray of the Sun: Poems About the Times We Feel Alone**. New York: Harper-Collins, 1995. 105p. $15.89. ISBN 0-06-023613-2. "On Education" tells the story of a creative boy who is educated to become like everyone else. "Lies" by Yevgeny Yevtushenko (trans. Robin Milner-Gulland and Peter Levi) warns adults that they must confront youth with life's hardships.

4. Hunter, Shaun. **Visual and Performing Artists**. New York: Crabtree Publishing, 1999. 48p. (Women in Profile). $8.95pa. ISBN 0-7787-0035-6. The volume includes complete profiles on Mexican artist Frida Kahlo and American artist Georgia O'Keeffe. It includes a brief profile of American artist Faith Ringgold.

5. Janeczko, Paul B. **How to Write Poetry**. See full booktalk below (p. 215). Janeczko suggests several structures that might help members of the group shape their thoughts and reactions.

6. Lobel, Anita. **No Pretty Pictures: A Child of War**. See full booktalk in Chapter 1 (p. 39). A professional artist tells about the horrible childhood that eventually unfolded her artistic talent.

Hamilton, Jake. **Special Effects in Film and Television**. New York: DK Publishing, 1998. 63p. $17.95. ISBN 0-7894-2813-X.

## *Summary/Description*

*Special Effects in Film and Television* explains how special effects enhance the story line and impact of a picture. Beginning with the contribution of Georges Méliès in 1902, the book discusses SFX developments up to Oscar-winning John Dykstra. It then predicts the future of SFX, which will include hydraulic seats, 3-D movies, and positioning of dead screen icons in modern movies. Beginning with the storyboard, Hamilton explains and illustrates concepts and terms that apply to camera effects, miniatures, projection, movement, crash landings, fire, water, natural disaster, and war. Movies and full color illustrations demonstrate the steps of each process.

## *Booktalk*

How were the snow walkers able to walk, and how is superman able to fly? How did Jim Henson's Creature Shop hide Pinocchio's strings? How can a movie build a gorilla family? How can an actor survive fire, flood, and war? Jake Hamilton answers all those questions on his special effects guided tour of movies like *Star Wars*, *The Wizard of Oz*, *Pinocchio*, *ET*, and *Jurassic Park.* He describes the step-by-step process of building a story and then dramatizing it with camera angles, stop-motion, matte painting, sugar glass, snow machines, wind machines, gelatin pellets, and computer software. When you read *Special Effects in Film and Television*, you'll learn how that larger-than-life character in Hollywood, special effects, is growing up.

## *Related Activities*

1. Choose a short story. Make up a storyboard and include the special effects you think you would need to carry it out. Then read or tell the story to the group. Use the "special effects" you have been able to create.

2. Plan a speech. Make up a series of pictures or charts that cue each idea in the speech. Then decide on the visual aids and the audience interaction necessary to communicate each point. Discuss your plan with another group member. Prepare any "special effects" that you need and practice your speech several times before delivering it to the audience.

3. Read *King Arthur*. Discuss what special effects techniques will be needed to communicate the legend as depicted in Rosalind Kerven's book.

4. Read any book in the Harry Potter series. Discuss what percentage of the story would require special effects and what these special effects would be.

5. *Star Wars: Incredible Cross-Sections*, *Star Wars: Episode I*, and *Star Wars: The Visual Dictionary* all contain characters and equipment requiring special effects. Lucas Film Ltd. Productions also

recommends *George Lucas: The Creative Impulse* by Charles Champlin. Using these books, start a scrapbook or journal of the special effects that you can now identify in movies and television programs.

## *Related Works*

1. Champlin, Charles. **George Lucas: The Creative Impulse**. New York: Harry Abrams, 1997 rev. ed. 232p. $39.95. ISBN 0-8109-3580-5. Lucas Films recommends Champlin's book, along with the four DK publications, for information about special effects.
2. Kerven, Rosalind. **King Arthur**. See full booktalk in Chapter 3 (p. 131). The illustrations suggest many special effects required to tell the story, with the tone established in Kerven's book.
3. Reynolds, David West. **Star Wars: Episode I**. See full booktalk in Chapter 3 (p. 138). The book shows the *Episode I* vehicles in minute detail.
4. Reynolds, David West. **Star Wars: Incredible Cross Sections**. See full booktalk in Chapter 3 (p. 138). The book shows the *Star War's* vehicles in minute detail.
5. Reynolds, David West. **Star Wars: The Visual Dictionary**. See full booktalk in Chapter 3 (p. 140). The book shows the equipment and characters of Star Wars.
6. Rowling, J. K. **Harry Potter Series**. See full booktalks in Chapter 3 (pp. 181–87). In Harry Potter's world, normal meets enchantment. It's not a world of technology, but special effects will be needed to bring Harry's story to the screen.

James, Laura. **Michelle Kwan, My Story: Heart of a Champion**. New York: Scholastic Inc., 1997. 166p. $4.99pa. ISBN 0-590-76356-3.

## *Summary/Description*

In *Michelle Kwan, My Story: Heart of a Champion*, Michelle tells about her life of hard work, focus, and joy. She began skating when she was five years old. When she was seven and a half, she decided she wanted to be an Olympic champion. By the time she was twelve, she had passed the senior women's test and had catapulted herself into a whole new level of competition. Throughout the book, Michelle credits her family, coaches, choreographers, and friends for her success. They encouraged her to work hard but also to balance herself on and off the ice. Her family reminded her to maintain the distinction between "discipline and pressure." Her friends, along with her family, helped her to keep her perspective and sense of humor. Her coaches and choreographer taught her the difference between a technician and an artist.

She starts her story with her disastrous program and the thought that getting back up is the most important part of both skating and life. Laura James communicates the warmth and personality of Michelle Kwan. Even the glossary of terms is a friendly and personal discussion of skating.

## *Booktalk*

Michelle Kwan is all grown up and ready to "go for the gold." In *Michelle Kwan, My Story*, Michelle shares her joy in skating and the hard work and focus it takes to get to the Olympics. For Michelle, success has meant balancing her life on and off the ice. Her biggest disappointments came when she lost that balance, that mental and emotional focus. In fact, she starts her story with her biggest failure, the 1997 U.S. Figure Skating Championships. Her greatest successes came, however, when she got back up after falling. One was the gold medal she won at Nationals, a year later.

In a sport that must combine the "tiger and butterfly," Michelle comes with a tiger personality. She has worked hard to develop the physical strength for the powerful, driving skating moves, as well as the delicate, artistic presentation. With both, she can fly on the ice and in life. Lucky for us, she can take her audience with her.

## *Related Activities*

1. Choose three other female contenders for the Olympic Gold Medal. Research their backgrounds. Discuss the traits these women share with Michelle Kwan.

2. Often women athletes must deal with the feminine stereotype. Research women athletes who have excelled and how their public has perceived them.

3. In Part 5 of *Ophelia Speaks*, three essays deal with "The Academic Squeeze." Each deals with handling pressure and outside judgments. Compare each girl's perception to Michelle Kwan's.

4. Analyze the pressures of your day. Using the chapter "Managing Time Effectively" in *Strategies for Studying*, set up goals and a time schedule. Each month, evaluate how you have met those goals and how effective your scheduling has been.

5. In *Rules of the Road*, the main character excels in sales and business rather than in athletics. What characteristics and attitudes do the real-life Michelle Kwan and the fictional Jenna Boller share?

## *Related Works*

1. Bauer, Joan. **Rules of the Road**. See full booktalk in Chapter 2 (p. 114). The main character encounters opportunities that help her become a winner personally and professionally.

2. Corbett, Sara. **Venus to the Hoop**. See full booktalk in Chapter 2 (p. 99). This nonfiction account tells the story of the 1996 Olympic Gold Medal Women's Basketball Team's task of balancing their physical power and feminine beauty.

3. Hunter, Shaun. **Great African Americans in the Olympics**. New York: Crabtree Publishing, 1997. 64p. $15.96pa. ISBN 0-86505-823-7. This volume profiles Debi Thomas, who won the Olympic Bronze Medal for figure skating in 1988.

4. Shandler, Sara. **Ophelia Speaks**. See full booktalk in Chapter 2 (p. 126). This collection of essays and poems by young women expresses the concerns and frustrations many share about the pressures of growing up.

5. Strudwick, Leslie. **Athletes**. New York: Crabtree Publishing, 1999. 48p. (Women in Profile). $15.96pa. ISBN 0-7787-0037-2. Strudwick fully profiles six athletes and briefly profiles ten athletes. One of the athletes profiled is Sonja Henie, who won gold medals in the 1928, 1932, and 1936 Olympics.

6. University of Victoria's Counseling Services. **Strategies for Studying: A Handbook of Study Skills**. Victoria, BC: Orca Book Publishers, 1996. 150p. $12.95pa. ISBN 1-55143-063-0. "Managing Time Effectively" gives an inventory survey, exercises, and sample charts to help plan time effectively.

Janeczko, Paul B. **How to Write Poetry**. New York: Scholastic, 1999. 117p. (Scholastic Guides). $12.95. ISBN 0-590-10077-7.

## *Summary/Description*

*How to Write Poetry* provides step-by-step advice about the poetry writing process, from gathering ideas and words to sharing finished poems. Each chapter includes a list of suggested materials, writing tips from other poets, "Try this . . ." sections, examples, revision guidelines, and a bibliography. Five "Poetcraft" sections provide descriptions, poems, checklists, examples, and exercises for the following techniques: sound, images, word choice, figurative language, and line breaks. Chapters 2, 3, and 4 focus on particular forms: acrostics, synonym poems of opposites, list poems, poems of address, persona poems, and narrative poems. Chapters 1 and 5 focus on preparation and presentation. At the end of the book, Janeczko provides a three-page bibliography of poetry books. The glossary distinguishes between terms discussed within the text and terms occurring elsewhere in the glossary. "Biographical Notes" describe the writing background of each of the writers mentioned. The index includes topics, techniques, and authors. It shows clear connections between poetry and prose, between modern and classical poetry, and between free and more structured forms.

## *Booktalk*

How would you like to

learn to talk to yourself?

make your own greeting cards?

recognize a friend in a special way?

liven up your prose?

Write some poems. Express yourself! *How to Write Poetry* suggests techniques to improve your expression but also warns you about some common mistakes writers make. Janeczko lets you warm up with some acrostic poems, do something different with some clerihews (some what?), and tell your own story or someone else's in a narrative poem. If you want to reflect on your day, encourage a friend, cheer on the school team, or become a poet laureate, *How to Write Poetry* is a fun and informative tool to help you.

## *Related Activities*

1. Write clerihews ("short rhyming poems about historical and literary figures") for each member of a school team or council.
2. Locate as many of the books recommended by Janeczko as possible. Compare the advice in those books with the advice in *How to Write Poetry.*
3. Develop a poetry library in your classroom.
4. Find "poems" or poetic expression in prose paragraphs. Develop a poem from a prose paragraph.
5. Janeczko uses examples to illustrate poetic terms. Make a scrapbook of poems that you find. Organize them according to the techniques that they illustrate.

## *Related Works*

1. Appelt, Kathi (text), and Kenneth Appelt (photographs). **Just People & Paper/Pen/Poem: A Young Writer's Way to Begin**. See full booktalk above (p. 195). The book includes poems by the author, pictures that reinforce the poem, an explanation of the process, and invitations for the reader to compose poems.

2. Bouchard, Dave (text), and Robb Terrence Dunfield (paintings). **If Sarah Will Take Me**. Victoria, BC: Orca Book Publishers, 1997. 30p. $16.95. ISBN 1-55143-081-9. Bouchard has used poems to accompany the paintings of Robb Terrence Dunfield.

3. Elmer, Howard. **Blues: Its Birth and Growth**. See full booktalk above (p. 201). This book illustrates, in the story of the blues, the marriage between sound and rhythm.

4. Hesse, Karen. **Out of the Dust**. See full booktalk in Chapter 1 (p. 30). The main character writes her thoughts in poetry. Related Activity 3 asks the reader to use Billie Joe's topics to write personal poems.

5. Lyon, George Ella (text), and Robert Hoskins (photographs). **Where I'm From: Where Poems Come From**. See full booktalk below (p. 217). Lyon explains how to write poetry from several starting points and then illustrates the process with her own poems.

6. Myers, Walter Dean (poem), and Christopher Myers (illus). **Harlem**. See full booktalk below (p. 241). *Harlem* illustrates several techniques explained in Janeczko's guide, including the blending of words, rhythms, and pictures.

7. Philip, Neil, ed., and Michael McCurdy (illus). **War and the Pity of War**. See full booktalk in Chapter 1 (p. 44). This book would be a good example of how the selection of color and illustration reinforces the tone of a poetry collection.

Lyon, George Ella (text), and Robert Hoskins (photographs). **Where I'm From: Where Poems Come From**. Spring, TX: Absey & Company, 1999. 99p. (Writers & Young Writers Series #2). $13.95pa. ISBN 1-888842-12-1.

### *Summary/Description*

*Where I'm From: Where Poems Come From* discusses poetry as a tool for recreating experiences and weaving together pieces of information. It is the second book in the Writers & Young Writers Series by Absey & Company. George Ella Lyon uses focus points such as objects, play, images, shape, other people's words, voices, and stories. She then explains, in an essay, how she herself has used these points to communicate her own experiences and information. She includes her own poems as illustrations and suggests writing exercises that result in poetic expression and poems. The volume should encourage reading, writing, and communication.

### *Booktalk*

Do you have to submit a personal essay? Explain who you are and how you feel? You may want to start with a poem or materials for a poem. George Ella Lyon will help you tell where you're coming from with *Where I'm From: Where Poems Come From.* She uses everyday objects and experiences that nobody ever thinks are too poetic. Then she shows how to transform them into messages that you and others will want to read and listen to. Lyon plants the seeds for some clear and entertaining self-expression that will help everyone grow into better writers and speakers.

## *Related Activities*

1. Complete a section in George Ella Lyon's book each week.
2. Add a chapter. Think of one more place that poems come from. Write an explanatory essay and poems.
3. Make up a scrapbook or journal containing the types of poems Lyon describes. You can use your own poems, those of your friends, or poems in other poetry collections. Choose or draw pictures to accompany the poems.
4. Read the poems you have written. Choose one or two of the poems and write a personal essay explaining yourself either for an employer or a school admissions department.
5. On page 2 of *How to Write Poetry*, Paul B. Janeczko quotes George Ella Lyon's description of her writing journal. As you read other writing books, note writing tips that you feel are helpful and worth keeping. Write them down in a separate writing guide or journal and classify the quotes by the writing skills that they address.

## *Related Works*

1. Appelt, Kathi (text), and Kenneth Appelt (photographs). **Just People & Paper/Pen/Poem: A Young Writer's Way to Begin**. See full booktalk above (p. 195). Appelt also uses poems as springboards for student writing.
2. Clinton, Catherine. **I, Too, Sing America**. See full booktalk below (p. 219). This anthology centers on the African American experience in America.
3. Giovanni, Nikki. **Shimmy Shimmy Shimmy Like My Sister Kate: Looking at the Harlem Renaissance Through Poems**. See full booktalk below (p. 236). This anthology centers on the poets and poems of the Roaring Twenties in Harlem.
4. Janeczko, Paul B. **How to Write Poetry**. See full booktalk above (p. 215). Janeczko talks about the entire process of writing poetry, including some technical terms associated with it.

5. Philip, Neil, ed., and Michael McCurdy (illus). **War and the Pity of War**. See full booktalk below (p. 44). This anthology centers on the experiences of war throughout the ages.

6. Shalant, Phyllis. **The Great Eye**. New York: Puffin Books, 1996. 150p. $4.99pa. ISBN 0-14-130072-8. The main character works out many of the problems in her life by writing poetry about them.

# TRUST

Clinton, Catherine (prose text), and Stephen Alcorn (illus). **I, Too, Sing America: Three Centuries of African American Poetry**. Boston: Houghton Mifflin, 1998. 128p. $20.00. ISBN 0-395-89599-5.

### *Summary/Description*

*I, Too, Sing America* includes thirty-six poems by twenty-five African American poets, and spans three centuries. Each poet reflects the concerns of the time and the universality of poetry. The topics include slavery, homeland, inspiration, identity, violence, patriotism, and fate. A beige and white quilt introduces each section, and a pastel illustration accompanies and interprets each poem. Clinton gives a short biography of each poet that explains the poet's significance within the African American community and literary heritage. She also explains and describes the poems she has chosen. Reading the poems in order provides a fuller picture of the American experience.

### *Booktalk*

Read "I, Too, Sing America" by Langston Hughes (p. 9). Discuss the following questions: What does the speaker tell us about himself? What does he like and dislike? Is he happy? Angry? Shy? Confident? Why does he talk about "company" and "kitchen"? Why does he talk about being "beautiful"? What does "Tomorrow" really mean? Who is the "they," and why will "they" be ashamed?

Show the picture on page 8. How does the artist see the poem? Why is the man dressed as he is? Why does he hold a dove? Why is the background made up of red and white stripes? Ask the students if they would have interpreted the poem in the same way.

*I, Too, Sing America* lets us hear the voices of twenty-five African American poets who sing about being inspired and black in America. Through their love, frustration, and anger they show us the importance of forging a whole country that respects the beauty, talent, and work of each person. Reading the book from beginning to end gives us an entirely new view of American history.

## *Related Activities*

1. Analyze the techniques used by the poets in *I, Too, Sing America.* Using some of those techniques write phrases, lines, or poems that express your own experience.

2. Ask another student to illustrate what you have written, draw illustrations yourself, or choose illustrations that interpret what you have written.

3. Choose four poems. Plan a choral reading of the poems that includes an overall title, transitions, and a concluding statement.

4. Construct a timeline of the poems and poets. Place it against a timeline of American history.

5. *I, Too, Sing America* draws from three centuries of American history. Choose one of the periods identified. Research African American life during that time period.

6. Choose one of the poets included in the anthology. Find more poems by that poet. Try to describe what characterizes the poems and poet in terms of style and content.

## *Related Works*

1. Cox, Clinton. **Come All You Brave Soldiers**. See full booktalk in Chapter 3 (p. 155). Clinton tells about African American life and courage during the American Revolution.

2. Elmer, Howard. **Blues: Its Birth and Growth**. See full booktalk above (p. 201). Elmer traces the history of the blues from its African oral tradition.

3. Giovanni, Nikki. **Shimmy Shimmy Shimmy Like My Sister Kate: Looking at the Harlem Renaissance Through Poems**. See full booktalk below (p. 236). Along with the poetry of Harlem Renaissance poets, Giovanni includes her own analysis and commentary based on the African American experience.

4. McKissack, Patricia C., and Fredrick L. McKissack. **Black Hands, White Sails: The Story of African-American Whalers**. See full booktalk in Chapter 2 (p. 103). The book explains the history of whaling in relation to slavery. It also comments on the rhythms that African Americans brought to whaling.

5. Myers, Walter Dean (poem), and Christopher Myers (illus). **Harlem**. See full booktalk below (p. 241). Walter Dean Myers's poem is a musical description of Harlem and its roots. You might read it out loud or set it to music. The pictures and poem text would be a suitable display for a poetry festival or black history celebration.

Myers, Anna. **Ethan Between Us**. New York: Walker & Co., 1998. 153p. $15.95. ISBN 0-8027-8670-7.

### *Summary/Description*

In *Ethan Between Us*, seventeen-year-old Clare recalls the summer Ethan came into her life. At fourteen, Liz and Clare were best and exclusive friends. But Ethan brought his haunting music, gentle personality, and good looks to their oil camp. As both girls became enamored of him, and Clare won him, the friendship between Liz and Clare crumbled. Clare lied to her parents and missed Liz's ballet recital to go on a date with Ethan. Liz read Clare's diary, discovered Ethan's mental illness, and spread rumors about him. Before Clare and Liz could take back their mistakes, Ethan was killed in a school fire. Now seventeen, both girls have realized that trust, loyalty, and love grow stronger between two people when those gifts are also given sincerely to many.

### *Booktalk*

Ask the group to whom they should give more loyalty, a boyfriend or a girlfriend. Ask who is more important in their schedules, a boyfriend or a girlfriend.

When Clare and Liz are fourteen, they are best friends. That summer, sixteen-year-old Ethan moves to their oil camp. He isn't like the other boys. He listens to them. He befriends outcasts. He plays beautiful music, and he hears voices. Both Clare and Liz would like to be his girlfriend but neither knows about the voices that drive him, the voices of his genius that could destroy him, as well as the people who love him. Their friendship may not survive. In fact, none of them may survive the summer and fall of lies, betrayals, and accidents that seem to surround the mysterious Ethan.

## *Related Activities*

1. Read "One Need Not be a Chamber to be Haunted" by Emily Dickinson. Discuss the following questions: Who is the speaker? What does the speaker mean by "Haunted?" How does capitalization and punctuation aid the poem's purpose? How do you feel the poem applies to *Ethan Between Us*?

2. *Kissing Doorknobs*, *When She Was Good*, and *Ethan Between Us* all deal with mental illness. Discuss how the mentally ill character is characterized in each novel and how that characterization affects the novel as a whole.

3. In *P.S. Longer Letter Later*, two very different seventh-grade girls maintain a long distance friendship. Compare their friendship to the friendship between Clare and Liz.

4. Read one selection about friendship from *Taste Berries for Teens* each day. Discuss it or write a journal entry in reaction to it.

5. Read "Touching" by Nissim Ezekiel (page 14 of *Life Doesn't Frighten Me at All*). Write down the many definitions of touch that Ezekiel uses in the poem. Compare your definitions with other definitions from the members of the group. According to the speaker, what place should touching have in our lives? Write down or discuss your reaction to the speaker's ideas.

## *Related Works*

1. Danzinger, Paula, and Ann M. Martin. **P.S. Longer Letter Later**. See full booktalk in Chapter 3 (p. 172). Two seventh-grade girls must share their joys and frustrations by long distance when one girl's family relocates.

2. Dickinson, Emily. "One Need Not be a Chamber to be Haunted." In **The Complete Poems of Emily Dickinson** edited by Thomas H. Johnson. Boston: Little, Brown, 1960. The speaker sees confronting the self as far more frightening than confronting an outside threat.

3. Ezekiel, Nissim. "Touching." In **Life Doesn't Frighten Me at All** by John Agard. New York: Henry Holt, 1989. The poem explores the many meanings of the word *touched* and how many ways a person can be touched.

4. Hesser, Terry Spencer. **Kissing Doorknobs**. See full booktalk in Chapter 3 (p. 148). The main character tries to keep relationships with friends and family while fighting obsessive-compulsive disease.

5. Mazer, Norma Fox. **When She Was Good**. See full booktalk in Chapter 3 (p. 176). A mentally ill older sister terrorizes and abuses her younger sister.

6. Youngs, Bettie B., and Jennifer Leigh Youngs. **Taste Berries for Teens: Inspirational Short Stories and Encouragement on Life, Love, Friendship, and Tough Issues**. Deerfield Beach, FL: Health Communications, 1999. 344p. $12.95. ISBN 1-55874-669-2. Part 2, "Friendship: Finding, Keeping and—Sometimes—Losing It," on pages 51–93 includes essays about why friendships are important and how a person can keep good friendships.

Rottman, S. L. **Hero**. Atlanta, GA: Peachtree Publishers, 1997. 134p. $14.95. ISBN 1-56145-159-2.

### *Summary/Description*

Sean Parker is an intelligent, angry, troubled ninth grader. His mother is an abusive alcoholic, and he sees his father as cold, distant, and uncaring. When Sean is sentenced to community service for a violation, he meets Dave Hassler, a tough World War II hero who holds Sean to high intellectual, moral, and social standards. Sean decides to accept hard work and responsibility rather than abuse. He now seeks the love and security that promise to come with his commitment. Sean Parker has grown up in a world without heroes, but with the help of Dave Hassler, he becomes one. In a final essay, Sean explains what *hero* means to him.

## *Booktalk*

Sean Parker's abusive mother is drinking herself to death. His father isn't around. Sean's own decisions could get him voted least likely to succeed in his high school. No one trusts him, even himself. Where can Sean go? The court sentences him to a farm where he can do community service. He must work for Dave Hassler, and Dave does hassle. He is the toughest man Sean has ever met. But, finally, Sean must learn the difference between a hard time and a bad time. Sean's new journey tests his physical, mental, and emotional strength. It also prepares him to live his own life, seeking the hero in himself and others.

## *Related Activities*

1. Read Sean Parker's essay, "My Hero Is . . ." aloud. Ask the members of the group to write down the ideas they hear in the essay. You might need to read the essay more than once. Ask each member to jot down notes about each of the ideas.

2. Discuss these ideas. Ask for the members' reactions to them. Ask them to cite specific examples to explain their reactions.

3. In *Hero*, *The Tuesday Cafe*, *A Fly Named Alfred*, *A Beautiful Place on Yonge Street*, and *The Great Eye*, each main character writes and talks about the writing process. List the principles each person has learned about writing. Discuss whether the same idea appears in more than one novel.

4. Sean Parker faces a series of tests in *Hero*. List these tests. Discuss how each test strengthens him.

5. Read "Just People," on pages 54–57 in *Just People & Paper/Pen/Poem: A Young Writer's Way to Begin*. Then complete the "Invitations" on page 91.

6. Read Chapter 14, "The Debate" in *Sirena.* Discuss how and why Sirena attacks the heroic stories Philoctetes tells. Discuss how these heroes differ from the hero Sean honors at the end of *Hero*. Discuss how they are the same.

## *Related Works*

1. Appelt, Kathi (text), and Kenneth Appelt (photographs). **Just People & Paper/Pen/Poem: A Young Writer's Way to Begin**. See full booktalk above (p. 195). The poem "Just People" describes the love between two non-heroes in a high school and how one of them brings recognition to the other killed in an accident.

2. Napoli, Donna Jo. **Sirena**. See full booktalk in Chapter 2 (p. 91). Sirena questions the heroes Philoctetes honors.

3. Shalant, Phyllis. **The Great Eye**. New York: Puffin Books, 1996. 150p. $4.99pa. ISBN 0-14-130072-8. Thirteen-year-old Lucy Rising uses writing to help her adjust to her changing life and the changing lives of the people she loves.

4. Trembath, Don. **A Beautiful Place on Yonge Street**. See full booktalk in Chapter 3 (p. 166). Harper Winslow falls in love at writing camp and meets more writing challenges. This is the third in the series.

5. Trembath, Don. **A Fly Named Alfred**. See full booktalk in Chapter 2 (p. 128). Harper Winslow begins writing for the school newspaper and initiates a column that gets him into trouble. This is the second in the series.

6. Trembath, Don. **The Tuesday Cafe**. See full booktalk in Chapter 1 (p. 23). When a judge gives Harper Winslow a writing assignment, he enrolls in a writing school, which gives him many more assignments and unusual experiences. This is the first in the series.

Tito, Tina E. **Liberation: Teens in the Concentration Camps and the Teen Soldiers Who Liberated Them**. New York: The Rosen Publishing Group, 1999. 63p. (Teen Witnesses to the Holocaust). $17.95. ISBN 0-8239-2846-2.

## *Summary/Description*

*Liberation* is divided into six chapters. The first chapter explains the background of the camps and the American liberation of those camps. Chapters 2 through 5 are personal narratives of concentration camp survivors and American soldiers: a fifteen-year-old boy, a sergeant, a secretary proficient in languages, and a Native American/African American. These narratives show how teenagers and twenty-somethings were locked into the Second World War both as victims and soldiers. The sixth chapter explains what happened to each person after the war. A map at the beginning of the book shows the parts of Europe and North Africa invaded by the Nazis and their allies. At the end of the book, a timeline shows the progression of the war and Jewish persecution (This timeline differs slightly from the rest of the books in the series.); a glossary explains German and military terms; and a source list includes books (basic and advanced), videos, and web sites for additional information. The book also includes a name and subject index and biographical information about the author and series editor. Pictures accompany each of the narratives. *Liberation* is one of eight books in the Teen Witnesses to the Holocaust series.

## *Booktalk*

Ask the group to describe the stereotypical teenage life. Then ask them to describe what a teenage life is really like.

In *Liberation*, former concentration camp prisoners and their liberators tell what their teenage lives were like when they confronted the Nazi horror. The prisoners saw their families die or disappear. They experienced typhus and dysentery. They were forced to hide in sewer pipes and latrines. The liberators saw walking skeletons who greeted their saviors with moans, tears, and sometimes silence. Both experienced and saw what they thought the world would never believe or understand because they themselves could not believe or understand it. At very young ages, they were asked to take on responsibilities that most people would not face in their entire lives. And, because they were so young, they were left to tell the story. *Liberation* allows us to realize that young people's strength and courage helped to rebuild the world after World War II.

## *Related Activities*

1. *Teenage Refugees from Bosnia-Herzegovina Speak Out*, *Hidden Children of the Holocaust*, and *The Lost Children of Berlin* are all nonfiction statements from people who have been part of significant world events in early adulthood. Discuss what common ideas, wishes, or elements appear in these interviews?

2. The Final Solution was essentially a form of ethnic cleansing. Research other conflicts that have involved conflict on the basis of race. What kinds of conditions surround such conflicts?

3. Using the bibliography at the end of the book as a start, explore the books, movies, and web sites listed. Divide the bibliography into fiction and nonfiction sources. On one day of each month, come together and discuss what you have read. Maintain an annotated bibliography that discusses the work's contents and the group's reaction to it.

4. Research Hitler's ultimate plan for eliminating and enslaving "inferior" people.

5. *Liberation* lists Generals Eisenhower, Bradley, and Patton. Research their roles in World War II and, more specifically, their roles in the liberation of the camps.

## *Related Works*

1. Baer, Edith. **Walk the Dark Streets**. See full booktalk in Chapter 3 (p. 153). The main character finds her life more and more restricted by Nazi policy and must finally flee to America.

2. Kustanowitz, Esther. **The Hidden Children of the Holocaust: Teens Who Hid from the Nazis**. See full booktalk in Chapter 3 (p. 158). People who, as teenagers, hid from the Nazis, tell their stories.

3. **The Lost Children of Berlin**. Produced by A&E Television Networks, 1997. 50 min. Color. $19.95. AAE-16117. Videocassette. Students from the same Jewish school reunite and tell their stories of hiding and persecution.

4. McKee, Tim, and Anne Blackshaw. **No More Strangers Now: Young Voices from a New South Africa**. See full booktalk in Chapter 2 (p. 77). Teenagers talk about the problems that have separated them and their hopes for the future.

5. Tekavec, Valerie. **Teenage Refugees from Bosnia-Herzegovina Speak Out**. The Rosen Publishing Group, 1997 rev. ed. 64p. (In Their Own Voices). $16.95. ISBN 0-8239-2560-9. Teenagers tell about their feelings about their country's conflicts and their own relocation.

Van Steenwyk, Elizabeth. **A Traitor Among Us**. Grand Rapids, MI: Eerdmans Books for Young Readers, 1998. 133p. $15.00. ISBN 0-8028-5150-9.

## *Summary/Description*

Thirteen-year-old Pieter becomes a courier for the Dutch Resistance during the German occupation of Holland. The Germans arrested his father a year before. His brothers both fight for the Resistance. Only Pieter is home to protect his mother. The town knows there is a traitor reporting to the Germans. Everyone who fights the Germans risks exposure and death. But Pieter wants to live up to his family's example, and he has fallen in love with Beppie, one of the main communicators for the Resistance. While Pieter is taking greater risks, his brother arrives with a wounded American soldier. But this soldier is also Dutch and a Jew. Pieter and his mother must protect the soldier and carry his messages. Pieter eventually leads the town's informant to the head of the Resistance and discovers that the traitor is his best friend's father. Thrown into the fighting on this dangerous journey, Pieter is saved by a German soldier. By the end of the novel, Pieter and the reader trust no stereotypes. The book begins with a map of the Netherlands and ends with a pronunciation guide.

## *Booktalk*

Discuss the following questions:

How many of you believe everything adults tell you? Why?

How many of you believe everything your friends tell you? Why?

What do you consider the best source of information?

Pieter, at thirteen, is a trusted courier for the Dutch Resistance. His brothers are fighting. The Germans have arrested his father, and his mother fears he will be shot. He too fears he will be shot, especially when his friend tells him there is *A Traitor Among Us*. As he carries his messages, he wonders if he can trust the doctor, his teacher, the minister, his uncle, his cousin, or even the beautiful Beppie, whom he loves. No place is safe, not even his home. He waits for the Germans to find him and kill him, but nothing is as it seems in Pieter's world. Nothing is as he has been told. The world, he is discovering, can be horrible, but surprising.

## *Related Activities*

1. In *The Hidden Children of the Holocaust*, Yvonne Kray Sokolow tells about hiding from the Nazis and working against them, just as Pieter worked against them. Research Resistance activities during World War II.

2. In *No Pretty Pictures*, Anita Lobel writes an epilogue that clarifies many of the events she did not know about as a child. Take on the role of Pieter and write the epilogue he would write fifty years after his wartime experience.

3. We think of adults fighting in war, but in World War II, many children performed significant deeds to save themselves and their families. The record and spirit of these deeds comes to us in fiction and non-fiction. Read *Walk the Dark Streets*, *The Hidden Children of the Holocaust*, *No Pretty Pictures: A Child of War*, and *Liberation: Teens in the Concentration Camps and the Teen Soldiers Who Liberated Them*. View *The Lost Children of Berlin*. Discuss why children and specifically teenagers became such a central and valuable part of the war experience.

4. In *Summer Soldier*, an eleven-year-old boy must fight a war when his father enlists in the army. Even though the times and circumstances are different in *Summer Soldier* and *A Traitor Among Us*, compare the two experiences and what the boys learn from them.

5. War often forces people to react to stereotypes rather than individuals. When reading *A Traitor Among Us*, list the number of times Pieter is surprised by a person who is different from his preconception. When reading and viewing the Related Works, list the number of times a character or person surprises you.

## *Related Works*

1. Baer, Edith. **Walk the Dark Streets**. See full booktalk in Chapter 3 (p. 153). The main character, with the help of her family, escapes to America from Nazi Germany.

2. Kustanowitz, Esther. **The Hidden Children of the Holocaust**. See full booktalk in Chapter 3 (p. 158). Chapter 6 tells the story of Yvonne Kray Sokolow, whose family moved to the Netherlands to escape the Nazi threat. She tells about delivering illegal newspapers for the Dutch Resistance.

3. Lindquist, Susan Hart. **Summer Soldiers**. See full booktalk in Chapter 3 (p. 160). Feelings of hate, fear, and prejudice bring World War I very close to home for an eleven-year-old boy and his friends.

4. Lobel, Anita. **No Pretty Pictures: A Child of War**. See full booktalk in Chapter 1 (p. 39). Lobel talks about hiding, as a small child, from the Nazis during the war.

5. **The Lost Children of Berlin**. Produced by A&E Television Networks, 1997. 50 min. Color. $19.95. AAE-16117. Videocassette. Students from the same Jewish school reunite and tell their stories of hiding, resistance, and persecution.

6. Tito, Tina E. **Liberation: Teens in the Concentration Camps and the Teen Soldiers Who Liberated Them**. See full booktalk above (p. 225). The book includes interviews with teenagers and young adults brought together under the most horrifying circumstances.

 Whelan, Gloria. **Forgive the River, Forgive the Sky**. Grand Rapids, MI: Eerdmans Books for Young Readers, 1998. 111p. ISBN 0-8028-5155-X.

### *Summary/Description*

Twelve-year-old Lily Star leaves her house on the Sandy River when her father drowns. She and her family move into town and live above their hardware store. Her mother had to sell the land to pay the father's debts, and now must work full time in the store to support her family. Lily is angry at the river for her father's death and also angry with the new owner of the land, who does not seem to appreciate it but fences it in so that others cannot enjoy it. The new owner, T. R. Tracy, is a former test pilot who has been crippled in a plane accident. He is angry at the sky and wishes to hide himself from the world. As Lily pushes to get back to her land, she confronts Tracy and her own grief. Then, Tracy must confront his anger and abandon his isolation. As they help each other to heal, they discover the strength of the human heart.

## *Booktalk*

Lily loses her father and her home all at once. Now a stranger fences in her land and shuts her out. Can she stay in town and forget about her river home? After all, the river killed her father. Why shouldn't she leave it behind?

T. R. Tracy loses his friends and his career as a test pilot all at once. Can he build a fence high enough to shut out the world? According to Tracy, nobody wants a loser in a wheelchair. As these two angry people struggle with their losses and each other, one must learn to *Forgive the River*; the other must learn to *Forgive the Sky*. Both learn to trust the future and themselves one day at a time.

## *Related Activities*

1. The death of loved ones often leaves a person angry and confused. Discuss the reaction to death of each of the characters in the following novels: *Forgive the River, Forgive the Sky*; *Out of the Dust*; *Sang Spell*; *Cowboy Ghost*; and *The Spirit Window*.

2. Read "Forgotten" by Cynthia Rylant, on page 14 of *Pierced by a Ray of the Sun*. In this poem, a girl describes the loss of a father. Discuss how the poem relates to *Forgive the River, Forgive the Sky*.

3. Often we fight with people who eventually help us. Discuss the results of the rocky relationships in the following novels: *Forgive the River, Forgive the Sky*; *Hero*; and *A Door Near Here*.

4. Read "The One-Armed Boy" by Joseph Hutchinson, on page 4 of *Pierced by a Ray of the Sun*. Describe the boy who is the focus of the poem. How is his missing arm a problem in his life? What other problems does he have? What does the speaker imply about the power of the human spirit? Compare the boy to Tracy in *Forgive the River, Forgive the Sky*.

## *Related Works*

1. Gordon, Ruth, ed. **Pierced by a Ray of the Sun: Poems About the Times We Feel Alone**. New York: HarperCollins, 1995. 105p. $15.89. ISBN 0-06-023613-2. In the "One-Armed Boy," on page 4, the speaker describes a boy who must deal with his physical handicap, a dysfunctional family, and cruel schoolmates. In "Forgotten," on page 14, a fourteen-year-old girl tries to figure out how she should feel about the death of the father who deserted her.

2. Hesse, Karen. **Out of the Dust**. See full booktalk in Chapter 1 (p. 30). The main character, who feels responsible for her mother's death, must come to terms with her own life and her new relationship with her father.

3. Naylor, Phyllis Reynolds. **Sang Spell**. See full booktalk in Chapter 3 (p. 187). After his mother's sudden death in a car accident, the main character is drawn into a mysterious world of lost souls that challenges him to find his true self.

4. Peck, Robert Newton. **Cowboy Ghost**. See full booktalk in Chapter 1 (p. 15). The main character must find the courage to deal with his tough, distant father and the loss of his brother.

5. Quarles, Heather. **A Door Near Here**. See full booktalk in Chapter 1 (p. 54). The main character falsely accuses a teacher of abuse and then finds that the teacher saves her sister's life.

6. Rottman, S. L. **Hero**. See full booktalk above (p. 223). A confrontational relationship between a juvenile offender and the farmer to whom he is assigned grows into a deep friendship.

7. Sweeney, Joyce. **The Spirit Window**. See full booktalk in Chapter 1 (p. 19). The main character must deal with the death of her grandmother and the preservation of the land that the grandmother loved.

## TEACH AND LEAD

Blatner, David. **The Joy of Pi**. New York: Walker & Co., 1997. 130p. $18.00. ISBN 0-8027-1332-7.

### *Summary/Description*

*The Joy of Pi* describes the struggle and fascination humankind has had with squaring the circle. It explains the relationship between circles and squares, the importance of Pi, the history of Pi, and the modern struggle with an ancient problem. It shows Pi figured to a million numbers, cartoons, jokes, and trivia (or "Pi on the Side"). *The Joy of Pi* also provides a bibliography for further reading, including a web site, and an index.

## *Booktalk*

Pie reflected in a mirror gives the value of Pi (p. 109). But who cares? For centuries, mathematicians have tried to square the circle. Pi is the answer. Computers have accelerated the study of the mystical, magical Pi, the "root of perfection." *The Joy of Pi* shows how computers have enabled people to carry the figure to the one-millionth digit. (See the last page of the book.)

Why is Pi so fascinating? The building you are sitting in right now could not have been built without Pi. You can figure out your hat size by using the circumference of your head and Pi. You can use Pi to figure the height of an elephant if you're brave enough to measure the diameter of his foot. The O. J. Simpson trial may have had a different conclusion if the FBI agent had used Pi. *The Joy of Pi* gives the history and the trivia of Pi, even a recipe for pumpkin Pi. Good reading.

## *Related Activities*

1. Have a Pi contest in your school. In "Memorizing Pi," the author tells how people have tried to memorize the staggering number of digits. A pie-baking contest and a Pi-memory contest would complement each other.

2. Some attempts at memorizing Pi have involved poems, musical scores, and stories ("Memorizing Pi"). Mathematics, English, and music enthusiasts can work together to create Pi poems, songs, stories, and essays.

3. Pages 116–18 contain examples of Pi mnemonics written in Dutch, French, Greek, Italian, Spanish, and Swedish. Write your own mnemonic in the foreign language of your choice.

4. Page 119 includes an MIT football cheer. Write a similar Pi cheer for an academic team.

5. Find as many everyday situations as possible that involve Pi. Ask each contributor to write an explanation of how Pi is involved. Post these examples on a bulletin board.

## *Related Works*

1. Agard, John. **Life Doesn't Frighten Me at All**. New York: Henry Holt, 1989. "A Wise Triangle" is a fantasy personification of a triangle who hides the fourth side. "Maths" is a schoolchild's expression of frustration with math.

2. Kraft, Betsy Harvey. **Sensational Trials of the 20th Century**. See full booktalk in Chapter 3 (p. 133). One of the sensational trials is the O. J. Simpson trial. The trial is also dealt with in *The Joy of Pi*.

3. Lindsay, Vachel. "Euclid." In **Contemporary American Poetry** by H. Lincoln Foster. New York: Macmillan, 1963. The speaker describes Euclid and his colleagues pondering the dimensions of a circle while a child, fascinated by its moon shape, watches.

4. Nemerov, Howard. "Grace to Be Said at the Supermarket." In **Sound and Sense: An Introduction to Poetry, 6th ed.**, edited by Laurence Perrine. New York: Harcourt Brace Jovanovich, 1982. The speaker sees geometry and science as a way to intellectualize our animal instincts.

5. Nemerov, Howard. "To David, About His Education." In **The Next Room of a Dream**. Chicago: University of Chicago Press, 1962. The speaker tells David that he must learn the abstract concepts to enter the adult world but should remember they are just false shields against confusion.

Fradin, Dennis. **Samuel Adams: The Father of American Independence**. New York: Clarion Books, 1998. 182p. $18.00. ISBN 0-395-82510-5.

## *Summary/Description*

The story of Samuel Adams is also the story of the American Revolution. Fradin acknowledges that this often forgotten but controversial man was both manipulator and hero. Adams twisted facts and made alliances so that he could affect the break from England. But while his methods were deceptive, his goal was selfless. He made no money from the Revolution, and he put principle above popularity. Adams wrote many of his letters under pseudonyms, gave his speeches to other revolutionary leaders, and destroyed most of his personal writing and correspondence. Founding a small group called the Sons of Liberty, he turned the concerns of a few into the overwhelming cry of a nation.

As the poorest patriot, he allied himself with John Hancock, the richest patriot. The alliance was successful and symbolic. The Battle of Lexington, the first battle of the Revolution, began because the British were coming to hang the charismatic Adams and Hancock. Both rich and poor joined to defend them and the principles they represented. The Articles of Confederation succeeded because of Adams's persistence and gave way to the Constitution because of his wisdom.

Fradin depicts a man who worried more about his country than himself, and whose memory carries on in the results of his labor rather than libraries, documents, or statues. Pictures, maps, and sample documents accompany the clear narrative. A bibliography provides additional sources, and an index provides easy access to the information.

## *Booktalk*

Samuel Adams couldn't hold a job, had a hard time supporting a family, and owned only one threadbare coat. His business was revolution. He was such a powerful leader that his British enemies called him the "Grand Incendiary" and the "Master of the Puppets." Adams was so charismatic that the British prime minister referred to the patriots as "Adams' Crew." Adams sparked the revolution, glued together the Articles of Confederation, supported the Constitution, and insisted on the Bill of Rights. He may have been the most dangerous man in American history. Ignoring his own poverty, illness, and personal tragedies, Samuel Adams earned the title of which he would be most proud, "The Father of American Independence."

## *Related Activities*

1. Write a dramatic scene based on Adams's plea for independence. (See page 126 in *Samuel Adams*.)

2. Pages 136–37 of *Samuel Adams* contain the speech Adams gave to the Congress at York in the most desperate days of the American Revolution. Rewrite that speech for a modern audience.

3. Samuel Adams's life is a record of American independence. Construct a timeline of his political life.

4. In *The Journal of William Thomas Emerson*, Mr. Wilson and his patriot group function much as Samuel Adams and his group functioned. After reading both books, explain the parallels in this nonfiction and "based on fact" account.

5. Read "Liberty and Peace" by Phillis Wheatley in *I, Too, Sing America.* Research any allusion that is unfamiliar. Discuss what these allusions add to the meaning of the poem. Describe the speaker and purpose of the poem.

### *Related Works*

1. **Benedict Arnold: Triumph and Treason**. Produced by A&E Television Networks, 1995. 50 min. Color. (Biography). $14.95. AAE-14017. Videocassette. The video describes how Arnold grew up, how he became a successful and envied military man, and how his personal life influenced his tragic decision to commit treason.
2. Cox, Clinton. **Come All You Brave Soldiers**. See full booktalk in Chapter 3 (p. 155). The book talks about the black man's war for freedom within the Revolution and how the American Revolution sowed the seeds for the American Civil War.
3. Denenberg, Barry. **The Journal of William Thomas Emerson**. See full booktalk in Chapter 1 (p. 12). William Thomas Emerson is hired by Mr. Wilson to spy for the revolutionaries.
4. Rinaldi, Ann. **Cast Two Shadows**. See full booktalk in Chapter 1 (p. 46). The novel shows differences between the Revolutionary War in the North and in the South.
5. Severance, John B. **Thomas Jefferson: Architect of Democracy**. See full booktalk below (p. 245). This biography includes the controversial Adams, Jefferson's contemporary.
6. Sterman, Betsy. **Saratoga Secret**. A young girl carries a letter to Benedict Arnold so that he may defeat Burgoyne's army.
7. Wheatley, Phillis. "Liberty and Peace." In **I, Too, Sing America** by Catherine Clinton. See full booktalk for *I, Too, Sing America* above (p. 219). Wheatley celebrates the American victory and the principles of freedom that it was supposed to symbolize.

## Giovanni, Nikki. **Shimmy Shimmy Shimmy Like My Sister Kate: Looking at the Harlem Renaissance Through Poems**. New York: Henry Holt, 1996. 188p. $16.95. ISBN 0-8050-3494-3.

### *Summary/Description*

*Shimmy Shimmy Shimmy Like My Sister Kate* celebrates the poets and the spirit of the Harlem Renaissance. Giovanni sees this period as one of the first flowerings of African American culture, possible because the people finally had control over their own bodies. Thus, they had the freedom to express themselves physically, emotionally, and intellectually by their own choice. The book begins with a poem by W. E. B. DuBois and ends with Ntozake Shange, so it extends beyond the time period usually associated with the Harlem Renaissance. Giovanni uses short essays throughout the anthology to explain the poets' place in African American life and her own reaction to the poets. The poems highlight how the African American must be private and public at the same time and how this creativity has helped in coping with those demands. Several of the selections might be considered appropriate for more mature audiences. The end of the book includes biographical notes, a bibliography for further reading, a general index, and an index of first lines.

## *Booktalk*

Spirituals, blues, and jazz are all freedom cries of a nation. *Shimmy Shimmy Shimmy Like My Sister Kate* contains those cries in poetry. Giovanni concentrates on a period in history called the Harlem Renaissance, a time when Harlem nurtured the poets, musicians, dancers, and professionals whose ancestors rose out of slavery "to higher ground." She also extends a little beyond those historical boundaries to what came before and what has followed. *Shimmy Shimmy Shimmy* celebrates the African Americans' freedom to control their minds, bodies, and talent.

## *Related Activities*

1. Using *I, Too, Sing America* and *Shimmy Shimmy Shimmy Like My Sister Kate: Looking at the Harlem Renaissance Through Poems*, group the poems by theme. What themes are most common? Discuss what these themes reflect about African American life.

2. Using *Blues: Its Birth and Growth,* research blues lyrics. Note the rhythm of the songs and discuss how those rhythms aid the author's purpose.

3. Read "Same in Blues" by Langston Hughes, on pages 50–51. Discuss what the poem has in common with the blues lyrics and rhythms you have found through Activity 2. Set the poem to music.

4. *Harlem* by Walter Dean Myers, expresses many of the feelings and ideas expressed in *Shimmy Shimmy Shimmy Like My Sister Kate: Looking at the Harlem Renaissance Through Poems* and *I, Too, Sing America*. List the poems and poets that share the images, ideas, and feelings expressed.

5. Use pictures and illustrations to complement your favorite poems from *Shimmy Shimmy Shimmy Like My Sister Kate.*

## *Related Works*

1. Clinton, Catherine (text), and Stephen Alcorn (illus). **I, Too, Sing America**. See full booktalk above (p. 219). This anthology of African American poetry spans three centuries and includes commentaries on each of the poets.

2. Elmer, Howard. **Blues: Its Birth and Growth**. See full booktalk above (p. 201). This thin volume traces the blues sound from its African roots to its place in mainstream America.

3. Grove, Vicki. **The Starplace**. See full booktalk in Chapter 1 (p. 4). Two girls form a close friendship in spite of the town's prejudice.

4. Hacker, Carlotta. **Great African Americans in Jazz**. New York: Crabtree Publishing, 1997. 64p. (Outstanding African Americans). $8.95pa. ISBN 0-86505-818-0. This book traces the connection between blues and jazz and features seven famous jazz performers. It briefly profiles six more.

5. Myers, Walter Dean (poem), and Christopher Myers (illus). **Harlem**. See full booktalk below (p. 241). The poem and illustrations paint a picture of the history and heart of the Harlem community.

Linnéa, Sharon. **Princess Ka 'iulani: Hope of a Nation, Heart of a People**. Grand Rapids, MI: Eerdmans Books for Young Readers, 1999. 234p. $18.00. ISBN 0-8028-5145-2.

## *Summary/Description*

In the late 1890s Princess Ka 'iulani looks forward to being the Hawaiian Queen. Through her mother, she is a Hawaiian chief. Through her father, however, she is a Scot. Her destiny will be to draw these two worlds, the Hawaiian and the Western, together. She will have to deal with overwhelming American business interests and the jealousies of her own family to bring the strategically placed Hawaiian Islands peacefully into the twentieth century. As a princess, she takes on this responsibility when she is seventeen. By the time she has accomplished her task, she is in failing health. At twenty-three, she dies. Born into privilege and indulgence, she lives personal and public lives of loneliness and loss. She never becomes queen, and she never marries. The physically delicate but steel-willed princess chooses duty over personal happiness to give her beloved people peace and freedom.

Sharon Linnéa has included "A Word About the Hawaiian Language," which gives definitions and pronunciation guides; a "Prologue," which sets the stage for the account; and a map, index, and annotated bibliography.

## *Booktalk*

Ask the following question: What does the word "princess" mean to you?

The tragic death of Princess Di has taught the world that princesses do not always live in a fairy-tale world. When Princess Ka 'iulani is ten years old she is surrounded by servants, beautiful clothes, doting parents, privilege, and safety. By the time she is seventeen, she has lost her adoring mother and is fighting to keep her Hawaiian Islands safe from Western greed. Beautiful and charismatic, she pleads with world governments and media to save her land. But her home is too small and too strategically placed to be left alone. As a descendant of a royal Hawaiian mother and a Scottish father, her destiny is to blend the two worlds blended in her own blood.

At seventeen, the fairy-tale princess becomes a brave woman who will sacrifice her personal happiness for the love of her country.

## *Related Activities*

1. Read Princess Ka 'iulani's speech to the press on p. xvii. Do not give the speaker's identity. Ask the audience to infer as much as possible about the speaker and the situation from what is said and how it is said. This activity would also be an appropriate booktalk.

2. Read the song to Ka 'iulani on p. 138. Ask the audience to infer as much as possible about the speaker and the situation from what is said and how it is said. This activity would also be an appropriate booktalk.

3. Read *The House of Pride*. Discuss the problems that London deals with in this short story collection. Discuss how these short stories relate to the factual information from *Princess Ka 'iulani: Hope of a Nation, Heart of a People.*

4. In Chapter 3 of Mark Twain's *Following the Equator*, Twain comments on the history and government of Hawaii as well as the leprosy that plagues the islands. Summarize Twain's view of the Hawaiian situation. Discuss how he places it in the larger context of government and politics in general.

5. Robert Louis Stevenson visited the Hawaiian Islands to recuperate from an illness. During this visit he wrote *The South Seas.* In Chapter 3, "The Maroon," he describes Tari (Charlie) Coffin. Read the passage that begins on page 21 with the words, "At the top of the den . . .". Finish the paragraph. In the paragraph, what information does Stevenson give the reader about Tari? What information does Stevenson give the reader about his own attitudes about the white man and the changes in the islands?

6. On pages xvii–xviii Princes Ka 'iulani reveals her disappointment and horror that the people who would overthrow her government are the sons of missionaries. On pages 182–84 of *Hawaii's Story by Hawaii's Queen*, Liliuokalani relates the circumstances surrounding "The Bayonet Constitution." Begin reading the first full paragraph with the words, "It has been known ever since that day . . ." and read to the end of the chapter. How do the details of her account characterize "the conspirators?"

7. On page 373 of *Hawaii's Story by Hawaii's Queen*, Liliuokalani makes her final appeal to the American people. Begin reading with the words, "Oh, honest Americans, As Christians hear me . . ." and read to the end of the book. Compare her appeal to Princes Ka 'iulani's on pages xvii–xviii. What does each passage reveal about the author?

## *Related Works*

1. Dyer, Daniel. **Jack London: A Biography**. See full booktalk above (p. 199). Dyer's biography includes London's fascination with and inspiration from the Hawaiian Islands.

2. **Hawaii's Lost Riches**. Produced by A&E Television Networks, 1998. 50 min. Color. (Treasure!). AAE-13046. $19.95. Videocassette. The film shows the wholesale theft of the Royal Family's treasures as the American planters took over the islands. It also includes the slow steps toward restoration.

3. **Hawaii's Vengeful Goddess**. A&E Television Networks, 1998. 50 min. Color. (In Search of History). $19.95. AAE-40405. Videocassette. This documentary tells the story of the goddess of the volcano and how her whims often determined the leadership of the island.

4. Liliuokalani. **Hawaii's Story by Hawaii's Queen**. Tokyo, Japan: Charles E. Tuttle, 1964. This controversial biography tells about royal life and the overthrow of the government.

5. London, Jack. **The House of Pride**. New York: Macmillan, 1912. This collection of short stories reveals London's perception of the Americans, Europeans, and Chinese who took over Hawaii. He pays special attention to the problem of leprosy, its source, and the cruel treatment of its victims, which eventually touched all levels of society.

6. Stevenson, Robert Louis. **The Works of Robert Louis Stevenson, Vol. VII**. New York: The Davos Press, 1906. This volume contains *In the South Seas*, which Stevenson wrote while he was he was in the South Seas trying to recover his health.

7. Twain, Mark. **Following the Equator: A Journey Around the World, Vol. 1**. New York: Harper & Brothers Publishers, 1899. Chapter 3 centers on Twain's reflections on the Hawaiian Islands, then known as the Sandwich Islands.

Myers, Walter Dean (poem), and Christopher Myers (illus). **Harlem**. New York: Scholastic Press, 1997. 30p. $16.95. ISBN 0-590-54340-7.

### *Summary/Description*

In *Harlem*, a celebration of the spirit, the pictures of Christopher Myers make a striking backdrop for the words of Walter Dean Myers. The poem lists the people, places, beliefs, pastimes, and feelings of Harlem in the language and rhythms of the community. The lists themselves provide allusions for research. The poetic comparisons Myers chooses depict Harlem as an integral part of the natural world. The entire picture book creates an experience, a walk through Harlem.

## Booktalk

Open to the first picture. It has no poetry. Discuss what is in the picture and what the images introduce or suggest. Continue to read parts of the poem and show the pictures. You may want to read one or two pages and then pass the book around or discuss the marriage of one of the sections and pictures. You may want to read the entire book aloud and show the pictures as you read. The students can then come back to the book to enjoy the pictures and text privately.

## Related Activities

1. Find a partner and complete a similar project involving poetry and art. Create your own mural.

2. Find other poems that talk about Harlem. You might start with "Harlem" by Langston Hughes in *I, Too, Sing America* and "Sonnet to a Negro in Harlem" in *Shimmy Shimmy Shimmy Like My Sister Kate.* Compare their tones, subjects, and purposes.

3. Research the allusions to people and places used in "Harlem." Report to the class and explain why those allusions are significant. Why, for instance, does the picture on the first page prominently display the Apollo Theater?

4. Use two copies of the book. Laminate the pages and use the pages in a classroom or hallway mural. Display other Harlem poems and artwork that illustrate their content or spirit.

5. Write a musical score for the Walter Dean Myers poem.

## Related Works

1. Clinton, Catherine (text), and Stephen Alcorn (illus). **I, Too, Sing America**. See full booktalk above (p. 219). The poem "Harlem" talks about what happens to a "dream deferred."

2. Elmer, Howard. **Blues: Its Birth and Growth**. See full booktalk above (p. 201). This book gives a brief history of the blues in America, beginning with its African roots.

3. Giovanni, Nikki. **Shimmy Shimmy Shimmy Like My Sister Kate: Looking at the Harlem Renaissance Through Poems**. See full booktalk above (p. 236). "Sonnet to a Negro in Harlem" by Helene Johnson celebrates the black woman.

4. Hacker, Carlotta. **Great African Americans in Jazz**. New York: Crabtree Publishing, 1997. 64p. (Outstanding African Americans). $8.95pa. ISBN 0-86505-818-0. This book gives seven full and six brief profiles of jazz performers.

5. Parker, Janice. **Great African Americans in Film**. New York: Crabtree Publishing, 1997. 64p. (Outstanding African Americans). $8.95pa. ISBN 0-86505-8222-9. This volume in the series contains profiles of Cicely Tyson and Keenan Ivory Wayans, both born and raised in Harlem.

 Rinaldi, Ann. **Mine Eyes Have Seen**. New York: Scholastic Press, 1998. 275p. $16.95. ISBN 0-590-54318-0.

### *Summary/Description*

Annie Brown, John Brown's fifteen-year-old daughter, lives on her father's Maryland farm in the summer of 1859. She is the lookout as Brown gathers his sons and supporters to raid Harper's Ferry. Although she is charged with the house chores, she is scholarly and reflective. Her father does not fully appreciate his daughters but does give Annie the job "to remember and tell what went on." Her summer is filled with conflict as she fends off curious neighbors, deals with the rowdy and restless group ready to launch the raid, and tries to sort out the feelings she has about her own father. *Mine Eyes Have Seen* integrates several historical accounts of John Brown and his mission through this character of Annie Brown, a person that John Brown himself was never able to value or see clearly.

### *Booktalk*

Annie Brown, at fifteen, must make personal decisions that betray her beliefs and shape her nation. As the daughter of John Brown, the abolitionist, she serves as the lookout while he and his men plan the Harper's Ferry raid. When John Brown's second wife refuses to come to the farm, Annie comes to help a man who really does not know her. She finds herself in a world of radicals and mystics and must sort out her feelings about her family and her father's mission. Although she takes on all the woman's work, her father tells her that her real job is "to remember and tell what went on here," perhaps the biggest job of all. When, at the end of the summer, she can say *Mine Eyes Have Seen*, she finds that she is "Annie Brown, all growed."

## *Related Activities*

1. Research abolitionism, Dunker, Quaker, the suffrage movement, Frederick Douglass, Dred Scott, and the Fugitive Slave Act. Explain how each was significant in the anti-slavery movement.

2. Read "The Battle Hymn of the Republic," "Nearer My God to Thee," and "Amazing Grace," all alluded to in *Mine Eyes Have Seen.* Discuss what these hymns communicate about God and about solving national problems.

3. Research the play *Richard III* by Shakespeare. Why is it appropriate that Annie refers to this play throughout the novel?

4. In Chapter 22, Annie reports, as fully as possible, what has happened at the Ferry. Much of the account reflects the speed of the communication and transportation of the day. What effect would today's transportation and communication have had on the event? Rewrite the chapter in the context of today.

5. Ann Rinaldi includes a bibliography on the last page of her novel. Locate some of these sources or similar sources and then tie the events of the novel to the historical information they find.

6. Read "Bury Me in a Free Land" by Frances Ellen Watkins Harper in *I, Too, Sing America.* Describe the speaker. List the scenes the speaker uses to support the poem's purpose. List the reactions to those scenes. Identify any pattern in the order of presentation. Discuss the irony of the title.

7. Read the lyrics of the song "John Brown's Body" in *War and the Pity of War.* It is sung to the tune of "The Battle Hymn of the Republic." Discuss how the vision of John Brown presented in the song compares with Annie's vision of Brown.

## *Related Works*

1. Harper, Frances Ellen Watkins. "Bury Me in a Free Land." In **I, Too, Sing America** by Catherine Clinton (text) and Stephen Alcorn (illus). See full booktalk above (p. 219). The poem is a series of images that show why the speaker wishes to be in a land free of slaves. The author moved in with John Brown's wife after the Harper's Ferry disaster.
2. Howe, Julia Ward. "The Battle Hymn of the Republic." In **Services of Religion** compiled by the Unitarian and the Universalist Commissions on Hymns and Services. Boston: The Beacon Press, 1937. Containing the title of the book, this hymn sees the coming of the Lord as a triumphant battle.
3. "John Brown's Body." In **War and the Pity of War** edited by Neil Philip and illustrated by Michael McCurdy. See full booktalk in Chapter 1 (p. 44). This anonymous composition glorifies Brown and is sung to the melody of "The Battle Hymn of the Republic."
4. Shakespeare, William. "The Tragedy of King Richard the Third." In **The Complete Works of William Shakespeare** edited by W. J. Craig. London: Henry Pordes, 1973. Richard the Third is both hero and villain.
5. United Presbyterian Church. **The Hymnbook**. New York: Presbyterian Church in the United States, The United Presbyterian Church in the U.S.A., Reformed Church in America, 1952. "Nearer My God to Thee" and "Amazing Grace—How Sweet the Sound" are both alluded to in *Mine Eyes Have Seen.*
6. Williams, Jean Kinney. **The Quakers**. See full booktalk below (p. 248). Williams discusses the role Quakers played in the abolition of slavery.

Severance, John B. **Thomas Jefferson: Architect of Democracy**. New York: Clarion Books, 1998. 192p. $18.00. ISBN 0-395-84513-0.

## *Summary/Description*

Severance presents Thomas Jefferson as a man of contradictions. He was against slavery but owned slaves. He condemned slave/owner fraternization but was accused of it. He wrote the Declaration of Independence but supported stable government. He was a leading political figure but preferred to be a scholar. He honored European thinkers but worked to eliminate European influence from North America. He shrewdly authorized the Louisiana Purchase but found his own life in financial shambles. He fought for the rights of the common man but opposed the idea that big government could ensure those rights. Severance expresses these contradictions in an objective, balanced style as he portrays Jefferson as a brilliant and responsible man living in tumultuous and changing times. The book includes "In Jefferson's Words," reflections on personal morality and government; an extensive bibliography of related works; etchings of Jefferson and his life and times; and a name and topic index.

## *Booktalk*

One would think that nobody would argue with the man who wrote the Declaration of Independence. But the document was so criticized and torn apart that Jefferson must have wondered why he bothered to write it in the first place.

Thomas Jefferson wasn't a public idol. In fact, today, we might not even notice him. Quiet and hardworking, he tried to give as much as possible to a nation in which he believed. He wasn't perfect and didn't try to be, but he did every job the best way he knew how, and some people in his time admired him for it. Many who came after him honored him for it. Severance takes the complicated story of a complicated man and tells it as simply and as completely as possible. For him, Jefferson is a man with whom we can identify and empathize.

## *Related Activities*

1. After reading the "In Jefferson's Words" section of *Thomas Jefferson: Architect of Democracy*, write a reaction to one of the quotations or plan to discuss or reflect on one of the quotations each day.

2. On page 24, Severance notes that Francis Bacon, Isaac Newton, and John Locke were Jefferson's heroes. These three men were philosophers during the Enlightenment. Research these men, their influence on the Enlightenment, and their influence on Jefferson.

3. Starting with the bibliography at the end of the book, continue to read about Jefferson and his world.

4. Lafayette, a French army officer and hero of the American Revolution, was Thomas Jefferson's friend. Research Lafayette's role in the Revolution and his reaction to its results, especially the issue of slavery. You may wish to refer to *Come All You Brave Soldiers*.

5. Severance opens *Thomas Jefferson: Architect of Democracy* with a description of Jefferson's demeanor as he delivered his "First Inaugural Address." Read Jefferson's "First Inaugural" and discuss what the speech reveals about the man and his relationship with his nation.

## *Related Works*

1. **Benedict Arnold: Triumph and Treason**. Produced by A&E Television Networks, 1995. 50 min. Color. (Biography). $14.95. AAE-14017. Videocassette. The video describes Arnold's life and treachery. He led British troops to capture the capital of Virginia and its governor, Thomas Jefferson.

2. Cox, Clinton. **Come All You Brave Soldiers**. See full booktalk in Chapter 3 (p. 155). Cox points out Jefferson's active participation in slavery and the often-unfair treatment of African Americans who risked their lives in the war.

3. Fradin, Dennis. **Samuel Adams: The Father of American Independence**. See full booktalk above (p. 234). The biographies of Jefferson and Adams reveal Jefferson to be the intellectual gentleman and Adams to be the pragmatic, irascible scrapper.

4. Jefferson, Thomas. "First Inaugural Address." In **The Literature of the United States, Vol. 1, 3d ed.**, edited by Walter Blair, Theodore Hornberger, Randall Stewart, and James E. Miller, Jr. Chicago: Scott, Foresman & Company, 1966. Jefferson underscores the rule of law over the rule of personality and his humble commitment to political and religious freedom under that law.

5. Rinaldi, Ann. **Cast Two Shadows**. See full booktalk in Chapter 1 (p. 46). The novel reveals the problem of slavery during the American Revolution.

Williams, Jean Kinney. **The Quakers**. Danbury, CT: Franklin Watts, 1998. 110p. $22.00. ISBN 0-531-11377-9.

## *Summary/Description*

*The Quakers* tells the story of The Children of the Light: their origins, development, service, relationship to U.S. history, and modern form. George Fox, at nineteen, broke away from the Puritan faith. He allowed women to preach and developed a new religious vocabulary. *Worship* became *meeting*, *excommunicated* became *disowned*, *converted* became *convinced*, *regulations* became *disciplines*. The changes in language reflected an entirely new perception of the relationship of religion to secular life, and Jean Kinney Williams tells how this gentle sect has influenced our own political policies and has grown into an international religion.

## *Booktalk*

A teenager, nineteen-year-old George Fox, founded *The Quakers*. His new ideas and beliefs helped to shape our nation and the world. In simple, clear language, Jean Kinney Williams explains how separation of church and state allowed the strong religious beliefs of the Quakers to express and act on social programs related to women's rights, land rights, slavery, and prison reform. The Quakers have influenced our Constitution, statehood, and modern views, and Williams shows how these Children of Light worship today and continue to influence the world.

## *Related Activities*

1. Research other religious groups' influence on American history.
2. Ask students how the information about Quakers supports the portrayal of Quakers in *Mine Eyes Have Seen* by Ann Rinaldi.
3. Complete a timeline of Quaker development.
4. Ask a minister or member of the Quaker faith to speak to the group about Quaker beliefs.
5. After reading *Moby Dick*, discuss Melville's image of the Quaker.

6. Develop a list of Quaker-affiliated schools in the United States. Choose one and research its founding and modern mission.

## *Related Works*

1. Hacker, Carlotta. **Scientists**. New York: Crabtree Publishing, 1998. 48p. (Women in Profile). $8.95pa. ISBN 0-7787-0028-3. The book includes a profile of Jocelyn Bell Burnell, Irish astronomer, who was educated in a Quaker boarding school and still maintains her Quaker affiliation today.

2. McKissack, Patricia C., and Fredrick L. McKissack. **Black Hands, White Sails: The Story of African-American Whalers**. See full booktalk in Chapter 2 (p. 103). The book explains how Quakers helped former slaves come from the Underground Railroad to the whaling industry.

3. Melville, Herman. **Moby Dick** edited by Charles Feidelson Jr. New York: The Bobbs-Merrill Company, 1964. (The Library of Literature). Melville depicts a Quaker as a tight-fisted businessman.

4. Murphy, Jim. **Gone A-Whaling: The Lure of the Sea and the Hunt for the Great Whale**. See full booktalk in Chapter 2 (p. 108). Murphy talks about the significant role of Quakers in the whaling industry.

5. Rinaldi, Ann. **Mine Eyes Have Seen**. See full booktalk above (p. 243). John Brown's daughter tells the story of the summer of preparation for his raid on Harper's Ferry.

# Author/Title Index

*Note*: Titles with booktalks are in boldface type.
Page numbers in boldface indicate sections with summaries and booktalks.

# Subject Index